Humans and Other Animals

A211
Philosophy and the Human Situation

The Open University

Humans and Other Animals

Rosalind Hursthouse

Walton Hall, Milton Keynes
MK7 6AA

First published 1999. Reprinted 2000, 2003, 2007.

Edited, designed and typeset by the Open University.

Printed and bound in Great Britain by Bell & Bain Ltd., Glasgow.

ISBN 0 7492 8751 9

This text forms part of an Open University course A211 *Philosophy and the Human Situation*. Details of this and other Open University courses can be obtained from the Course Reservations Centre, PO Box 724, The Open University, Milton Keynes MK7 6ZS, United Kingdom: tel. (00 44) 1908 653231 .

For availability of this or other course components, contact Open University Worldwide Ltd, The Berrill Building, Walton Hall, Milton Keynes MK7 6AA, United Kingdom: tel. (00 44) 1908 858585, fax (00 44) 1908 858787, e-mail ouwenq@open.ac.uk

Alternatively, much useful course information can be obtained from the Open University's website

http://www.open.ac.uk

1.4

Mixed Sources
Product group from well-managed forests and other controlled sources
www.fsc.org Cert no. TT-COC-002769
© 1996 Forest Stewardship Council
FSC

The paper used in this publication contains pulp sourced from forests independently certified to the Forest Stewardship Council (FSC) principles and criteria. Chain of custody certification allows the pulp from these forests to be tracked to the end use (see www.fsc-uk.org).

Contents

READINGS

Preface

Acknowledgements

I am grateful to members of the Open University Philosophy Department, and to the external assessor, Michael Clark, for comments on earlier drafts of this material. Particular thanks are also due to Shirley Coulson, the course manager, and Peter Wright, the editor, not only for comments, but also for much practical help in getting the book into its final form.

Grateful acknowledgement is made to the following sources for permission to reproduce material in this book: Singer, P. (1993) *Practical Ethics*, 2nd edn, Cambridge University Press; Regan, T. (1985) 'The case for animal rights', in Singer, P. (ed.) *In Defence of Animals*, Blackwell Publishers Ltd; Midgley, M. (1983) *Animals and Why They Matter: A journey around the species barrier*, Copyright © 1983 Mary Midgley, Penguin Books Ltd; Scruton, R. (1996) *Animal Rights and Wrongs*, published by Demos, 9 Bridewell Place, London EC4V 6AP; *Animal–Human Relationships*, RSPCA (1995): Midgley, M., 'Animals and the philosophers', by permission of Dr Mary Midgley; Clark, S.R.L., 'A view of animals and how they stand', by permission of Professor S.R.L. Clark; Singer, P., 'The ethics of animal liberation: a summary statement', by permission of Professor Peter Singer; Regan, T., 'The rights view', by permission of Tom Regan; Rollin, B., 'A philosophical approach to animal rights' by permission of Professor Bernard Rollin; Linzey, A., 'Theology and animal rights', by permission of Andrew Linzey; Ryder, R., 'Speciesism', by permission of Dr Richard D. Ryder.

How to use this book

This book consists of six chapters and you will be working on it, and the associated Readings, for the next six weeks. However, unlike the previous book, the chapters do not correspond to a week's work, and you should be careful to follow the Study Plan. Marginal references are to entries in the set book *Thinking from A to Z* (Warburton (1996)). You should look up any that are unfamiliar as you go along.

Exercises are included throughout; those with answers at the back of the book are indicated, the others have answers and discussion immediately after the exercise. Many are of the sort you have become familiar with, but some are much longer and a word should be said about how to use the answers and discussion that follow them.

The unfamiliar sorts of exercise are intended to teach you techniques for reading and critically evaluating philosophy and the answers and discussion take up quite a bit of space. As you progress through the book, you may find you catch on very quickly and that the answers and discussion seem rather laboured. But, remember, these long answers and discussion are there for those who need them; if you do not, then please skip them. Anyone who has not been getting high grades does need them and is well-advised to work through them patiently, despite their length.

The concentration and time required for these longer exercises may result in your losing track of where you are going as you study. You can reorientate yourself by looking back to the objectives at the beginning of each chapter and ahead to the summary at its end. The contents page is also useful for this.

STUDY OBJECTIVES

By the end of Weeks 7–12 you should:

- Have a good knowledge and understanding of some of the most important philosophical arguments against much of our treatment of animals.
- Be able to offer arguments for and against the main positions discussed.
- Have understood the three approaches to moral questions current in contemporary moral philosophy and appreciated some of the differences between them.
- Have had practice in a range of reasoning techniques.
- Have mastered the basic reading method for most philosophical texts.

Study plan

The reading for each week is outlined below. It might be a good idea, before you start work, to put the bookmark at the end of each week's reading, so that you can see where you are aiming to get to.

Study Week	Chapters	Readings
Week 7	Chapter 1	(1) Singer
Week 8	Chapter 2 Chapter 3 to p.85	
Week 9	Chapter 3 continued Chapter 4 to p.118	(2) Regan
Week 10	Chapter 4 continued Chapter 5 to p.154	(3&4) Midgley
Week 11	Chapter 5 continued Chapter 6 to p.177	(4) Midgley continued (5) Scruton
Week 12	Chapter 6 continued Revision test	Re-reading some (5) Scruton (6) RSPCA Information

Monitoring your progress

It is often difficult to monitor your own progress; so spend five minutes doing the exercise below now and it will provide you with something to look back on in six weeks to see how far you have progressed.

EXERCISE 1
The morality of vegetarianism

If you are not a vegetarian, write a brief paragraph in answer to the question 'Why are you morally justified in not being a vegetarian?' (The last sentence of your paragraph should be 'Therefore, I am morally justified in not being a vegetarian.')

If you are a vegetarian on grounds of health or personal preference, write a brief paragraph in answer to the question 'Why is anyone morally justified in not being a vegetarian?'

And if you are a vegetarian on moral grounds, write a brief answer to the question 'Why should everyone be a vegetarian?'

Revision test

Another way in which you can monitor your progress would be to do the revision test for each chapter (pp.196–207) as you finish each one, but without putting notes on the page so that you can use it again when you are revising for the exam. Only turn to Reading 6 when you have completed your work on this book in week 12.

The Utilitarian Defence of Animals

OBJECTIVES

When you have worked through this chapter, you should:

- Have grasped the content and point of the principle of charity.
- Have a good knowledge of Peter Singer's view on our treatment of animals.
- Have developed your ability to read long extracts from philosophical works by applying the basic reading method.

Introduction

So far in this course we have considered an important aspect of our relations with our fellow human beings; the extent to which our individual liberty should be curtailed so that we can all live together. But, as I began writing this book, the newspapers were filled with descriptions of demonstrators trying to prevent the export of live animals across the English Channel. Comparisons were drawn in the media with the actions of hunt saboteurs, and with the extreme actions of some 'animal rights activists' who have vandalized or bombed laboratories at which experiments on live animals are carried out. Now, on the arguments you met in Book 1, it would seem that all of these actions on the part of the 'animal liberationists' must be straightforwardly wrong. After all, they are all attempts to curtail the freedom of other human beings, and those other human beings are not doing anything that harms people or adversely affects their interests. They are, on the contrary, contributing towards providing people with tasty, cheap food, or just enjoying themselves (and keeping down the fox population) or pursuing medical knowledge which will relieve human suffering. How could interfering possibly be justified?

premises
assumption

If we take it as a **premise** that morality or ethics is solely concerned with our actions in relation to each other, then it would, indeed, be very hard to find an argument to justify such interference. But, although many people are inclined to agree that 'morality deals only with our relations to each other' when they consider the question in isolation, a few obvious counter-examples to that general claim usually make them change their mind. Most people will agree that it is wrong to torture animals; that when we see small boys about to set fire to a petrol-doused cat, what we see is small boys about to do something wrong, which they should be prevented from doing and taught not to do. Most will also agree that the wanton slaughter of animals is also wrong. Though many will want to defend hunting as a sport, they distinguish hunting from wanton killing. Shooting flying ducks, one after another, fishing or angling – that is sport, they say, and a fine activity. But mowing down a hundred ducks sitting on a lake with a rapid-fire automatic, or dynamiting a whole lakeful of fish, just for the hell of it – that would be wanton slaughter and wrong.

All argument has to start somewhere, from some premises which, in the context of *that* argument, are not argued for. In this book, we shall be taking it as a premise (a) that ethics is *not* solely concerned with our actions in relation to each other and, as a related premise, (b) the claim that *some* of our treatment of animals is morally wrong.[1]

We should note that premise (b) is very modest, i.e. claims very little. As long as you accept that, for example, the boys torturing the cat would be wrong, you agree with it. You can think that there is nothing wrong with not being vegetarian, support hunting, be in favour of experimentation on live animals, see nothing wrong in the fur trade, think quite generally that human beings and their moral claims are hugely more important than animals and any moral claims that might be made on their behalf... and still agree with premise (b).

The reason it is important to get the premise out in the open is this. For much of this book, we shall be looking at the arguments of two contemporary philosophers, Peter Singer and Tom Regan, who are in the vanguard of the 'animal liberation' movement – and they are both radical. They want to convince us that we should become vegetarians (if we are not already). They want to convince those of us who hunt, or wear furs, or buy cosmetics that have been tested on animals, that we should stop doing so. They want us to curtail drastically, or even abolish entirely, the use of animals in science. They are, in a word, extremists – and the difficulty with extremism is that it tends to provoke extreme responses. Faced with someone arguing (as both these philosophers do) that animals are in some sense *equal* to human beings, that they matter morally as much as human beings do, those who regard this as an absurd position are likely to find themselves taking up an extreme position in opposition to it. Instead of saying, reasonably and cautiously, that animals matter, but not as much as human beings do, some will insist roundly that animals do not count at all, that they just do not matter, that it is ridiculous to make moral claims on their behalf – quite forgetting that we ourselves are prepared to make a moral claim on the tortured cat's behalf.

Mary Midgley, a more moderate animal liberationist whose arguments we shall also consider, draws a useful distinction between what she calls the 'absolute' and the 'relative' dismissal of animal claims – moral claims made on behalf of animals. On the absolute view, she says, 'animals are not a serious case at all, but fall outside the province of morality altogether' (Midgley (1983), p.10). She illustrates the view by quoting from an early book by Peter Singer (Singer (1975), p.67) describing – 'an American television programme in 1974':

> Robert Nozick asked the scientists whether the fact that an experiment will kill hundreds of animals is ever regarded by scientists as a reason for not performing it. One of the scientists answered 'Not that I know of'; Nozick pressed his question: 'Don't the animals count at all?' Dr A. Perachio, of the Yerkes centre, replied, 'Why should they?' while Dr. D. Baltimore, of the Massachusetts Institute of Technology, added that he did not think that experimenting on animals raised a moral issue at all.

> On this view, claims on behalf of animals are not just excessive, but downright nonsensical, as meaningless as claims on behalf of stones or machines or plastic dolls.
>
> (Midgley, op. cit., p.10)

She contrasts absolute dismissal with relative dismissal:

> Humanitarians occupied with human problems do not usually dismiss animal claims as just nonsensical, like claims on behalf of stones. Instead, they merely give them a very low priority. The suggestion is now that animals, since they are conscious, are entitled to *some* consideration, but must come at the end of the queue, after all human needs have been met. I shall call this idea relative dismissal... to distinguish it from absolute dismissal. As we shall see, the distinction makes a good deal of difference in practice, since many claims on behalf of animals do not compete with real human needs at all, and therefore do not seem to stand in the same queue. Englishman baiting bears were not in the same position as Eskimoes killing them in self-defence.
>
> (Ibid., p.13)

Absolute dismissal will not be ignored in what follows, but we shall be concentrating on arguments against it rather than any defence of it. Near the beginning of her book, Midgley says it would be useful if any reader who was feeling fairly dismissive about animals' claims could use a particular example of cruelty to an animal as a test to decide whether their dismissal was actually absolute or merely relative, and that seems a good idea for a reader of this book too.

Reading 'animal liberation' philosophy

One of the objectives of Book 1 was that you should have gained confidence in your ability to read long extracts from philosophical texts. In this book, the aim is to increase that ability substantially by concentrating explicitly on *reading techniques*. Introducing these at the very outset might have been rather daunting, but now you have gained some confidence, you should find them easy to relate to your recent experience and the application of them to the readings in this book quite straightforward. Indeed, you may have already been employing at least some of them.

The first reading technique can readily be related to the reading you have done on freedom, but is particularly pertinent to the readings in this book, that is, to reading philosophers with whose conclusions you may strongly disagree, for example, Singer and Regan, extreme animal liberationists that they are. 'But,' someone might wonder, 'why are we not reading sensible philosophers arguing for reasonable views we can agree with?'.

One answer is that you have to be prepared to engage with writers you strongly disagree with as well as those that are arguing, comfortably, for such desirable institutions as toleration and freedom of thought and expression. Another answer is that we shall be trying to play the role of 'sensible philosophers arguing for reasonable views' ourselves, by trying to pin down just what we think is wrong with Singer's and Regan's arguments. We may be certain in advance that there must be *something* wrong with them, given the conclusions they reach, but pinpointing what it is will be no easy task.

I believe that one of the most interesting upshots of engaging critically with philosophers' arguments is what one so often learns about one's own thoughts or beliefs – and this is equally so whether one initially agrees or disagrees with them.

Before I first read Singer and Regan I believed that whether or not to be a vegetarian just wasn't a serious moral issue, that using animals in scientific experiments was obvious common sense, and it had simply never occurred to me that there might be anything morally wrong with buying a fur coat. But after I had read them critically, had come up with a number of objections to them, and had read their responses to such objections, I found myself puzzled. My conviction that there was not much wrong with our treatment of animals remained unshaken (it took other authors I read later to do that) but I was puzzled about the grounds of my conviction. 'I *know* it's all right for me to eat meat and wear fur coats,' I said to myself, 'but *why* is it all right?' What *did* I think about why it was all right? I wasn't sure.

Briefly continuing this psychological autobiography, I should tell you frankly that I eventually converted to vegetarianism. I tell you this because I think that, on such an issue, it is disingenuous if not downright dishonest of an author not to declare her cards, and I will say further that yes, I should be very happy if I converted you to vegetarianism. But that is very different from saying that that is what I am aiming to do. I say that what I am aiming to do is to give you a good knowledge of some of the most important philosophical arguments against much of our treatment of animals *and* objections to those arguments and leaving you to make up your own mind; I am *not* aiming to convert you.

All that I ask is that you read me in the light of the principle I am about to describe. And it does not matter if you approach reading Singer and Regan with the conviction that they must be wrong – as long as you read them in the light of this principle. For it governs finding out what a writer is *really saying*. Once you have found that out, you may make of it what you will – that is your freedom.

The principle of charity

The principle of charity, roughly, requires that we try to find the best – the most reasonable or plausible – (rather than the worst) possible interpretation of what we read and hear, i.e. of what other people say. What does this high-sounding injunction amount to in practice?

At its most mundane level, consider ordinary conversation containing, as we say, 'slips of the tongue'. My aunt is 85; like many people of her age, she tends to muddle up names, skipping generations. She is talking about 'Jack' – my son, she says, saw him last week, such a splendid boy, so interested to hear he has decided to give up the law and go in for social work. But my son's name is Jason; 'Jack' was my father's name, and he is, alas, long dead. So there is my old aunt, rabbitting on about having seen Jack, and how proud I must be of him, and what they talked about... What do I do? Do I *interpret* my aunt as making a number of completely barmy claims about my long dead father? Or do I – knowing that she saw Jason just last week, that he has indeed decided to give up the law and go in for social work, that he told me he and his great aunt discussed it and so on – effortlessly, indeed, quite unthinkingly, but charitably, assume that when she says 'Jack' she means 'Jason'? Of course I do. Anyone would. Thereby I act in accordance with the principle of charity.

This sort of example is so mundane that it is hard to see how the principle could embody anything important. But it is important because our capacity to communicate with each other – the very possibility of language – rests on our willingness to aim to interpret what others say as, if not true, at least reasonable rather than barmy. When I interpret my aunt's utterances as being quite reasonable ones for her to make about my son Jason rather than crazy ones about my long dead father Jack (though maybe she has some details wrong) it is not just a matter of my being nice to her, but of my keeping the channels of communication open. If I neglect the principle of charity, I shall just interpret what she says as ravings and guarantee that she fails to communicate to me what she wants to say.

How does the principle work in practice applied to reading philosophy?

In some respects, very straightforwardly. If, at first glance, a philosopher appears to be contradicting himself, the principle requires that we look for a charitable interpretation in which he does not do so. After all, asserting a contradiction is about the most unreasonable, implausible, idiotic thing a philosopher (rather than say, a poet) could do. Uncharitably ascribing self-contradiction to a philosophical writer might seem to be a mistake that no one is likely to make, but in fact it is quite common. One way in which it comes about is through failing to notice when a writer is playing **devil's advocate** against her own argument, putting forward the strongest objection she can, in order to prepare the ground for going on to show that she can meet the objection.

devil's advocate

This mistake can be avoided by the most straightforward application of the principle of charity. (Naturally, one might, after careful reading and sustained analysis of a whole reading, conclude that a writer was inconsistent, or contradicting herself in an unobvious way. But that is very different from interpreting two adjacent paragraphs in such a way that one obviously contradicts the other. In the first case, we assume that the writer, reasonable and intelligent as he is, is fallible. In the second we assume, uncharitably, that he's an idiot.)

Since so much philosophy consists of arguments, applying the principle often involves trying to find an interpretation according to which the writer is producing good, ideally, even **sound arguments**, and this, too, is quite straightforward. If the writer seems, at first glance, to be relying on an obviously false premise, the principle suggests that we try to think of an interpretation of the premise which makes it at least plausible, one that someone might reasonably hold, that will still support the conclusion the writer wants. Or if, at first glance, she seems to be drawing a recklessly broad conclusion which could easily be refuted by a counter-example, the principle suggests that we try to think of an interpretation of the conclusion which

sound arguments

makes it at least plausible. And, further, we should be looking for interpretations of the premises and conclusion which preserve their connection. If, at first glance, the apparent premises do not seem to provide any support for the conclusion, which apparently just comes out of nowhere, the principle suggests that we try to find an interpretation of either, or both, according to which the writer is giving reasons for what she says.

Here is an (unrealistically brief) example. Suppose an animal liberationist produces the following one-sentence argument, say, in a letter to a newspaper. 'Our treatment of animals is wrong', he says, 'because all life is sacred.' If we laid that out as premise and conclusion we would get.

Premise All life is sacred.
Conclusion Our treatment of animals is wrong.

rash generalization

The premise, as stated, is obviously false, a **rash generalization** that is easily refuted by counter-example – e.g. 'A cabbage's life is not sacred'. But, being charitable, we can easily come up with a more plausible premise which the writer would probably be happy with – say, 'All animal life is sacred' or even 'All sentient animal life is sacred'. Of course, many of us will not agree with that premise either, and think it too is open to refutation by counter-example, but it is more plausible than what we started with.

An uncharitable interpretation of the conclusion would be to take it as saying that all our treatment of any sort of 'animal' is wrong – another rash generalization easily refuted (killing insects so tiny I can't see them is not wrong; feeding my cat is not wrong). But a charitable interpretation is easy to find. Although insects and such like are, strictly, animals and not plants, by the word 'animal' we usually mean larger creatures, and often mammals, so charitably we should suppose that the conclusion is about animals in that sense – dogs and cats, sheep, cows, chickens, chimpanzees, elephants, maybe fish, maybe not. And, finally, the premise is about the sanctity of *life*, and the writer has given it as a reason for his conclusion about 'our treatment' of animals being wrong. So, charitably, we should interpret the conclusion in such a way that it connects with that premise. Of course he doesn't mean such treatment as my feeding my cat: he means treatment that involves killing or destroying animal lives – such things as killing animals for food or sport or their fur and using them in scientific experiments.

EXERCISE 2
The principle of charity

Write down a one or two-sentence answer to each of the following questions.

1 What does the principle of charity tell us to do?

2 Give an example of the principle applied to something you have read (including this book, if you like).

3 If, when you first read a piece of philosophy, it seems to you that the author is saying one thing in one paragraph and the complete opposite in the next paragraph, what should you do? reread & check whether they were playing devils advocate.

4 Give an example of how the principle might be applied to an argument.

5 Can you think of an objection to applying the principle when reading philosophy? (An answer is given in the section that follows.)

Check your answers against those at the back of the book before reading on.

Applying the principle when reading philosophy: two scenarios

'But', you might reasonably object, 'isn't it important in philosophy to read critically? Yet how can I read something critically, keeping a sharp eye out for mistakes in reasoning, ambiguities, suppressed premises and so on if, at the same time I'm being charitable and letting the writer off the hook all the time?'

This is a good question, and serves to remind us that the principle of charity must be applied with discretion, not mechanically – and not always.

What is the point and purpose of the principle of charity in relation to reading philosophy? Well, used properly, it helps to avoid making weak criticisms of what you read. And that will help you on the one hand, to produce better arguments, and on the other, to learn more from what you read.

What is a 'weak criticism'? We have everyday terms for it, such as '**pedantry**' and 'nit-picking', but lots of sound philosophical criticism certainly looks like nit-picking to the untrained eye and you want to know when it is and when it isn't. Roughly speaking, a *weak criticism* is one that the writer could have easily escaped by modest changes to what she said – changes which, in being modest, do not affect the main thrust of her argument.

pedantry

So, consider a variant on the brief example above again. Suppose a reader is fairly dismissive of animal claims and wants to criticize a one-sentence passage in which the author argues 'much of our treatment of animals is wrong because all life has value; it all counts for something'. If he ignores the principle of charity he can, as we have seen, knock down this pathetic little argument very easily. 'So, according to the author, it's wrong to kill cabbages is it!' But, if one is aiming to engage seriously in philosophical argument about the rights and wrongs of our treatment of animals, that's a cheap shot – and an uncharitable interpretation. Why not interpret her as meaning 'all *sentient* life'? Then the 'main thrust' of her argument is preserved – that is, she still has an argument (albeit a very small one) for the conclusion that much of our treatment of animals is wrong. So the cabbage counter-example is a weak criticism.

And look at what has happened to the 'fairly dismissive' reader who has gone for the weak criticism! In his eagerness for the cheap shot, he has completely overlooked a more plausible argument against much of our treatment of animals. How would he argue against someone who said 'Much of our treatment of animals is wrong because animals' lives (though not as important as ours) count for something'? By moving to absolute dismissal and saying that no, animals' lives just don't matter at all, there is nothing wrong with killing them in their thousands just for the hell of it? Well, perhaps this is indeed what he thinks, but the chances are quite high that he does not.

So, if he produced the weak criticism in an essay he probably wouldn't do well. His tutor would say that he should have considered the more plausible argument, and might well accuse him of 'setting up a **straw man**' or even of **irrelevance** – his criticism didn't go to the heart of the argument. And, more generally, he would have *failed to learn* – in this case, that there is an argument against much of our treatment of animals that is quite tricky to shoot down – unless one moves to the extreme of absolute dismissal. And all because he didn't think charitably.

straw man

irrelevance

What you are doing in this course is reading real philosophy – long passages, indeed whole articles and sections of books – written by professional philosophers, and the chances are high that, however much you might disagree with their conclusions, you have something to learn about plausible arguments they have for them. And you will cut yourself off from the possibility of this learning if you do not try to apply the principle of charity, because you will just overlook the arguments that really are there, in the reading.

Let's go back to the good question above – 'How can I simultaneously read critically and yet be charitable?' – and imagine yourself reading carefully, with concentration, a philosophical passage or an article in the course arguing for a conclusion you completely disagree with. In doing so, you are already applying the principle of charity to a certain extent because you are taking what the writer is saying seriously. But you will undoubtedly be reading critically, on the hunt for things that are wrong with the arguments, because you are dead against the conclusion. Applied to a greater extent, the principle of charity has the effect of channelling your desire to find objections, targeting it on strong criticisms instead of weak ones.

And that is how, when you are reading something you strongly disagree with, it is possible to read critically *and* apply the principle simultaneously.

But what if you are in total agreement with a philosopher's conclusions? Given that only a small proportion of the population is vegetarian, this may not be a problem for you reading Singer and Regan, which is why it is so important to introduce you to the principle before you read them. In any case its relevance is not limited to this book; in other areas of philosophy you may find yourself reading writers you strongly agree with.

When that is so, in order to read critically, we need, if anything, to try to apply a contrary principle of **devil's advocate**. For when we support someone's conclusions, it may be particularly hard to spot mistakes in the reasoning or to identify such things as ambiguities – we are being charitable unconsciously. So in this sort of case we need to fight against it, playing devil's advocate and trying to pick holes.

devil's advocate

So this is the sort of case in which the principle of charity should not be applied. A related case is your own writing. When you re-read what you have written you should not only be grudging but downright mean, and nit-pick all you can. Charity does not begin at home!

EXERCISE 3
Reading critically

Write down one or two sentences in answer to each of the following.

1 What does the principle of charity help you to do?

2 What is a weak criticism?

3 Describe a scenario in which you should apply the principle. Give a reason why you should.

4 Describe a scenario in which you shouldn't apply the principle. Give a reason why you shouldn't.

Check your answers against those at the back of the book before reading on.

The basic reading method

Introductions to philosophy standardly emphasize the importance of reading philosophy 'carefully'. But, for many people, all that means is reading slowly and underlining a lot – and what many find discouraging is that, conscientiously doing this all through a course, they still don't seem to get any better at mastering what they read. So how does one get better? How do professional philosophers read?

I don't know that I would have been able to articulate what I do. But fortunately I found that the writer of an excellent American text book (Peter Windt, *An Introduction to Philosophy: Ideas in Conflict,* 1982) had done it for me and I am going to introduce you to his method. The method involves multiple readings of the philosophical text and at first sight may seem rather time-consuming. But as Windt emphasizes, 'it involves skills which can be developed, and with practice most students can move through the various stages more quickly and efficiently than on their first few attempts' (Windt (1982), p.50).

Windt divides reading philosophy into three stages.

1 Skimming.

2 The reading outline.

3 Critical evaluation.

Skimming

The aim of skimming is to give you a *rough* idea of what the author is up to. What you are hoping to pick up as you skim is a rough idea of (a) what his topic is and (b) what his main conclusion about it is. Very often, in the reading for this course, you will know about (a) already because the course author will have told you. So you will be hoping to pick up (b) and, since you are reading philosophy, also (c) a *rough* idea of at least some of his arguments to that conclusion.

There are three rules to help you to do this successfully.

1 Skim with *the right questions in mind,* explicitly looking for answers to them. In what follows, I am going to help you with this by giving you 'the right questions' every time, so all you have to do is apply the rule.

But where do you look for these answers? At the beginning and end of every paragraph. Hence the second rule for skimming is:

2 Read just the first one or two and the last one or two sentences of each paragraph *only.*

Sometimes you won't even need to do that – just the first or last few words will do. Some writers, such as Mill, are admirably clear and provide obvious signposts indicating what they are doing: 'The objection likely to be made...' (Mill, *On Liberty*, 1985 edn, pp.78–9) – that's all you would need to notice at the beginning of that paragraph; 'I answer, that...' – that's all you would need to notice at the beginning of the next. Mill summarizes his four principal arguments for preserving freedom of expression in three paragraphs, beginning 'Firstly', 'Secondly' and 'Thirdly' – and that's all you would need to notice at the beginning of them. Since the fourth argument appears in the middle of the paragraph, you wouldn't pick it up while skimming – but that's all right. You are aiming for a rough idea of some of the author's arguments, and picking up that Mill has at least three is a good enough nugget of information to get from skimming.

Sometimes the first or last sentence, on its own, just isn't enough to make any sense, and then you have to read on, or go back a further one. *But*, when you are skimming, you must try to resist doing more. If, having read a maximum of two at the beginning and two at the end, you are still in the dark about what that paragraph is about, just mentally label it 'something-or-other' and press on.

The third rule for skimming is:

3 Use what you already know.

You will not usually be asked to read an author about whose views you know nothing. You will usually have been told something, often just before you read, and, the further you go on in the course, the more knowledge you will accumulate. This third rule serves as a handy reminder to use this knowledge and I will illustrate its application later on.

Having skimmed, you should have answers to 'the right questions' and they will give you your rough idea of what the author is up to in the reading. Armed with this rough, but none the less helpful idea, you go back to the beginning and set off on the second stage.

The reading outline

At the second stage you do indeed read carefully. The aim is to produce 'a reading outline' which covers every paragraph so that you wind up with a thorough understanding of what the author has said. Note that you are still not aiming to criticize anything he says, but instead to give as sympathetic an interpretation as possible. If you are sympathetic anyhow, give your sympathy full rein; if you are not, apply the principle of charity as conscientiously as you can.

At this point, people's preferred practices differ. I'm a note-taker myself; when I settle down to master an article paragraph by paragraph, I write little labels, or one or two-sentence summaries which cover sometimes just one paragraph, sometimes three or four at a time, such as (labels) 'Introduction', '1st argument against ...', 'objection' or (sentences) 'Our interest in eating flesh is a relatively minor one'. But some people prefer to mark up the text itself; they write the labels in the margin beside the relevant paragraphs, and they underline or highlight the bits of the text that I would quote or paraphrase in my notes.

If you prefer to do the second, I will issue a word of warning. When you take notes, sheer exhaustion tends to keep them brief and thereby (with a bit of luck and skill) relevant. But underlining or highlighting is easy, and students tend to wind up underlining far too much. You are trying to produce an *outline,* so aim to restrict yourself mostly to underlining no more than one sentence per paragraph, if that. Your skimming has already provided you with a rough idea of what to concentrate on – don't get distracted.

These first and second stages cover what I shall call 'doing a *full* reading' of an extract. It is only after we have done a full reading that we shall get to the third stage.

Critical evaluation

Windt describes this stage as involving reading the piece yet again. First, he says, analyse all the details of every section. Then 'formulate some critical opinion about the success of that particular section and its contribution to the aims of the whole piece'. Then review 'all the results to see what you think about the major contentions of the whole piece' (Windt, op. cit., p.57).

This is a counsel of perfection for students beginning philosophy. It might be something you did nearer the end of the course if you had an essay explicitly on a particular reading. But, in general, you are not expected critically to evaluate the readings on your own, as Windt's third stage requires. Rather, we provide a substitute for the third stage, expecting you to follow the course author's discussion with understanding. Now this does not usually involve re-reading the whole piece. It involves returning to, and re-reading, certain parts of it with great attention to detail, or reviewing particular sections, to see whether or not, for instance, they are subject to the same objection, or raise the same problem. And by the time you have done that a few times, you will have *really* mastered the reading.

The rest of this week's work will involve applying the first two stages to a Reading from Peter Singer's *Practical Ethics.*

Singer in defence of animals

People often speak of moral concern about our treatment of animals as something that developed only as recently as the 1970s. At the very least, they must mean (applying the principle of charity) 'in Western human thought' because societies influenced by Jainist, Hindu and Buddhist thought have been vegetarian on moral grounds for thousands of years. But even as a claim about Western thought, it is not strictly true. Ancient Greeks and Romans who argued for vegetarianism on moral grounds included the Pythagoreans, Ovid,

Plutarch and Porphyry; famous vegetarians (on moral grounds) include Leonardo da Vinci, Benjamin Franklin (though he lapsed) and George Bernard Shaw, and writers who have deplored much of our treatment of animals as cruel, or exploitative, or unjust include Montaigne, Voltaire, Mandeville, Pope, Coleridge, Blake, Schopenhauer, Bentham, Shelley, Lewis Carroll, Robert Browning and C.S. Lewis.

It is not even quite true to say that the *growth* of moral concern about our treatment of animals is a recent development in Western moral thought. Concern has grown at least once before, in the nineteenth century, which saw the founding of anti-vivisection societies in both Britain and America, the founding of what later became the Royal Society for the Protection and Care of Animals and various vegetarian societies, and a modest rush of changes in legislation governing the treatment of animals.

However, what is true is that the nineteenth-century campaign rather fizzled out, and little was subsequently heard of moral claims on behalf of animals – until the 1970s. Since then, the animal liberation movement has grown apace, to the extent that, at least in Britain, it has made a perceivable difference in our society. If you are over forty, you might remember how many people used to wear real fur coats in the winter; you don't see many now in Britain. British supermarkets now offer free-range chickens and free-range eggs; they didn't twenty years ago. People working in university laboratories in Britain used to experiment on living creatures without any formalized constraint; now their experiments (supposedly) have to be approved by 'ethics committees'. In some circles at least, vegetarianism has increased dramatically. I never knowingly encountered a vegetarian at the philosophy conferences I went to twenty or more years ago; now they are quite common, and at some ethics conferences (particularly conferences on animal and environmental ethics) they are the rule rather than the exception.

The philosopher Peter Singer is one of the founding fathers of this modern animal liberation movement and perhaps the most famous. He was one of the earliest in the field in the 1970s, and the most influential. In 1971 there appeared a collection of articles by some of the very first people in the field called *Animals, Men and Morals* (Godlovitch, et al. (1971)). It was far from being a standard, establishment, philosophy collection (edited by two philosophy graduate students, containing articles by two novelists and other non-philosophers) and this fact, added to its very radical message, might well have lead to its being generally ignored. But Singer made the book, and its radical message, famous by reviewing it in an article – 'Animal Liberation' – in the *New York Review of Books* (Singer (1973)), that, at one blow, gave the 'animal liberation' movement its name and conferred philosophical respectability on it. Within two years, Singer published his own *Animal Liberation: a new ethics for our treatment of animals* (Singer (1975)) and has written numerous books, chapters of books, and articles in the area ever since.

Singer argues for a radical change in our treatment of animals on the basis of utilitarianism, so, in preparation for the reading, do the following exercise on utilitarianism.

EXERCISE 4
Utilitarianism

Which statement, in each of the following pairs, best expresses the views of a utilitarian?

1(a) Actions are right in proportion as they tend to promote happiness, wrong as they tend to produce the reverse of happiness.

(b) Actions are right if they are in accordance with God's law; wrong if they are forbidden by God's law.

2(a) Some actions, such as killing people, lying, and breaking promises are wrong even if they have beneficial consequences.

(b) The end justifies the means.

3(a) Freedom from coercion and interference is a natural right.

(b) Freedom from coercion and interference is right because it has beneficial consequences.

4(a) Coercive, paternalistic, intervention is right because it is the most effective way of increasing overall happiness.

(b) Coercive, paternalistic, intervention is wrong because it infringes people's liberty.

5(a) When I am trying to decide what to do I must consider the interests of all those affected by my decision, weigh them up, and adopt the course of action most likely to maximize the interests of those affected.

(b) When I am trying to decide what I ought to do I must consider the interests of all those affected by my decision and also whether I have any special duties or responsibilities in relation to any of them.

6(a) When I am trying to decide what I ought to do I must consider what the consequences of my action are likely to be.

(b) When I am trying to decide what I ought to do I must consider *only* what the consequences of my action are likely to be.

And finally, is the following statement true or false?

7 Utilitarianism is a consequentialist view.

Singer standardly contrasts utilitarianism with a theory which maintains that morality, or ethics, is a system of rules such as 'Do not lie', 'Do not kill', 'Do not steal', etc. An obvious difficulty about regarding ethics as a system of such rules is what is the right thing to do when the rules conflict? Which rule do you apply? Singer regards it as one of the great advantages of utilitarianism that it avoids this problem. He says:

> there is a long-standing approach to ethics that is quite untouched by the complexities that make simple rules difficult to apply. This is the consequentialist view. Consequentialists start not with moral rules but with goals. They assess actions by the extent to which they further these goals. The best-known... consequentialist theory is utilitarianism. The classical utilitarian regards an action as right if it produces as much or more of an increase in the happiness of all affected by it than any alternative action, and wrong if it does not.
>
> The consequences of an action vary according to the circumstances in which it is performed. Hence a utilitarian can never properly be accused of a lack of realism, or of a rigid adherence to ideals in defiance of practical experience. The utilitarian will judge lying bad in some circumstances and good in others, depending on its consequences.
>
> (Singer (1993), p.3)

The 'classical utilitarians' to whom Singer refers are the nineteenth-century ones, Bentham and Mill, who produced the classic statement of the principle of utility – 'the Greatest Happiness Principle'. It is, perhaps, a reflection of how much less optimistic we are nowadays than the British Victorians that modern utilitarians such as Singer tend to think more in terms of minimizing pain and suffering than maximizing happiness, a view known as 'negative utilitarianism'.

Another, more important, difference between Mill and Singer is that the latter explicitly mentions a 'principle of equality' as part of his utilitarianism, whereas there is no explicit mention of equality in Mill's statements of his utilitarianism. This is not at all because Mill thought that equality was unimportant; rather he thought that a principle of equality was:

> involved in the very meaning of Utility, or the Greatest Happiness Principle. That principle is a mere form of words without rational signification, unless one person's happiness, supposed equal in degree (with the proper allowance made for kind), is counted for exactly as much as another's. Those conditions being supplied, Bentham's dictum, 'everybody to count for one, nobody for more than one', might be written under the principle of utility as an explanatory commentary.
>
> (Mill, J.S. (1962 edn), p.319)

For reasons that will rapidly become obvious in the reading, Singer wants to make it absolutely explicit that when, as a utilitarian, I weigh up the interests of those who may be affected by my action, I must give those interests *equal* consideration. For his purposes, this is too important to be left implicit 'in the very meaning' of the greatest happiness principle.

'Equality for animals?'

Given the above background material, it is now time to embark on your first attempt to apply the basic reading method to a Reading from Singer. Since this is the first attempt, I think it would be best if you tackled the Singer Reading in two halves. What I am going to do shortly is ask you to do a full reading (but not yet a critical evaluation) of just the first fourteen paragraphs of the Reading, i.e. go through the first two stages of Windt's method.

Stage 1: skimming

If you can't remember what skimming involves, and what three rules you should follow when doing it, look back at pp.20–1. The questions I suggest you should have in mind are:

1 What view is Singer defending (or arguing for)?

2 What is his argument based on?

3 How does speciesism come in?

Having skimmed, you should be able to write down at least one complete sentence that begins something like this:

> Singer is defending (or 'arguing for') the view that...

Depending on how good you are at skimming, that sentence may be more or less detailed, and you might be able to write down one or two more, such as completed versions of:

> His argument is based on...
>
> He compares... to...

Stage 2: the reading outline

Then you do a careful reading, aiming to produce an outline of the passage which covers every paragraph so that you wind up with a thorough grasp of what the author has said. Then (and only then) you will be ready to read my discussion. After that, we'll go through the same procedure with the second half, and that will complete your work for this week.

READING
Singer

Even with what you know of utilitarianism and the background information on Singer above and in the Readings, you will probably still need to do more than skim the first paragraph in order to orient yourself. I would suggest reading it quite carefully and then skimming. You should not need to spend more than *five minutes* on the skimming.

Embark on a full reading of the first fourteen paragraphs of Reading 1 now.

Reading 1, paragraphs 1–14

Skimming

By skimming this Reading (and using what you knew already) you should have picked up that

> Singer is arguing for the view that much of the suffering we inflict on animals is wrong

and that

> His argument is based on the principle of equality.

Using more of what you know already about utilitarianism you might have been very thorough and written down:

> His argument is based on the (negative) utilitarian idea that we should minimize suffering, and on the principle of equality.

Given the introduction to the Reading, you should have picked up that

> He compares speciesism to racism,

and, if you are a really good at skimming, you will have picked up the idea that

> he says it is speciesism not to take the interests, or suffering, of animals into account, or not to extend the principle of equality to them, just as it is racism not to take the interests of members of races other than one's own into account.

The reading outline

Numbers refer to paragraphs. Words in quotation marks are bits of the text you might have underlined or highlighted. (I regard the following as a rather minimal outline – yours may be much fuller, but it certainly should not be slighter.)

1–3 Introduction: 'the principle of equal consideration of interests' 'cannot be limited to humans'.

4 Statement of 'the argument for extending the principle of equality beyond our own species', from humans to non-human animals.

5 'The capacity for suffering [is] the vital characteristic that entitles a being to equal consideration'.

6 'Sentience... is the only defensible boundary'.

7 Speciesism is like racism.

8 Conclusion and an objection: 'you can't equate the suffering of a person and a mouse'.

9 Reply. (I wouldn't necessarily expect you to outline the reply, but you might well identify it by underlining 'We should still apply the principle but the result... is... to give priority to relieving the greater suffering'.)

10 Further clarification of the reply.

11 Further complications. 'Non-human animals and infants and intellectually disabled humans are in the same category' as far as justifying experiments is concerned. (There is rather a lot packed into this paragraph and an adequate outline need not cover much of it. But you really should have picked out that startling claim.)

12 Summing up of the discussion of the objection in (8), and a further point – 'Sometimes animals may suffer more because of their limited understanding'.

13 Another objection: 'comparisons of the sufferings of different species are impossible to make' and reply – 'Precision is not essential'.

14 Topic of killing animals postponed for a later chapter. (There is not really any need for more under (14), since what we are concentrating on now is *this* chapter and hence the infliction of suffering on animals. We could add:

> *Conclusion* 'Pain and suffering are bad and should be prevented or minimized irrespective of the... species of the being that suffers'.)

I hope that your reading outline, like mine, picked out *major claims* – e.g. in 1–3, 5–7 and 11 – and the places where Singer (playing **devil's advocate**) considers *objections* or counter-arguments to what he is saying – e.g. in 8 and 13 – and then gives *replies* – e.g. in 9 and 13. (If it did not, then you have not yet quite caught on to what is involved in producing a reading outline which extracts the bones of the philosophical writer's arguments. Don't worry; this will come with time.)

devil's advocate

DISCUSSION

By now you may feel that you have a clear grasp of what Singer is saying in these first fourteen paragraphs. In case you do not, I am now going to run through it again. Recall that Windt's 'third stage' of the reading method – the 'critical evaluation' – involved reading a piece yet again, analysing all the details of every section (p.22 above). Reading my discussion can be regarded as your substitute for this third reading and analysis (though I do not promise to analyse *all* the details). Remember that, throughout the discussion, I am just summarizing and elaborating on what Singer says, emphasizing charitable interpretations. I am not necessarily endorsing a single sentence of it.

1–3 Singer begins with a clear statement of what he has done and is going to do. Having argued, in the previous chapter of his book, that we should accept the principle of equal consideration of interests applied to our fellow humans, he will now argue that we cannot limit its application to humans; we must extend it beyond our own species. So that's a *major claim* in the Reading, and our first thought about it should be 'So what *is* the argument? Why must we extend the principle beyond our own species?' We don't think this aggressively (principle of charity), but in a spirit of interested enquiry.

4 The argument, or answer to that question 'Why?', is introduced in this paragraph where, rather than giving the argument, Singer describes it. 'It amounts to no more than a clear understanding of the nature of the principle of equal consideration of interests'. We understand that this principle implies that we must not give unequal weight to the interests of people of different races, or different intelligence; what we may not have understood is that it implies that we must not give unequal weight to the interests of people and animals. Why?

5 Because it is the capacity for suffering that entitles a being to equal consideration, not race, nor being able to reason, nor being able to talk. Why?

Because if something – a being – has the capacity for suffering (and maybe enjoyment or happiness too) it must have an interest in not suffering (and an interest in enjoying itself or being happy too). And the principle of equality, or equal consideration of interests just says: give interests – *all* interests – equal consideration.

6 What sort of being, or creature, is utilitarianism concerned with then, when it bids us to maximize the interests of those affected by our actions, and to give equal consideration to those interests? Well, any being or creature *with* interests of course: the 'only defensible' boundary line of concern is the line between non-sentient things (like stones) which do not have interests and sentient things (which do). And the latter class includes not only us human beings, but many species of animals – certainly nearly all the ones we eat, hunt, kill for their fur and use in science. ('Certainly nearly all' not 'certainly all' – fruit flies are used in science quite a lot, but it is doubtful that they are sentient in the sense of having the capacity to suffer or enjoy.)

7 Any attempt to draw the boundary line of concern *through* the class of sentient beings is arbitrary and violates the principle of equality. Why? Well, what happens if you draw the boundary line of concern *through* the class of sentient beings, putting, for example, rational sentient beings on one side and non-rational sentient beings on the other? You say that the interests of those on one side of the line are of concern, but those on the other side are not (or are of less concern). But then you are not giving *all* the interests equal consideration. You are saying some matter more, or have more weight than others. And so you are violating the principle of equality. Drawing the boundary line between rational sentient beings and non-rational ones would be one example. Racism is another. And drawing the boundary line between human sentient beings and non-human sentient beings is just another – and is speciesism. Once you have clearly understood the principle of equal consideration of interests, it is obvious that it applies not just to human beings but to all sentient beings.

This may seem so simple that it should not take so long to establish. Why not just say, 'If morality is concerned with furthering interests (or minimizing pain or suffering) then it is concerned with further animals' interests as well as humans' interests, because they are all *interests*'? Surely, that's all the argument amounts to. This is more or less what Singer said at the outset: 'The argument... is... so simple that it amounts to no more than... the principle of equal consideration of interests' (paragraph 4). But he is undoubtedly right to spend so long on it, for a strange, but obvious, fact about us is that we often find it very hard to bring to consciousness what our sincerely spoken words commit us to. People have been saying, with passionate sincerity, 'I believe all human beings are equal' at least ever since the Stoics (from the third century BC) and simply not noticing that this committed them to the equality of slaves and their 'owners', poor and rich, blacks and whites, natives and immigrants, men and women. And, before Singer wrote, many people who had subscribed to utilitarianism, had said, with passionate sincerity, that morality was about maximizing happiness and minimizing suffering – and simply not noticed that this committed them to minimizing animal suffering as well as human.

8 Having concluded his argument for extending the principle of equality to non-human animals, Singer then turns to clarifying what the principle means in practice. This is necessary, because, when he refers to the principle briefly, as he often does, it can seem much crazier, or absurd, than in fact it is – to an uncharitable reader that is. It is worth noting that the objection Singer considers here is a perfect example of a 'weak criticism' that someone could only make if they were failing to apply the principle of charity. 'The principle of equality applies to animals'; it supports 'equality for animals' and 'equal consideration of animals' interests' – on an uncharitable reading, this is interpreted as meaning that the interests of all animals now have equal weight, leaving us with no way of choosing between the suffering of humans and, say, mice. 'But!' the uncharitable reader says triumphantly, 'that's obviously crazy/absurd – a human dying of cancer suffers much more than a mouse dying of cancer, and we ought to relieve the human before the mouse, not give them equal consideration the way Singer says we should'. (The objection here is a form of the **absurd consequences move**.)

absurd consequences move

9–12 But the objection *is* a weak criticism because Singer can escape it so easily, without undermining the main thrust of his argument. All he has to do is state his principle more fully – in the way that any charitable reader would have taken it anyway. The principle in full is that the suffering of one sentient being is to be counted equally with the *like* suffering of any other being. (We might recall (p.25) Mill's careful qualifications on Bentham's principle of equality, that 'everybody is to count as one, nobody for more than one'; that 'one person's happiness, *supposed equal in degree (with the proper allowance made for kind)* is counted for exactly as much as another's. *Those conditions being supplied,* Bentham's dictum' is just part of the very meaning of the utilitarian principle.) What has been described as 'crazy/absurd' is a case in which the suffering is not 'like' because the suffering of the human is much greater. Different species have different physiologies, nervous systems and mental capacities so it should not be surprising that when they undergo the same things – cancer, a slap, being overpowered and confined – they experience different amounts of suffering. Sometimes a human would suffer more than a non-human animal would in the same circumstances (as in the cancer case); sometimes (an important, easily overlooked point) less, as in the case of being confined. Sometimes the difference is the result of their different mental capacities (as in those two cases); sometimes the result of their different physiologies (the slapped baby, the slapped horse.)

In paragraph 11, is Singer in trouble once he admits what a difference the superior mental capacities of human beings make? Won't he have difficulty in arguing against the use of non-human animals in painful scientific experiments? Suppose that we must do the experiments, on utilitarian grounds, to relieve suffering. Isn't there an obvious argument, on utilitarian grounds, for using non-human animals rather than humans? After all, if the scientists let it be known that they were going to use us, we would all suffer acutely from terror, whereas the non-human animals don't know and hence do not suffer in that way. So their suffering and ours would not be the same: ours would be greater.

This, I think, should not be called a weak criticism because, even on the most charitable reading of Singer, it is an objection to the main thrust of his argument that comes up very naturally, and most of us are rather startled by his reply. This is that, manifestly, not *all* human beings have these superior mental capacities. *If* their not suffering anticipatory terror is an obvious reason for using non-human animals, it is equally (if we are to avoid speciesism) 'an obvious reason' for using infants and intellectually disabled human beings as well.

Many find it impossibly hard not to abandon the principle of charity at this point. How can one be charitable to someone who is claiming that we should use orphans or the intellectually disabled for scientific experiments? But before one withholds the principle, one had better be sure that the author really is making the claims in question. *Is* Singer claiming that we ought to be using orphan infants and intellectually disabled human beings in scientific experiments the way we use animals? The principle clearly requires that we make every effort to interpret him in such a way that he is not making such an outrageous, 'crazy', claim. And there is such a charitable interpretation to hand. We can interpret Singer, not as aiming to downgrade infants and the intellectually disabled to the moral level of experimental animals, but as aiming to upgrade experimental animals to the moral level of some of those helpless, innocent human beings we think of as most in need of our protection and concern, namely orphan infants and the intellectually disabled.

Indeed, once this interpretation has occurred to us, we might be rather struck, looking back, at how cautious paragraph 11 is. When you first read it, however hard you are trying to apply the principle of charity, you perhaps tend to think 'Good grief! He's saying we should use babies and the intellectually disabled for experimental purposes. The man's a raving Nazi!' But when you look at it again, in the light of the charitable interpretation, you should notice that you can't find a single sentence that does say that. '*If* we use this argument to justify experiments on non-human animals...' he says. He does not endorse the argument here. But will he elsewhere?

Reading 1, paragraphs 15–29

Although we shall still be reading the second half of the Reading charitably, we do not want to forget this question about Singer's views on the infants and the intellectually disabled humans. We should keep it at the back of our minds while we go on to a full reading of the next set of paragraphs (15–29), keeping a look out for whether he says anything more about it or relevant to it.

READING
Singer, part 2

The question you are seeking to answer as you skim is simply 'What is Singer arguing against?' Having skimmed you should be able to write down at least one complete sentence of this form:

> Singer argues against... and...

which, depending on how good you are at skimming, could be quite brief or more detailed.

How successfully did you skim last time? Would you have done better if you had used what you knew already? If so, try to make a point of using it this time. How successful was your reading outline? If it was very unlike mine, try to bring out explicitly where arguments, objections and replies occur.

You should not need to spend more than two minutes on the skimming.

Please embark on a full reading of Reading 1, paragraphs 15–29.

Skimming

Singer is so helpful with his sub-headings that you can get quite a good idea of what he is on about in these paragraphs just from noting them (and using what you know) which takes a matter of seconds. The sub-headings make it clear that he is going to discuss animals as food and their use in scientific experiments. And, from the first fourteen paragraphs, you would not expect him to argue in favour of these. So, reading nothing but the sub-headings you could come up with:

> Singer argues against our using animals for food and in experiments

and that would be enough. This indicates that, if you spent more than two minutes on the skimming, you are making unnecessarily heavy weather of it. It would be a good idea to try practising it on other things you read.

If you read just a little more than the sub-headings, looking at the beginnings and endings of paragraphs, you might have come up with more detail, such as:

> Singer argues against our using animals for food but not for total vegetarianism and for a great reduction in the number of experiments performed on animals but not a total ban.

To have got this would be really excellent.

Reading outline

15 Introduction to the discussion of our use of animals for food.

16–17 First argument against using animals for food. *Our* ('citizens of industrialized societies') interest in eating flesh is 'a relatively minor interest', a luxury – we like it, but we don't need it.

18 Second argument against using animals for food. 'Animals are made to lead miserable lives so that their flesh costs less'.

19 What follows from these arguments (practical upshots). We should not eat meat 'unless we know... [it] was not produced by factory farm methods' nor eggs unless they are free range.

20–1 *These* arguments 'do not take us all the way to a vegetarian diet'. What if the animal has not suffered at all (an objection someone might make to Singer)? Further argument which 'brings us close to a vegetarian way of life'. (I wouldn't necessarily expect you to outline the argument because it is not easy to find a single bit to underline and so you would have to paraphrase.) We ('those of us living in cities') can't know an animal has not suffered.

22 Introduction to the discussion of our use of animals in experiments.

23–5 Argument against many experiments on animals – many 'are not necessary to prevent human suffering' (22), they do not 'relieve more suffering than they inflict' (24).

26 Conclusion (which then serves as a premise for the next step) – 'the benefits to humans are either non-existent or uncertain, while the losses to members of other species are certain and real'.

Conclusion from that: these experiments are wrong.

27 An objection – what if 'thousands [would] die' unless one animal was experimented on? (Note that this is an attempt to refute Singer by the **absurd consequences move**). Reply – use the animal.

absurd consequences move

28 A hypothetical question for the objector – would you use a brain-damaged orphan to save thousands? (Note that this is a form of the ***tu quoque*** or **companions in guilt move**.) Further argument against many experiments on animals – those for which 'experimenters are not prepared to use... human beings at an equal or lower level of sentience etc.' This shows a speciesist bias.

tu quoque

companions in guilt move

29 Concluding remarks: similar arguments can be used against 'the fur trade, hunting in all its different forms etc.'

DISCUSSION

As before, what follows here is a discussion of what you have just read. Again, remember that I am summarizing and elaborating on what Singer says, not endorsing any of it.

The first half of Singer aimed to show that failing to give equal consideration to the suffering of animals was speciesist and hence wrong. The aim of this section, as its title indicates, is to show that some of our practices are speciesist, that is, that they violate the principle of equal consideration of interests, and are hence wrong.

15 The first practice to be considered is our use of animals for food.

16–17 The Inuit (Eskimo) might be able to defend their use of animals for food as non-speciesist by claiming that their interest in surviving is greater than that of the animals they kill. But our only relevant interest is in luxury. Meat eating is not a necessity for us. (Indeed – though Singer does not say so here – much medical evidence supports the view that we would be healthier if we didn't eat meat.) It cannot even be defended on grounds of efficiency. The use of animals for human food in our society reflects our willingness to allow our minor interest in luxury to override the major interests of the animals in question; it is thus speciesist, because we are not allowing the interests of the animals to count with their real weight.

18–19 Moreover, in using animals for food, we do not merely kill them, but make many of them suffer terribly in order to make their flesh available at the lowest possible cost. What, morally, ought we to do about this? 'Stop these practices' – but note that Singer does not go on to advocate anything extreme such as sending letter bombs to the owners of battery farms or attempting to prevent the export of live veal calves. He recommends only that we stop these practices by withdrawing our support from the factory farmers; if enough of us do this, the practices will cease. So we should not buy factory-farmed meat or battery-farm eggs.

19–21 The arguments so far support being a vegetarian if the only shops you can get to sell nothing but factory-farmed meat, poultry and eggs. But if (as many shops now do) they offer you a choice between factory-farmed and free-range you might, for all that has been said so far, just become a discriminating shopper, not a vegetarian. So Singer considers a further argument.

devil's advocate

He admits that the lives of free-ranging animals do not involve anything like as much suffering as those of animals reared in factory farms. But, in order to bring them cheaply to our dinner table, suffering *is* inflicted on them – and their interests thereby ignored. And this is speciesism – not taking their interests into account. (True, we not only make them suffer but kill them, but he is not talking about killing yet.) Well (playing **devil's advocate**) what if there are some 'green' small-scale farmers who do not inflict any of this suffering on their animals and kill them 'humanely' (as we say); then, pending the discussion of killing, it seems that Singer would have no objection to what they do. Nor would he object to our eating the meat they produced – *if* we knew it was produced without suffering. But there's the rub for most of us. Unless we personally know the farmer we buy the meat from, how could we know such a thing? We can't, so to avoid speciesism most of us should become vegetarian.

ad hominem **(in the second sense)**

22 This introduction to the subject of experimenting on animals could be read as an ***ad hominem*** argument demonstrating the inconsistency of some scientists who experiment on animals. There are those who seek to distance themselves from what they are doing by insisting that the other animals are not like us, that there is an absolute and fundamental difference between them and us. But, in many cases, there would not be any point to their experiments if this were true! To be consistent they must agree that the animals they are experimenting on *are* like us – insofar as, for instance, they suffer, or feel stress, or want food when they have not eaten for some time.

23–5 The comfortable belief that all, or most animal experiments are 'vital' is simply false. Many are unnecessary (testing new cosmetics, food colourings, shampoos); many do not benefit humans at all; many just might, conceivably, somehow, one day, but no better. And animals suffer in them, often quite terribly. A few, illustrative examples lead him to the conclusion that:

26 many experiments cannot be justified on the grounds that they relieve more suffering than they cause. They are not needed to, or just do not, relieve much human suffering and they cause a lot of animal suffering. So – final conclusion, using that as a premise – our use of animals in all such experiments is speciesist; the interests of the animals are not being considered at all, for if they were, there would be no human interests that had any chance of outweighing them.

27 An objection often made to anti-vivisectionists takes the form, as I noted, of an attempt to reduce their position to absurdity. 'You say we should not use animals in experiments?' they say. 'You have to be wrong. What if thousands of humans could be spared frightful suffering by experimenting on just one animal. It would be absurd to say that was wrong.' But this fails as an objection to Singer. Whoever said, 'We should never use an animal in an experiment, ever, no matter what beneficial consequences would result from doing so, because it is intrinsically wrong'? Not Singer the utilitarian, the philosopher who believes that an act is right if it produces the best consequences. As an objection to Singer, this would be attacking a **straw man**, and violate the principle of charity. **straw man**

28 Singer then neatly turns the question back on his opponents. Are they really convinced it would not be wrong to experiment on the one if that means saving thousands from suffering? Would they like to think again? What if the 'one' were an orphaned human being with severe irreversible brain damage? If the opponents now say experimenting on the orphan would be wrong, even to save thousands, then either they have lost their rhetorical question or revealed themselves to be blatant speciesists.

Singer then generalizes the point. Consider all the experiments that actually would relieve more suffering than they caused. These would be justifiable on utilitarian grounds. But they would be justifiable as experiments on some human beings too. Utilitarianism demands that we minimize suffering and the principle of equality demands that the animals' suffering be taken into account too. So if an experiment that would relieve more suffering than it caused could use either an irreversibly brain-damaged human or, say, a cat, and the cat would suffer more than the human, then the experimenter should use the human. If he is not prepared to, then, to avoid speciesism, he should not be prepared to use the cat either.

I will admit that it is not clear to me what Singer's conclusion means – 'If this bias [speciesism] were eliminated the number of experiments performed on animals would be greatly reduced'. Does he mean they would be reduced because, free of speciesism and accepting utilitarianism, the experimenters would use lots of humans instead – same number of experiments, but far fewer on animals? Or does he mean that, upgrading experimental animals to the moral level of some particularly helpless human beings, the scientists will realize that they are not dedicated utilitarians, cannot stomach inflicting suffering in order to relieve it and drastically cut down on their number of experiments – hence far fewer on animals? We will return to this puzzle in the next chapter.

29 Singer concludes by listing the many other areas in which he thinks our current practices embody speciesism and claims that the philosophical questions raised by these are basically the same as those already considered.

Conclusion

In this chapter, we have looked at some of Singer's arguments against much of our treatment of animals, those that emphasize the amount of suffering involved in it. In accordance with the principle of charity, we have concentrated on getting clear about what he actually says (and does not say) before beginning to criticize him. It is to that task that we shall turn in the next chapter.

Chapter summary

Reading philosophy

Reading philosophy necessitates reading carefully. This often involves applying the principle of charity, ensuring that we find a reasonable or plausible interpretation of what the author is saying. If we are being charitable, we will not interpret the author in such a way that she is open to weak criticisms, nor will we be ready to ascribe self-contradiction to her, nor to put words in her mouth and interpret her as saying implausible things that she did not say. A good method for mastering a particular piece of philosophy is to skim first and then to do a reading outline.

Singer in defence of animals

We have been applying both the principle of charity and the reading method to a piece by Peter Singer. Singer argues against our using animals for food in the way most of us (not necessarily the Inuit or 'green', humane farmers) do. He also argues against our use of animals in experiments. In both cases, he appeals to the negative utilitarian principle that we ought to minimize suffering, and to the principle of equality. The latter claims that the interests or suffering of one sentient being (e.g. an animal) are to be counted equally with the like suffering of any other being (e.g. a human). Singer believes that limiting the principle of equality to human beings is speciesism, which is akin to racism and sexism and thereby wrong.

Much more broadly, but still accurately, we might say the following: that Singer argues against much of our treatment of animals on the grounds that such treatment results in a great deal of animal suffering, and that animal suffering *matters*: it is something that, morally speaking, we ought to take seriously.

Further reading

Peter Singer's first book *Animal Liberation: a new ethics for our treatment of animals*, Random House, 1975, is still a stirring – and for many, a disturbing – read, containing many details of what was, at the time, common practice in animal experimentation and factory-farming. It emphasizes his rejection of speciesism, rather than his utilitarianism. Richard Ryder's *Victims of Science: the use of animals in research*, revised edn, National Anti-vivisection Society, 1983, first published 1975, also argues against speciesism and describes the history of animal experimentation as well as current practice at the time. The extent to which things have not changed very much can be gathered from *Brute Science,* by Hugh La Follette and Niall Shanks, Routledge, 1996.

Notes

[1] Human beings are, of course, animals themselves – hence the title of this book – and some writers make a point of talking always of the contrast between us and 'non-human animals'. I have followed the more standard convention of using the word 'animal' to mean 'animals of other species than the human'.

Criticizing Singer

OBJECTIVES

When you have worked though this chapter you should have:

- Developed your ability to criticize a philosophical position.
- Appreciated the relative strengths and weaknesses of various criticisms of Singer's position.
- Understood Singer's utilitarian position on killing.
- Become familiar with absurd consequences moves and grasped how to work out whether they set up a straw man.
- Understood what is involved in playing author's advocate.

In this chapter we shall be considering, in some depth and detail, criticisms that can be made of Singer's position on vegetarianism and on using animals in science. We shall also be exploring further two issues remaining from the previous chapter – what does he say about killing animals and where does he stand on using humans instead of animals as experimental subjects?

Singer's argument to vegetarianism

In the previous chapter you were encouraged to become more pro-active and independent in your reading, but in this chapter you will try to develop your ability to criticize what you have read. Instead of being told what the major criticisms of Singer are and then considering them, you will be given a set of exercises concerning criticisms. We will begin by tackling his argument about vegetarianism (Reading 1, paragraphs 15–21), leaving his argument against using animals in experiments until later.

EXERCISE 5
Criticizing Singer on vegetarianism

The point of this exercise, and the long discussion that follows it, is to encourage you to assess some ways of objecting to Singer, developing your ability to set about criticizing a philosophical position. The exercise including the discussion, which will involve looking back at parts of the exercise, reconsidering your answers, and thinking about what you have learnt, may well take an hour.

I am going to give you a list of possible initial responses to the instruction 'Tell me how you would set about criticizing what Singer says (in the reading) about vegetarianism'. They are all one-sentence responses which you should grade according to how well they represent good ways to set about philosophical criticism. Grade the responses according to the following system but note that you don't have to be particularly charitable.

A = excellent.

B = very good.

C = promising initial response which *might* turn into something good – though it might well turn into something bad.

D = not much good/poorish.

F = bad.

1 This is all rubbish; there's nothing wrong with me not being a vegetarian.

2 There may be something in what he says – it all sounds quite reasonable – but I am not convinced.

3 I am a vegetarian for religious reasons, so, although I agree with Singer's conclusion, I do not accept his argument.

4 I shall construct a counter-example to Singer's conclusion, to show it is false.

5 I shall construct a counter-example to Singer's argument, describing a set-up in which his premises are true but his conclusion false and thereby show that his argument is invalid.

6 I shall argue against his premise that animals suffer much as a result of our using them for food, thus showing that, even if his argument is valid, we do not need to accept his conclusion, because the argument is not sound.

7 How do we know that animals can feel pain?

8 I shall argue against his premise that equal consideration should be given to the like interests of *all* sentient beings, regardless of species (thus showing... etc.)

9 I shall construct an argument showing that Singer's conclusion is false, because we are all morally justified in eating meat if we want to.

10 Animals eat each other, so why shouldn't we eat them?

Check your answers against those at the back of the book before reading on.

DISCUSSION

You might like to practise skimming on this discussion before reading it thoroughly. You are looking for a rough idea of why I give the grades I do to some of the responses and what is going to happen at the end of the discussion. The discussion ends on p.45.

I have allowed different answers to half the questions because most are the ones in which I give the harsher grades because of the special knowledge I have as a teacher of philosophy, which I do not expect you to have. As I explain in the discussion, experience has taught me that certain ways of starting off nearly always develop badly, and I want to warn you off them.

1 F. It is not a *critical* response at all but just switching off and immediately abandoning the working hypothesis required by the principle of charity.

2 F. It counts as bad to me, because, like 1 it is not in accordance with the instruction. Indeed, I take it to be the same response as 1 merely disguised as sweet reasonableness. (*Why* aren't they convinced if it is so reasonable? If they have an objection to it let's hear it.) Being excessively charitable, you might have imagined that, in its sweet reasonableness, it isn't as bad as 1.

3 D. I would say it is not much good: it's too like 2. In what way is this person applying the working hypothesis of the principle of charity? *Why* doesn't she accept Singer's argument I want to know? What's her objection to it? (For all we know, she hasn't got one: if she bothered to treat him with charity, she might wind up with two arguments for her vegetarianism, her own and Singer's!)

4 D. I might *just* allow this to be a promising initial response. But more likely it is doomed to failure and is going to develop into a really weak criticism (p.17). Singer's conclusion, properly spelt out, was, after all, no broad, unqualified generalization. It wasn't 'No one should ever eat meat'. It is easy to find counter-examples to that, e.g. 'People who must eat meat or starve are morally justified in eating meat'. But Singer explicitly considers just such an example (the Inuit (Eskimo)) and accepts it. Nor will it do to construct the case in which the 'green' humane farmer and her family eventually kill their pampered pig and eat it. He has explicitly considered this sort of example too and accepted it – pending the discussion of killing. (The green farmer knows the pig hasn't suffered.) Nor will it do to construct the case in which I pick up the dead rabbit or pheasant from the road and take that home for the pot. He hasn't considered that sort of case but it is easy to imagine someone accepting it on Singer's behalf, because it does *not* show that his conclusion is false. However we express his conclusion, we know that it principally concerns

'those of us living in cities' – most of *us* – and does not go so far as to say that even those of who live in cities should *never* eat meat. His conclusion is, roughly, '*Most* of us should be vegetarian *most* of the time' – and it is very hard to come up with counter-examples to that sort of claim.

5 A. This is excellent according to me. Only as an *initial* response of course – the attempt may prove a failure. But all the responses are initial; comparing them, this is as good a way to set about criticizing Singer's argument as one could possibly have.

6 F. It may sound very harsh, but I would mark this downright bad, though I wouldn't expect you to. Why? Not so much because the facts about the suffering many animals undergo as part of the food-production process are well-known and available to everyone (though they are) but because someone who starts off this way is immediately turning away from philosophical argument and embarking on a long listing of (putative) **empirical** facts – about animal husbandry, laws governing the transport of animals, checks on battery farms, and so on. The objection is going to need pages of such material to be well-grounded – and none of it will be philosophy. But philosophy is what we are doing. So this would be a downright bad way to start. If you disagree with an author's empirical premise, the best way to start is just let him have it as a supposition, and look for something else to criticize. (Of course, if you can't find anything else wrong, you may have to come back to it as a last resort. But you usually can.)

empirical

7 D. I call this poorish, though once again, I am relying on my special knowledge. One criticism you could have made of it is that it does not really follow the instruction 'Tell me how you would set about criticizing Singer's argument'. To obey that instruction, it should mention the relevant part of his argument and say something like 'I shall argue that Singer's premise that animals can feel pain is questionable'. Then, as an *initial* response, it does not suffer from the same fault as 6, for someone who responds this way *might* be thinking of producing a philosophical argument for the view that animals cannot suffer. (We shall be looking at such an argument in a later chapter). So you might well have given it a C.

I mark it lower, for several reasons. For a start, any student who is aiming to come up with an abstract philosophical argument to the conclusion that animals can't feel pain is aiming not just to run but to break the 400-metre hurdle record before they can walk. The chances are quite high they will get distracted into arguing for a different conclusion – 'We can't *know* that animals feel pain' – and fail to notice that their argument also supports the conclusion that I can't know that any human apart from me feels pain either. (This is a common mistake.)

Moreover, it is likely that this student is not thinking of producing an abstract argument but *is*, in fact, going to suffer from the same fault as 6, i.e. produce a long list of (putative) empirical facts to show that animals do not feel pain. This time they will be about physiology or the way the brain works and how different our brains are from animal brains and so on. Once again, denying or questioning such a premise should be a last resort.

8 A. Excellent; same comments as for 5.

9 B. Good, but not as good as 5 and 8. Why not? Well, suppose the initial response is developed as well as it possibly could be, so we wind up with a really good argument supporting the conclusion that we are all morally justified in eating meat if we want to. Suppose I produce this argument. Can I, or you, conclude 'Well, that's done Singer in'? No, because I haven't 'done Singer in'. All I have produced is a stand-off situation, or a draw or a stalemate. Here's this (we are supposing) good argument of mine to one conclusion. Here's this other (we are assuming, by the principle of charity) good argument of Singer to a contrary conclusion. That's all we have so far – nothing to support the conclusion that my argument is *better* than Singer's. That's still an open question. (One thing we know for sure – it's not better just because it has reached the conclusion most of us want.)

Of course, my argument *might* be better – in (as always) either or both of two ways. (a) Maybe all my premises are more plausible than at least one of his. (b) Maybe my argument is valid whereas his is not. (Or, maybe they are both strictly invalid, but mine contains less serious flaws than his.) So to show that my argument is better, I have to argue for (a) or (b). (a) is going to involve arguing against one of Singer's premises – so I might as well go straight for 5. (b) is going to involve finding a flaw in his argument – so I might as well go straight for 8. After all, if I cannot pull off something at least akin to 5 or 8, my laborious attempts at 9 are really wasted effort. So I had better have a go at one of them.

10 F. Bad – not least because it is so unclear what it means. Is it asking why we shouldn't behave the way animals do? Surely not. Are we meant to understand it as claiming that we are justified in eating animals because they eat each other? That seems odd – we are justified in eating cows, sheep and chicken because lions and tigers do? There are various other silly things it could mean, and one that, though rather poor, is not actually silly, which we will consider later.

What can you learn from this exercise?

Although I gave you a way of marking yourself on this exercise, your marks are far less important than what you can learn from it. There is at least one very simple general rule you can take away from it, namely: when you set about criticizing someone's argument, aim to begin with 'I shall argue ...' or 'I shall construct a counter-example/an argument ...' – do *not* begin the way 1, 2, 3, 7 and 10 began. Although this is a simple, even a mechanical, rule, it is a very useful one to follow.

However, as some of the grades indicate, it is no guarantee of success. Having begun in that mechanical way, you then have to consider how you are going to go on. The discussion yields another fairly simple general rule which will sometimes save you from going astray, namely – do not begin by arguing against an author's empirical premises; look for something else to criticize first and only argue against an empirical premise as a last resort. (Cf. the discussion of 6 and 7. We will look at a qualification on this rule in the next few pages.) But if you can argue against a non-empirical premise (as in 8) that is, quite generally, an excellent way to begin.

As the grades indicate, constructing a counter-example (describing a set-up in which the premises are accepted as true but the conclusion is false) to show that the argument is invalid is also, quite generally, an excellent way to begin.

As the grades do *not* indicate, constructing a counter-example to the conclusion is quite often a good way to begin, comparable to 9. (Can you see why it is like 9? Constructing such a counter-example is a way of showing – a mini-argument to show – that the conclusion is false.) It was not a good way to begin in this particular case, because of the qualified nature of Singer's conclusion – 'Most of us should be vegetarian most of the time'. What 4 reminds us of is the importance of the principle of charity – if you aim to construct a counter-example to an author's conclusion, be very careful to get his conclusion right – as the principle of charity requires.

These are the general points you can learn from the exercise. What I hope is that you may also have learned some more specific points about your own objections to Singer, if you had, yourself, come up with some of the same responses 1–10. This concludes the exercise and its extended discussion.

Further objections

The preceding exercise suggested some approaches to criticizing Singer. We have seen that one of the best, 8, opted for arguing against his premise that equal consideration should be given to the like interests of all sentient beings –

what we might call the 'anti-speciesism' premise. Although you may feel certain that this premise *is* false, it turns out to be surprisingly hard to argue against, and I am delaying discussion of it until much later (Chapter 5). The other excellent approach, 5, opted for showing that Singer's argument is invalid. This too is tricky, but we will shortly look at two attempts. Before we do so, we will explore a few more poorish objections to get them out of the way.

The pseudo-Darwin objection

I said above that the vague 'Animals eat each other, so why shouldn't we eat them?' question might have been groping for something that, though rather poor, was not actually silly. We could try turning it into something more like 9 – an argument for a conclusion that was the opposite of Singer's. How would that work? Something like this:

Premise 1	By the Darwinian law of natural selection, stronger, fitter-for-survival creatures prey on weaker, less fit-for-survival creatures.
Premise 2	In using animals for food the way we do, we are just doing what is natural.
Conclusion	We are all justified in eating meat if we want to.

Unfortunately, though we have turned 10 into a good approach, the argument is distinctly poor. Here is what Singer says about it:

> [it] makes two basic mistakes, one a mistake of fact and the other an error of reasoning. The factual mistake lies in the assumption [Premise 2] that our own consumption of animals is part of the natural evolutionary process. This might be true of a few primitive cultures which still hunt for food, but it has nothing to do with the mass production of domestic animals in factory farms.
>
> Suppose that we did hunt for our food, though, and this was part of some natural evolutionary process. There would still be an error of reasoning in the assumption that because this process is natural it is right. It is, no doubt, 'natural' for women to produce an infant every year or two from puberty to menopause, but this does not mean that it is wrong to interfere with this process. We need to know the natural laws that affect us in order to estimate the consequences of what we do; but we do not have to assume that the natural way of doing something is incapable of improvement.
>
> (Singer (1993), pp.71–2)

There are several interesting points to note about Singer's reply. One is that he does not bother to attack the empirical Premise 1 which is, as a matter of fact, quite wrong about what Darwinism says (as you will see later in the course, in Book 4) – fleas prey on us but are hardly, thereby, stronger and fitter-for-survival. The second is that he *does* attack Premise 2 as an empirical premise, but in a special way. Look at the way he does it. Unlike an attack on Premise 1, which would call for a lengthy discussion of Darwinism (my parenthetical remark about fleas is just a clue about how such discussion proceeds), he can dispose of Premise 2 in a single sentence. His attack on the 'mistake of fact' in Premise 2 does not need to call on pages of facts about human beings' consumption of animals. What it does is point to the obvious gap between saying 'Strong fit animals (e.g. human beings) naturally prey on less fit animals (e.g. chickens)' and 'Strong fit animals (e.g. human beings) naturally buy less fit animals (e.g. chickens) at the supermarket'. If you can 'knock off' an empirical premise in a single sentence, that is worth doing. (This is the qualification on the simple rule about not attacking empirical premises that I mentioned above.)

But the third thing to notice is that, even with a one-sentence refutation of the empirical premise, Singer does not think that the argument rests there. What is really important is the 'error in reasoning', to which he devotes a whole paragraph. *That* is the really important thing. (And just how important this particular error in reasoning is, again, is something you will be studying in Book 4.)

Absurd consequences objections

There are several objections to Singer which aim to show that his conclusion has **absurd consequences**. These too can be regarded as a version of the approach in 9 – as an argument to show that Singer's conclusion is false. So as an *approach,* it is good – but whether or not it works is a different matter.

absurd consequences move

EXERCISE 6
Absurd consequences

Consider the following three attempts to show that Singer's conclusion has absurd consequences and decide in each case whether it is a good criticism, or whether its sets up a **straw man**.

straw man

1 Of course, other things being equal, it would be morally preferable to reduce animal suffering. But other things are never equal. Questions about human diet involve not only the interests of individual animals, but also vital environmental and human concerns. On the one hand, as Singer points out, it might be more efficient if food suitable for animal consumption were not fed to meat-producing animals. On the other hand, a mass conversion of humanity to vegetarianism would represent an increase in the efficiency of the conversion of solar energy from plant to human biomass with the likely result that the human population would continue to expand and, in the process, to cause greater environmental destruction than might occur otherwise. The issue is an enormously complex one, and

cannot be solved by any simple appeal to the claim that animals have interests which deserve equal consideration.

(a) Good criticism.

(b) Straw man: misrepresents Singer as arguing for a mass overnight conversion to vegetarianism rather than each of us joining a collective practice that will, we hope, slowly but surely change our economic and social organization, as we keep a watchful eye on the environment.

2 Singer seems unaware of the fact that there are many circumstances in which using animal food products is not a luxury, as he says, but a necessity. Anyone who works in healthcare knows that these are frequently essential to building up or maintaining patients' strength when they are fighting cancer, recovering from major surgery, or trying to get past anorexia. Are we supposed just to let these people die?

(a) Good criticism.

(b) Straw man: misrepresents Singer as claiming that human interest in surviving cannot override interests of animals, a claim he explicitly disavows when considering the case of the Inuit.

3 It's easy to see that Singer has never had to cope with feeding three children and a husband, let alone at the end of working day and on a tight budget. My children would love to be vegetarian – if that meant eating nothing but sweets, crisps and chips! As it is, I'm grateful if I can get them to eat chicken – and unlike Singer, I can't afford to buy free range unless I force my family to go without lots of other things. It costs three times as much in case he hasn't noticed. If I were in Singer's position, then I might well be vegetarian, but as things are, it's completely impractical. Besides, I don't think I have any right to impose vegetarianism on my children and husband even if I could!

(a) Good criticism (though not very well expressed.)

(b) Straw man: misrepresents Singer as arguing for my forcing other people to be vegetarian, rather than my just becoming vegetarian myself.

Check your answers against those at the back of the book before reading on.

Two attempts to show that Singer's argument is invalid

As I said above, trying to show that Singer's argument is invalid is tricky. It requires describing a set up in which his premises are true, but his conclusion false and if we try to set about doing that in a vacuum, we usually do not know where to start. What is more usual is that we start with a rather inchoate idea that there is something wrong with the argument somewhere which, without our realizing it, can be developed into this excellent form of criticism. But the development often takes quite a lot of patience. I think that 3 is on to something, but, as you will see, it takes some teasing out.

The 'No woman is an island' objection

One reason why 3 is not well expressed is that it is not clear what the 'absurd consequence' is supposed to be. (A really good statement of an absurd consequences move should begin with something like 'Singer's position has the absurd consequence that ...') As a guess, it is 'Singer's position has the absurd consequence that I ought to become vegetarian and thereby impose my vegetarianism on others'.

Suppose Singer defends himself as in 3(b), maintaining that this is attacking a straw man. 'I am saying that *you* ought to become vegetarian', he says, 'not that you ought to impose your vegetarianism on anyone else'. But then one can see that the writer of 3 has a good point. Unless you live alone, it is difficult to become a vegetarian without 'imposing' it, in some sense, on anyone else. It is difficult to draw a line between the actions that only affect yourself and those that also affect others (cf. Book 1, pp.68–70). People who live together usually eat together and share their meals. Neither insisting that everyone else joins you in vegetarianism nor sitting at table with a bowl of lentil soup while everyone else is eating Christmas turkey makes for familial or social unity. If I become vegetarian, the people I share my life with just *are* affected; I shan't be able to avoid imposing it on them.

This makes 3 into quite a nice absurd consequences move. But, as Nigel Warburton notes, the 'problem with using the absurd consequences move is that ... one person's absurdity is another's common sense' (Warburton (1996), p.2). Why couldn't Singer just say that the woman writing in 3 should impose her vegetarianism on her family? She says she thinks she has no right to do so, but, as a utilitarian, Singer is not concerned with rights, only with the consequences of actions. If she imposes vegetarianism on her family, animal suffering will be reduced as a consequence – so she ought to do it.

At this point, you may be able to see how we could turn this objection into a more powerful one – an objection that takes the form of showing that Singer's argument is invalid. Suppose we did not bring in rights but accepted Singer's utilitarianism and brought in the interests of the woman's family.

A utilitarian will judge eating meat bad in some circumstances and good in others, depending on its consequences. When we are deciding what to do, we should weigh up the interests of those *affected* by our decision. If my becoming vegetarian is going to affect my children and partner seriously, making the children unhappy and bewildered ('*Why* can't I have chicken on my birthday') and my partner angry and alienated, then it may well be that, on utilitarian grounds, I should not become vegetarian – or at least, not yet, or overnight. And the same will be true of anyone else whose decision to become vegetarian would affect those they live with in a similar way – so they should not become vegetarian, or at least not yet, or overnight.

This is shaping up to showing that Singer's argument is invalid. If we take his conclusion to be 'Most of us should be vegetarian most of the time' then his position has taken a severe knock. Although, as I said above, it is not easy to find counter-examples to qualified generalizations that begin with 'Most' rather than 'All' it looks as though we are coming close to finding one. For 'most of us' do indeed live together and eat together, and whether we are the main cook or a member of the family making demands on the main cook, it seems that Singer will have to admit that his conclusion has been refuted – on the basis of his own premises. Singer's premises are:

Premise 1	We should aim to minimize suffering (the utilitarian premise, which we have used).
Premise 2	We should give equal consideration to the suffering of animals (the principle of equality, or anti-speciesism premise, which we have not denied).
Premise 3	Animal suffering is involved in enabling us to eat meat (which we have not denied).
Premise 4	For most of us, the minor 'suffering' involved in *our* becoming vegetarian is outweighed by the suffering of the animals involved.

We have not denied Premise 4. What we have done is showed that it is not strong enough to do the job Singer wanted it to do. It may well be true of most of us, individually, that *I* wouldn't suffer much, if at all, and nor would you, nor Nigel, nor Janet... – but our families would, and quite possibly enough to override the suffering of the animals involved. So Singer's premises could all be true and the conclusion false. Far from its being the case that most of us should be vegetarian most of the time, it turns out that most of us should go on the way we are, to avoid upsetting our families.

Evaluating the objection

How good an objection to Singer is this? Its overall strategy – showing his argument to be invalid – is excellent, but does it work in this case? The way to assess it is to think of what Singer could say in reply. Remembering that Singer is aiming to convert us, to get us to change the way we behave in relation to eating animals, try to think of what he could say to escape the objection.

Singer could easily escape this objection by amending his conclusion to 'Most of us should aim to cut down on eating meat and favour free-range products, encourage those we know to do the same, and eventually become vegetarian'. And now the question is: Does this leave the main thrust of his argument intact, showing that, ultimately, this objection winds up as a 'weak criticism' (p.17)?

I would say that was rather a moot point. The amended conclusion is much less radical than the bold 'most of us should become totally (or nearly totally – there's still the case where you run down the pheasant accidentally) vegetarian immediately' – we might say that it amounts to a substantial concession, and that the criticism, far from being weak, has hit home.

But, being honest, we should admit that even the amended version is pretty radical for most of us. It is still insisting that most of us should change the way we behave in relation to eating animals. Statistics indicate that many, if not most of us are cutting down on eating meat, but few of us are entertaining the idea of becoming total vegetarians eventually. And most of us are not using the money we save on not buying meat to buy free-range chicken and eggs rather than battery-produced ones, as Singer would clearly require, because we are cutting down on health grounds rather than moral ones. So even the amended version of Singer's conclusion, if we are honest about it, is an uncomfortable one for most of us, and we cannot claim that we have managed to find a powerful objection to *that.*

So I would conclude that 3 is a good objection – it hits Singer where it hurts one might say, forcing a substantial concession out of him – but not, ultimately, a conclusive one; he still has a well-supported position which is an uncomfortable one for most of us.

Playing author's advocate

In the above discussion, I relied on a technique in argument to which we should give a name – 'playing author's advocate', on the model of playing **devil's advocate**. It was this: several times, in the course of discussing a particular objection to Singer, I brought in something that *he could say* in reply, to show that, according to him, the objection failed in some way. I spoke as his advocate.

devil's advocate

You might think that playing author's advocate is just applying the principle of charity and that certainly shows that you have caught on to its basic idea. But it really is a little different and that is why it needs a name of its own. The principle of charity is a principle governing interpretation of what an author actually says, making sure that you do not interpret him as saying, for example, 'No one should ever eat meat' when he does not. It concerns getting what the author means right before you go on to criticize him. But playing author's advocate is going beyond interpretation and the identification of an author's arguments – 'What Singer argues is this...' or 'The way Singer replies to this objection is...' It is actually thinking of arguments or replies for yourself – 'What Singer *could* argue or reply is this...' – on the author's behalf.

EXERCISE 7
Playing author's advocate

1 Turn back to pp.42–3 and look at the discussion of 4. In which of the three objections to the three counter-examples am I playing author's advocate?

2 Turn back to p.51 and look at the second paragraph beginning 'Singer could easily escape...'. Am I playing author's advocate here? Yes or no?

3 Suppose that I had said that Singer could escape the objection by amending his conclusion to 'A few of us should aim to cut down on eating meat'. Would I have been playing author's advocate? Yes or no?

Check your answers against those at the back of the book before reading on.

The 'I do not cause any suffering' objection

We have just developed the 'no woman is an island' objection into an attempt to show that Singer's argument is invalid. Such an attempt requires showing that, even if we accept Singer's premises, we do not have to accept his conclusion, because it does not follow – in this case, we argued that Singer's conclusion would be false. As we saw, Singer could produce an *amended* conclusion which escapes this objection. Can we show that the argument leading to the amended conclusion is invalid? The premises are as before:

Premise 1	We should aim to minimize suffering.
Premise 2	We should give equal consideration to the suffering of animals.
Premise 3	Animal suffering is involved in enabling us to eat meat.
Premise 4	For most of us, the minor 'suffering' involved in our becoming vegetarian is outweighed by the suffering of the animals involved.

but the conclusion is now:

Conclusion	Most of us should aim to cut down on eating meat, encourage those we know to do the same, and eventually become vegetarian.

It looks a tough proposition, but let's try the following. Look again at Premise 2.

When are we supposed to give equal consideration to the interests of animals? Well, when we are deciding whether what we are about to do is right or wrong of course – that's what moral principles are for, to provide us with moral reasons for and against acting in certain ways. Are we supposed to give equal consideration to the interests of animals *whenever* we are deciding whether what we are about to do is right or wrong? No, because a lot of the time what I am thinking of doing isn't going to have any effect on animals at all. Should I tell a hurtful truth or not? Put bottles in the bottle bank or not bother? Give to Oxfam or not? I have to decide, but I don't have to consider the interests of animals while doing so, because whatever I do isn't going to affect them.

So here I am, a town-dweller in the supermarket, shopping for dinner. Should I buy meat or not? Singer requires that I take the suffering of animals in the food-production process into account. But hold on – why should I? What is in front of me is not a live animal, confined and terrified, whose suffering I should take into account. In front of me are just a lot of pieces of inanimate meat. The suffering of the animals that went into producing them is all in the past and nothing I do one way or the other can make it better or worse. If I buy a piece of meat, I buy something which is the result of suffering, but I don't cause any animal to suffer. My buying the meat won't affect the interests of any living animal, any more than my telling someone the truth or not bothering with the bottle bank will. So I don't have to consider the interests of animals here and now, even according to Singer, because *my* action is not going to affect them. *I'm* not causing any suffering. So I buy the meat and take it home and we eat it.

And every other town-dweller can go through the same reasoning, and wind up buying the meat and eating it, and be morally justified in doing so, even granted Singer's premises. So all we town-dwellers are morally justified in eating meat most of the time if we want to, and not aiming to change, even granted Singer's premises. So his premises can be true and his conclusion false. So the argument is invalid.

Evaluation of the objection

What do you think of this objection? I think it has the distinct air of being a cheat in some way and we should consider whether we can play author's advocate against it. Is there something in Singer himself that counts against it?

In paragraph 18, discussing the horrors of factory-farming, Singer says (my italics):

> To avoid speciesism we must stop *these practices.* Our custom is all the support that factory farmers need. The decision to cease giving them that support may be difficult, but it is less difficult than it would have been for a white Southerner to go against the traditions of his society and free his slaves; if we do not change

> our dietary habits, how can we censure those slave holders who would not change their own way of living?

And at the end of paragraph 20, where he has discussed the animal suffering still involved in the process of free-range food production, he says:

> the principle of equal consideration of interests implies that it *was* wrong to sacrifice important interests of the animal in order to satisfy less important interests of our own; consequently *we should boycott the end result* of this process.

These quotations clearly count against the objection. But how, precisely? It is not easy to work it out.

It seems to me that, playing author's advocate, they can be used to identify what is rather hypocritical and/or morally irresponsible about my reasoning in the supermarket. I have not denied Premise 3 – that animal suffering is involved in enabling us to eat meat – but I have turned a blind eye to it. True, my buying the meat doesn't make any difference to the animals that have already suffered. And true, whether or not I buy this piece is not, on its own, going to have the slightest effect on British factory-farming, let alone global factory-farming – future animal suffering will not be diminished one jot by my buying some cauliflower and nuts instead. But (new premise) we don't assess our actions as right or wrong solely in relation to their direct, individual, consequences. We sometimes think of ourselves as being part of a movement or group, each of whose individual actions makes no difference at all but whose collective endeavour has substantial consequences. We do this when we vote. We do it when we contribute to charities such as Oxfam, or contribute to the office collection for someone's leaving present. Quite a few of us did it when, prior to Mandela's presidency, we boycotted South African goods. And when we think of ourselves and our actions under this aspect we say, for instance, that it is right to support certain endeavours, to be party to certain practices, wrong to support others and be party to them – not because of the consequences of each individual action, but because of the consequences of a collective practice.

So Singer would not say that, in the supermarket, I ought to consider the animals that will suffer as a direct consequence of my buying meat, and hence not buy it – which is open to the objection that there are no such animals. He would say that I ought to consider the general practices and processes that bring this meat to the supermarket, and realise that, according to the principle of equal consideration, these practices and processes are wrong. And *then* I should realise that I should not be a party to these wrong practices and processes but join the movement that is boycotting their end result, in the hope that eventually, through our collective endeavour, the practices and processes wither away.

And if that is how I, and every other town-dweller, should be reasoning, according to Singer's premises, then my objection fails.

Development of the 'I don't cause any suffering' objection

The objection can be developed further – though in a way that has more to do with Singer the author than what he says in the Reading.

Looking in the Reading for what counted against the objection, I quoted the two bits (from paragraphs 18 and 20) where we are being encouraged, as I put it, to join a collective endeavour, not merely to consider the direct effects or consequences of our own individual actions. Playing author's advocate, I construed this as introducing a further, very plausible premise – that we do not always assess our actions as right or wrong according to their direct, individual consequences. Sometimes we assess our actions (contributing to Oxfam, buying goods produced by child-labour) as right or wrong according to whether we are being party to, or boycotting, particular collective practices which have certain consequences.

Given just the Reading, I think that was a good piece of author's advocacy; the two bits of text lend themselves to it, and it provided a powerful and plausible block to the rather hypocritical objection.

But it must now be said that it is not clear that Singer himself – the author of not only this Reading, but the whole book from which it comes, and many other books and articles besides – can be allowed this advocacy. For in the first edition of *Practical Ethics,* and in many of his other writings, he emphasizes a particular version of utilitarianism which he espouses. And that version is 'act' or 'direct' utilitarianism.'[2] He insists that when I decide what I ought to do on a particular occasion, *all* that I am to take into account is:

> the interests of all those *affected* by my decision. This requires me to weigh up all these interests and adopt the course of action most likely to maximise the interests of those *affected.* Thus at least at some level of my moral reasoning I *must* choose the course of action which has the best consequences, on balance, for all *affected.*
>
> (Singer (1993), p.13; my emphasis throughout)

So, once again, if my buying particular bits of meat for my family does not affect any animal, only my family, I can buy the meat, and we can reinstate this objection. We insist that Singer's premises include *his* utilitarian premise and hence that *he* can't have the new one I saw in the two bits of text (paragraphs 18 and 20) without being inconsistent. But without the new premise, which introduces 'rule' or 'indirect' utilitarian, he will be open to the objection, hypocritical as its reasoning appears. I could play author's advocate on behalf of an indirect utilitarian, but not on behalf of Singer, the direct utilitarian. If he is appealing to indirect utilitarianism in those two bits of text, he has lapsed into inconsistency.

There is no suggestion that Singer might have got his empirical facts wrong, or even be appealing to non-utilitarian values. The suggestion is rather that, despite the above quoted claim, from the beginning of the *Practical Ethics,* that he is relying solely on just one specific form of utilitarianism – the 'direct' form – he is sometimes relying on a different form, namely 'indirect' utilitarianism.

Evaluation of the development

This does not seem much of a criticism. Why not rely on different forms of utilitarianism? And, in fact, in the second edition to *Practical Ethics* (perhaps indeed in response to the above charge of inconsistency) Singer adds a parenthetical comment on the above quotation:

> I say 'at some level in my moral reasoning' because... there are utilitarian reasons for believing that we ought not to try to calculate these consequences for every ethical decision we make in our daily lives... we must also consider whether the effect of a *general practice* (of doing the sort of thing direct utilitarianism would lead one to on this occasion) will benefit all those affected...
> (Singer (1993), pp.13–14; my emphasis)

So this development of the objection is weak – Singer has a ready reply. But it has been worth going through, because it is worth discovering that Singer is prepared to use both direct and indirect utilitarian reasoning – a point we shall rely on later when we look at his argument about experimenting on animals.

Conclusion

We have now looked at a number of objections to Singer's argument to vegetarianism. Few of them have been much good. The best was the development of the 'no woman is an island' objection, which at least showed that Singer would have to amend his conclusion. But the amendment I suggested – 'Most of us should aim to cut down on eating meat and favour free-range products, encourage those we know to do the same, and eventually become vegetarian' – is still one that few want to accept. Hence, pending someone else's coming up with an even better objection, we have an apparently valid argument whose conclusion applies to nearly everyone – and which most do not want to accept. What other avenue of escape is still open to us?

Well, we have not considered any argument against Singer's utilitarian premise. (This would be another excellent approach, since it involves arguing against a non-empirical premise.) We will look at a version of this in a later chapter. Nor have we considered what may seem the obvious target – the 'anti-speciesism' premise that equal consideration should be given to the like interests of *all* sentient beings. But, as I said above, I am delaying discussion of this until much later.

So it rather looks as though, if we are to escape Singer's amended conclusion about vegetarianism, we shall have to argue against at least one of the two fundamental premises which form his ethical approach. But before we do this we should critically evaluate Singer's position regarding animal experimentation to see if we meet the same problems there.

The argument about using animals in experiments

The following exercise asks you to put what you have learnt from the first section of this chapter to use. I suggest you spend at least half an hour on it before you read the discussion.

EXERCISE 8
Singer on animal experimentation

Re-read paragraphs (22)–(28) of the Singer reading, and, in the light of what you have just learnt, try to write down, in one sentence each, a number of ways in which you would (or should) set about trying to criticize what he says. You might like to look back at the ten initial responses to his argument about vegetarianism on pp.42–5 and also at the end of the discussion on 'What can you learn from this exercise?' (p.45).

DISCUSSION

Very straightforwardly, you could have begun your list with the two excellent approaches from the discussion of vegetarianism, namely:

1 I shall argue against Singer's utilitarian premise, thus showing that, even if his argument is valid, we do not need to accept his conclusion, because his argument is not **sound**.

sound argument

2 I shall argue against his anti-speciesism premise (thus showing... etc.).

You could also, very straightforwardly, have added the other excellent approach, namely:

3 I shall construct a counter-example to Singer's argument, describing a set-up in which his premises are true but his conclusion false, thereby showing that his argument is invalid.

If you did, then you clearly have absorbed one of the most important points from that section. If you thought about putting it down but then realized you had no idea how to set about doing such a thing in this case, and so decided not to, that is an equally intelligent response.

The other approach you could have added straightforwardly is:

4 I shall argue that Singer's position has an absurd consequence.

Once again, if you did, then you have absorbed an important point; but if you thought of it, but did not put it down because you could not think of an absurd consequence, that is equally good.

Beyond these four, I cannot make any simple predictions about what you are likely to have written down. I will begin by discussing some really poor responses.

Poor responses

I hope it is clear that, as before, anything analogous to the first three responses in Exercise 5 is no good – because they do not engage with Singer's argument. A good criticism of an argument must, at the very least, engage with one of his premises, or his conclusion, or the question of whether the premises really do support the conclusion.

I also hope that you did not write down:

> I shall argue against Singer's premise that animals feel pain, distress or stress.

This is not a good way to start, for the same reason as before (p.43) and in this case, for a further one. A number of experiments on animals crucially depend on the assumption that animals *do* feel pain, distress or stress – remember the *ad hominem* argument in paragraph 22 (p.36)?

And, finally, I hope that you tried to turn any objection you thought of into something that began 'I shall argue...' or 'I shall construct ...' which engaged with Singer's argument. Here is an example of a poor response which fails to do that:

> 'We are now all benefiting from the results of past experiments on animals.'

This is quite often voiced as an objection to anti-vivisectionists, but no amount of charity can turn it into anything that looks like an objection to Singer – how does it engage with his arguments?

absurd consequences move

Is it supposed to be setting up an **absurd consequences move**? If it had begun 'I shall argue that Singer's position has the absurd consequence that...' the person who made it would have been forced to think about how to fill in the '...', and how can they do so? Perhaps:

> 'Singer's position has the absurd consequence that we should not, now, benefit from experiments on animals that have been done in the past.'

That would, indeed, be an absurd consequence, but I can find nothing in Singer to suggest that he wants to claim it. It is attacking a **straw man**.

straw man

hypocrisy

Is it a charge of **hypocrisy**? That it would be hypocritical of Singer to claim that he is not vastly relieved to be living in Australia, now, where he is reaping the benefits of centuries of research on animals and so... well, and so what? So he must believe that there was nothing wrong with past experiments on animals despite all the suffering they caused and being inconsistent? But why must he believe that when he is talking about our *current* practices? In Britain, we are still reaping the benefits of our rich industrial past which employed child labour. Must we believe there was nothing wrong with it? Is it hypocritical of us to object to any current use of it?

The only point I can get out of this objection is the thought that, to be consistent, Singer should deeply regret a whole lot of past animal suffering, but that, enjoying its fruits, he obviously can't – it would be hypocritical of him. But that is not much of a thought. As a utilitarian, he has no reason to regret any experiments which have produced benefits to humans which outweigh the suffering to the animals involved. He is concerned about the others, and I expect he does regret them, as surely most of us would.[3]

Attacking Singer's premise about current animal experiments

Now let us look at a slightly better response, which attacks one of Singer's premises – not the utilitarian or anti-speciesism ones, but the one that emerges as a subsidiary conclusion in paragraph 26, namely:

> In these cases and many others like them, the benefits to humans are either non-existent or uncertain, while the losses to members of other species are certain and real.

Someone might begin an objection by saying: 'I shall argue that Singer's claims about the extent to which animals suffer in experiments or are used in unnecessary ones are greatly exaggerated and out of date'. (The intuitive thought, needing to be turned into an objection that begins 'I shall argue against Singer's premise that...', might be something like 'Things are nothing like as bad as Singer makes out' or 'Singer is unfair to scientists'.)

Anyone who sets about arguing against Singer in this way needs to be very careful to avoid the hazards involved in arguing against an **empirical** premise. Can the premise be disposed of quickly, or will it require turning away

empirical

from philosophical argument and embarking on a long listing of (putative) empirical facts – this time about the many changes in the law governing the treatment of experimental animals, the existence of ethics committees at all universities and research institutes whose job it is to scrutinize all proposed research involving living animals and reject those that are not necessary, the proven (?) integrity and concern for animal suffering of the members of such committees and so on? I repeat – if you disagree with an author's empirical premises, the best way to start is just to let him have them as a supposition and look for something else to criticize.

Nevertheless, if you work in a laboratory that does animal experiments, or know well someone who does, you may know that some of Singer's claims *are* somewhat out of date – his examples in paragraph 25 would quite possibly no longer serve as examples of things that are still going on in British and North American universities. *Practical Ethics* was first published in 1979 and since then – to a fair extent as a result of his writings – the laws in Britain and the US have been tightened up a lot. (Although we are reading the second edition (1993), paragraph 25 has come over unchanged from the first edition.) And someone who knows this may want to insist that Singer *is* wrong about his facts and that this point is too important to be brushed aside. After all, if we allow people false premises they can produce a valid argument for any conclusion they like!

This is a reasonable point. But it will still not make this objection into a good one.

Evaluating the objection

Remember that the point of attacking a premise is to show that we need not accept the author's conclusion even if his argument is valid. To see why this objection will not work, we need to think hard about what Singer's conclusion about using animals in experiments is.

A rather odd thing about the second half of the Singer Reading – which certainly did not strike me until I had subjected it to the full-scale critical evaluation that Windt recommends – is that it is not at all easy to say what Singer's conclusion is. He never states it explicitly. But we saw how important it was to be clear about this when we were doing the critical evaluation of the first half – get his conclusion wrong and it is all too likely that one's arguments against it will turn out to be attacking straw men. So what is it?

We can be sure that it is not that *all* experiments using animals are wrong – as a utilitarian, Singer will certainly want to say that animal experimentation is right in some circumstances and wrong in others, depending on its consequences. Is his conclusion then that *most* experiments using animals are wrong? Well, even that is not quite clear. If that was what he wanted to prove, you would expect his premises to include something like the following:

Premise In *most* experiments using animals, the benefits to humans are either non-existent or uncertain, while the losses to members of other species are certain and real.

But, when we look at paragraph 26, we get the more cautious 'In these cases, and *many* others like them, the benefits to humans,' etc. So it looks as though his (unstated) conclusion will be similarly cautious, something like:

Conclusion *Many* experiments on animals are wrong.

Now if that is his conclusion, what does he need as a premise about experiments using animals? Nothing stronger than:

Premise In *many* experiments using animals, the benefits to humans are either non-existent or uncertain, while the losses to members of other species are certain and real.

So that is the empirical premise we have to show is false if we want to escape his conclusion.

Now let us look again at what one could hope to show by citing facts from one's own experience working in a laboratory, or about changes in the law in the UK and US or about the existence of ethics committees and so on. No one could be in a position to prove that only *very few* such experiments are done nowadays. Who amongst us knows everything about what is going on in the US military (protected as it is by the US equivalent of the UK's Official Secrets Act – interestingly, Singer's paragraph 24 is new to the second edition)? Who is in a position to establish the integrity of the members of nearly every ethics committee? Who is intimate with all the details of what is done to animals in Eastern European institutions, which do not (yet) have ethics committees? (It is known that some experimenters in Britain actually get colleagues in Eastern Europe to do 'dodgy' experiments for them which would not be allowed here.) Even the most knowledgeable of us cannot muster enough facts to show that *very few* such experiments are done nowadays. To claim that would be to make a **rash generalization**. But only such a strong generalization could serve as an objection to Singer's premise. So the objection fails.

rash generalization

'Scientists must be at liberty to pursue the truth'

There is another, rather more fruitful way, of attacking Singer's premise that in many experiments on animals, the benefits to humans are either non-existent or uncertain. It is, I think, an objection that would be forced to make several substantial concessions to Singer, but would aim to salvage more in the way of animal experimentation than it seems likely he would be happy with.

Suppose the objection concedes (a) that using animals to test cosmetics is entirely unnecessary and (b) that some experiments that would not pass conscientious ethics committees' tests are wrong (so many of the experiments in military institutions are probably wrong, and so are many done in Eastern Europe, and it is wrong of scientists elsewhere to be party to the wrongful ones done there). That would still leave a large amount of animal experimentation in the UK and the US untouched, which Singer would no doubt want to see stopped, because the benefits to humans – he would say – are either non-existent or uncertain.

But now the objection makes a general – and plausible – claim about the relation between the whole scientific endeavour and particular scientific discoveries, namely this: we very rarely know in advance how useful a particular scientific discovery will eventually turn out to be. It may be obvious that, considered in isolation, it is extremely unlikely that it will ever be of any benefit to humans. But scientific experiments do not occur in isolation; they occur as part and parcel of world-wide scientific endeavour. To assume, of any particular experiment, that some scientist, somewhere, someday, will not find something in it that sets her off on a track that eventually results in great benefit to humans is to make a fatal assumption of infallibility.

With the mention of infallibility, we can see that this argument relates to Mill's arguments in Book 1 (pp.80–8). The claim is that scientists must be left at liberty to pursue scientific truth for its own sake, without having to justify each experiment as something that will provably or even quite probably benefit humans to an extent that outweighs the suffering to animals involved. Why? Because this is the most – indeed the only – effective means of ensuring that science does indeed minimize human suffering. Just as history brims with examples of suppressed views which turned out to be true, so the history of science brims with examples of scientific discoveries which turned out to be useful in ways that no one at the time ever expected.

Science, it might be said, is a package deal. If we want it to be pursued, wholly, or even in part, on the utilitarian grounds that, as a general practice, it is enormously beneficial, the general practice is what we have to accept. We have to opt for 'indirect' utilitarianism. We cannot apply 'direct' utilitarianism to each individual experiment or research programme saying '*This* one will not have particular beneficial consequences for humans, which will outweigh the suffering of the animals involved' because we cannot know what the long-term consequences are going to be. And, as we saw earlier (p.56), Singer has admitted that indirect utilitarianism is sometimes what we should use to assess actions as right or wrong.

We can see now how important it was to establish this point about him earlier. He *has* to be an indirect utilitarian about the general practice of eating meat – because, as a direct utilitarian, he would be open to the objection that no living animal suffers as a consequence of my buying meat at a supermarket. But, as an indirect utilitarian, he must accept the objection that many *apparently* unnecessary experiments which cause animal suffering should be allowed – because the general practice of science is so beneficial.

Evaluation of the objection

EXERCISE 9

Must scientists be at liberty to pursue the truth?

The objection shows which of the following:

1 Singer is completely wrong about our experiments on animals; they are all justifiable, because the general practice of science is justifiable.

2 Singer implies that many of the experiments using animals in universities and research institutes in the UK and the US are wrong, but this is false. Most of our current scientific practices in these countries are completely justifiable, because conscientious ethics committees rule out extreme abuses and most of the remaining general practice is justifiable.

3 Singer is forced to make a substantial concession: he must admit that many experiments in the UK and the US are justifiable as part of the general practice of science. But he can still produce an amended version of his conclusion which is quite radical.

Check your answers against those at the back of the book before reading on.

Playing author's advocate, we must consider whether Singer has a response to this objection that will still leave most of us feeling uncomfortable. And the amended conclusion we found for him when considering vegetarianism suggests one quite readily. He could, contrary to 2, continue to deny that most of our current scientific practices in the UK and the US are justifiable, despite the existence of ethics committees and the justifiability of the general practice.

Consider again the claim that, according to utilitarianism 'the end justifies the means' (see Exercise 4, 2(b), p.24 above). This has its uses as a catch phrase, but it also has its dangers – it is easy to misinterpret it. Contrary to what is sometimes carelessly thought, it does not mean that utilitarianism says that the end justifies any means; it only justifies those that are necessary to secure the end. Yes, the end of minimizing suffering justifies the general practice of science. And yes, the end of securing the general practice of science justifies the means of not judging each experiment individually but letting a whole lot through as part of that practice. Letting some apparently useless ones through is necessary. But we must not forget the overall aim of minimizing suffering. We should be looking for the ways in which we could maintain the general practice with the smallest possible amount of animal suffering. And, by and large, we are not doing that.

How much money and effort goes into finding alternatives to using animals, Singer could ask? A little, but not much. How much money and effort is directed towards avoiding the unnecessary reduplication of experiments in different institutions? Again, a little, but not much. How much money and effort goes into changing human lifestyles so that we do not bring suffering on ourselves and then turn to science for cures? Quite a lot but still not as much as there would be if less were directed towards experiments on animals.

'Most of our current scientific practices' embraces a much wider field than the individual experiments. 'The scientific endeavour' is not merely world-wide, but embodied in a set of complex institutions, which involve the teaching and training of future scientists, the funding of research, and the direction of research resources in particular directions. The ways in which all this is currently done could be radically changed, in a way that, within a matter of years, greatly reduced the number of experiments performed on animals, without any corresponding damage to the general practice of science.

So we could take Singer's conclusion to be something like:

Conclusion We should aim to reduce animal experiments wherever possible straight away. We should also seek alternatives, avoid unnecessary reduplication, change our lifestyles if they are unhealthy, encourage those we know and our children to do the same – and reduce the number of animal experiments perforce by directing more research resources into finding ways to do all those things and hence away from experiments using animals.

And, as before, that is still quite a radical conclusion.

Conclusion

So, as with the best objection to Singer's argument about vegetarianism, I would say that the 'scientists must be at liberty to pursue the truth' objection is a good one, but not, ultimately, conclusive. It forces Singer to make substantial concessions by appealing to indirect utilitarianism. But it has to concede that quite a lot of experiments using animals *are* wrong (p.62) and it still leaves him with a conclusion that calls for a radical change in the way we think and live.

Remaining issues: experimenting on humans

Indeed, we should recall at this point that, given Singer's anti-speciesism premise, his conclusion threatens to be astoundingly radical – for it seems that amongst the alternatives we should be seeking is experimenting on human beings. Is Singer indeed claiming this?

Discussing paragraph 11 (pp.32–3), I drew attention to how cautiously it was expressed, and said that we could, charitably, interpret Singer not as aiming to downgrade infants and the intellectually disabled to the moral level of experimental animals but as aiming to upgrade experimental animals to the level of some of these helpless, innocent human beings we think of as most in need of our protection and concern.

Of paragraph 28 (pp.37–8) I said that it was not clear to me what hope Singer was expressing when he said that the elimination of speciesism would greatly reduce the number of experiments performed on animals. Did he mean that, upgrading experimental animals, no decent, honest scientist would perform any seriously pain-inflicting experiments on animals, but only those, if any, that they would be prepared to perform on human beings, such as themselves or volunteers? Or did he meant that, downgrading humans, scientists would reason that a large number of experiments hitherto performed on highly developed animals would both be more accurate, and cause less suffering if performed on severely brain-damaged humans?

Singer himself has something to say which supports the charitable interpretations. A few pages after the Reading you have read he says:

> It is... important to remember that the aim of my argument is to elevate the status of animals rather than to lower the status of any humans. I do not wish to suggest that intellectually disabled humans should be force-fed with food colouring until half of them die – although this would certainly give us a more accurate indication of whether the substance was safe for humans than testing it on rabbits or dogs does. I would like our conviction that it would be wrong to treat intellectually disabled humans in this way to be transferred to nonhuman animals at similar levels of self-consciousness and with similar capacities for suffering. It is excessively pessimistic to refrain from trying to alter our attitudes on the grounds that we might start treating intellectually disabled humans with the same lack of concern we now have for animals, rather than give animals the greater concern that we now have for intellectually disabled humans.
>
> (Singer (1993), pp.77–8)

But, reassuring as this may sound, charity can only go so far, and we should look with grave suspicion at Singer's choice of example. Naturally, as a good utilitarian, he denies that *any* sentient creature should be force-fed with food colouring. New food colourings, like new cosmetics, are quite unnecessary on utilitarian grounds. 'There is no need to develop new ones that might be dangerous' (paragraph 23). But so what? What we are worried about is whether or not he is suggesting that some intellectually disabled humans should, for example, be restricted, whatever their preferences, to food high in cholesterol until they die, to discover the details of how such a diet affects human heart disease, or whether such humans should be infected with HIV so that various treatments could be tried out on them to see what, if anything, works.

That is, we want to know where Singer, as a utilitarian and anti-speciesist, stands, on experiments *which will contribute to a reduction in suffering which outweighs the suffering of those creatures involved in the experiments. Will* he say that the intellectually disabled must, given his premises, count as justifiable experimental subjects along with cats, pigs, etc.? On this all-important question he remains disconcertingly silent.

Note, however, that some clues about what we could say on his behalf emerge from his discussion of killing, which we will now consider briefly.

Remaining issues: Singer on killing

You may have wondered why, in paragraph 14, Singer delays the topic of killing animals to a later chapter of his book. The answer is that, before he can address that topic, he needs to discuss the utilitarian approach to killing in general, which takes all of Chapter 4, and only then can he turn, in the chapter after that, to the topic of killing animals. The utilitarian approach to killing is rather startling, because, according to utilitarianism, there is nothing wrong with it.

Recall that 'a utilitarian can never properly be accused of a lack of realism, or of a rigid adherence to ideals in defiance of practical experience. The utilitarian will judge lying bad in some circumstances and good in others, depending on its consequences' (Singer (1993), p.3). And what goes for lying also goes for killing. Killing is good or right when it furthers the interests of those affected; only bad or wrong when the consequences will be the reverse.[4] However, just as Singer was at pains to emphasize the point that beings with different mental capacities have different capacities for suffering, in this context he emphasizes the point that they have different 'interests' too.

He begins by drawing a technical distinction many philosophers use between the term 'human being' and the term 'person'. A *human being*, in the precise, biological sense, is defined as a member of the species Homo sapiens, which is something that can be determined scientifically by the nature of their genes. A *person* is defined as 'a rational and self-conscious being'.

EXERCISE 10
Human beings and persons

To test your understanding of these stipulative definitions, answer the following questions. Answer 'yes' or 'no' without worrying about possible complications.

1 Is a human baby (a) a human being, (b) a person?

2 Are you (a) a human being, (b) a person?

3 Is someone in an irreversible coma (a) a human being, (b) a person?

4 Is a normal adult chimpanzee (a) a human being, (b) a person?

5 Are all human beings persons?

6 Are all persons human beings?

Check your answers against those at the back of the book before reading on.

What is the significance of this distinction? Its importance for Singer lies in the fact that, other things being equal, it will usually be more wrong, on utilitarian grounds, to kill a person than a non-person (a being that is merely sentient, such as a snail or a baby). He says,

> A self-conscious being is aware of itself as a distinct entity, with a past and a future... A being aware of itself in this way will be capable of having desires about its own future. For example, a professor of philosophy may hope to write a book demonstrating the objective nature of ethics; a student may look forward to graduation; a child may want to go for a ride in an aeroplane. To take the lives of any of these people, without their consent, is to thwart their desires for the future. Killing a snail or a day-old infant does not thwart any desires of this kind, because snails and new-born infants are incapable of having such desires.
> (Ibid., pp. 89–90)

A *person* has an interest in continuing to exist, so that it can do all the things it desires to do in the future. And that interest must be taken into account when we do our utilitarian calculations.

But what about non-persons – those who are not rational, self-conscious beings? On this question, Singer finds himself driven to a rather odd position. Non-persons have no desires or preferences about their future to be frustrated by their being killed. So what is wrong with killing them? An obvious answer seems to be, if we think about maximizing happiness, that if they had been left alive to enjoy their simple pleasures, there would have been that much more pleasure around in the world than there would be if we had killed them. But then two questions arise.

1 What if the being in question is going to suffer rather than enjoy itself?

2 What if, having killed one such being, we immediately (or soon after) replaced it with another that was going to have the same amount or more pleasure?

Singer's answer to the first question, as you might expect, is that the being in question should be killed.

And his answer to the second, rather odd, question is, consistently, that there is nothing wrong with painless, stress-free killing in such a case. So with respect to the killing of chickens, ducks and fish (he is not sure whether cattle and sheep are persons or not), he accepts that this would not be wrong – *as long*, that is, as the killing is done painlessly, and the animal is replaced by another whose existence will contain as much pleasure as the one who is killed would have had.

Does this sound like a position that a dedicated 'animal liberationist' should rest content with? Many would say 'No' (and when we come to consider Tom Regan's views we will find that he says 'No'). For although the utilitarian requirement to minimize suffering still condemns much of our currrent practice with regard to animals, Singer's utilitarian position on the killing of non-persons still permits a great deal of exploitation of at least those animals which are non-persons.

Recall his earlier point (paragraph 20) about humane farmers, where he admits the possibility that animal flesh could be produced without suffering and notes that 'one problem is, of course, that using them as food involves killing them'. 'This is an issue', he says, to which he will return when he has discussed the value of life in the next chapter of his book. But now we have seen the upshot of that discussion. Where the killing of non-persons is concerned, it does not present a problem for using animals as food, as long as the killing is painless and stress-free and we breed sufficient replacements.

The same argument would justify painless experimentation on animals that were non-persons. True, the experimentation would, we may suppose, result in their untimely death, but, as before, this is not a problem as long as we breed sufficient replacements. Indeed, we might envisage the future scenario in which utilitarian scientists skilled in genetic engineering make a particular point of developing new forms of chimpanzees and dolphins (definitely persons in Singer's view), sheep and cattle (quite possibly persons in his view), etc. which were definitely non-persons. Then they too could be painlessly used and killed, as long as they were replaced. And, of course, the farmers and the suppliers of laboratory animals will *want* to replace them, because they will be marketable.

This scenario is not entirely far-fetched. (Pigs are intelligent and emotional creatures, and it has already proved financially worthwhile to breed exceptionally stupid ones which suffer less in factory-farming conditions, because the distress of the intelligent ones affects the quality and quantity of their flesh. Enormous and very stupid mice have proved very useful too.) But it seems a very odd one for an animal liberationist to allow – and, as it turns out, Singer eventually reaches a position which would rule it out.

Commenting on his own argument regarding the painless killing of a non-person and its replacement by another that will have the same amount or more pleasure, Singer notes that '[a]s a piece of critical moral reasoning, this argument may be sound'. But, he goes on,

> at the level of practical moral principles, it would be better to reject altogether the killing of animals for food, unless one must do so to survive. Killing animals for food makes us think of them as objects that we can use as we please. Their lives then count for little when weighed against our mere wants. As long as we continue to use animals in this way, to change our attitudes to animals in the way that they should be changed will be an impossible task. How can we encourage people to respect animals, and have equal concern for their interests, if they continue to eat them for their mere enjoyment? To foster the right attitudes of consideration for animals, including non-self-conscious ones, it may be best to make it a simple principle to avoid killing them for food.
>
> (Ibid., p.134)

Singer is here reverting to his indirect utilitarianism (cf. p.56), considering the effects of a general practice. Although direct utilitarianism would allow each individual act of painlessly killing an animal that was a non-person for food and replacing it with another, indirect utilitarianism suggests that, as a general practice, this will merely continue to foster our general speciesist attitude to animals as beings whose interests matter little in comparison with ours.

Experimental subjects again

Now that we have seen what Singer says about killing, let us return to the question I raised on p.66: must Singer (as a utilitarian and anti-speciesist) say that infants and the severely intellectually disabled count as justifiable experimental subjects along with, say, chickens? For, if so, then many of us will want to say that his position has a consequence for which 'absurd' is too trivial a word.

EXERCISE 11
Singer's advocate

Can you, playing author's advocate, think of any way in which Singer could avoid being committed to such a consequence?

DISCUSSION

It looks as though we could use indirect utilitarianism again. On his behalf, we could say that 'at the level of practical moral principles, it would be better to reject altogether' the use of human beings in experiments. Although direct utilitarianism (combined with anti-speciesism) would allow many individual cases of using a human non-person rather than an animal, the general practice (we could plausibly suppose) would foster callous attitudes to 'useless' human beings akin to those displayed by the Nazis.

But where would this reply leave him in relation to the use of animals in experiments? Doesn't his anti-speciesism commit him to saying that it would be better to reject that altogether too? For surely it is speciesist to reject all experiments on humans but accept some on animals. But if he bans all experiments on animals too, how can he be a utilitarian? A utilitarian, committed to minimizing suffering, can hardly propose banning all experiments on living subjects, when the scientific endeavour has such beneficial consequences. Can we play author's advocate here too?

Conclusion

I believe that there is no straightforward answer to this question, because Singer wears two hats. There is Singer the animal liberationist, the practical man who wants to change our attitude to the way we treat animals and think about our treatment of them. Here are most of us, buying cheap meat from the supermarkets, buying cosmetics, food colouring, and various other domestic products without looking to see whether it is labelled 'This product has not been tested on animals'. Here are most of us refusing to sign campaign documents, or subscribe to movements, against the use of animals in science because we think their use is necessary and only cranks protest about it. And he is campaigning to change us. As a campaigner, he has a brilliantly simple argument, namely the following:

Premise 1	What most of us are being party to is a huge amount of animal suffering which could be substantially reduced if we changed.
Premise 2	Our suffering matters morally, but animal suffering matters morally too.
Conclusion	Most of us should change.

As a campaigner, he has been (along with others) very effective in emphasizing and detailing the facts that support Premise 1. And, as I noted in the last paragraph of the preceding chapter (p.39), Singer's argument in the Reading could very broadly, but still accurately, be summed up in the above way.

But there is also Singer the academic philosopher. This is the man who wants to give a particular argument for Premise 2, the man who thinks that it is best argued for by appealing to utilitarianism and the principle of equality. This is the man who aims to give a general account of when actions are right or wrong, who appeals now to direct utilitarianism, now to indirect utilitarianism, who denies that there is anything intrinsically wrong with killing, who draws the distinction between persons and non-persons, who insists on the anti-speciesist version of the principle of equality and the idea that babies and the intellectually disabled (as non-persons) have the same moral status as hens.

As people who are studying philosophy, we are, inseparably, concerned with Singer in both his guises. As seekers of important truth, as we are in any academic discipline, we are seeking to know whether we should change – or are right to have changed if we have already. 'Have I got the *right* attitude to animals?' is the question each of us should be honestly seeking an answer to. And then Singer's 'brilliantly simple' argument should surely give most of us reason to think we do not.

But, given the content of that question, we cannot separate it from the further question 'What are the philosophical arguments that can be given in support of the attitude I have, and what are the arguments against it? Should I, in particular, accept Singer's detailed arguments, based on some version of utilitarianism and his version of the principle of equality?' And we may well decide that a reasonable answer to that last question is 'No'.

Chapter summary

In this chapter we have been exploring criticisms that might be made of Singer's arguments. Applying the principle of charity, and playing author's advocate, we have aimed to avoid weak criticisms; this frequently involved either taking careful note of what Singer's conclusions were, or amending them on his behalf.

Singer's argument to vegetarianism

We began by considering his argument for vegetarianism, and developed the 'no woman is an island' objection. But then, on his behalf, we amended his conclusion to 'Most of us should aim to cut down on eating meat and favour free range products, encourage those we know to do the same, and eventually become vegetarian' (i.e. most of us should change) and escaped that objection.

We then considered the rather hypocritical '*I* do not cause any suffering' objection, and saw that Singer could escape it by appealing to indirect utilitarianism. We concluded that the remaining promising criticisms were to attack at least one of the two premises which form his ethical approach – the utilitarian premise and the anti-speciesism premise that equal consideration should be given to the like interests of *all* sentient beings.

The argument about using animals in experiments

We then turned to considering his argument about using animals in experiments. We saw that empirical appeals to ways in which scientific practices have improved since Singer first wrote in 1979 will not work, since Singer's conclusion should, charitably, be taken to be 'Many (not 'most') experiments on animals are wrong'. We then explored the idea that science is a package deal and argued that allowing scientists to pursue scientific truth without having to justify each individual experiment was the only effective means of ensuring that science does, indeed, minimize suffering. We concluded that, as an indirect utilitarian, Singer must accept that many *apparently* unnecessary experiments which cause animal suffering should be allowed, because the general practice of science is so beneficial.

Playing author's advocate, we amended Singer's conclusion to meet this objection. I suggested 'We should aim to reduce animal experiments wherever possible straight away. We should also seek alternatives, avoid unnecessary reduplication, change our lifestyles as they are unhealthy, encourage those we know and our children to do the same, and reduce the number of animal experiments perforce by directing more research resources into finding ways to do all these things and away from experiments using animals (i.e. most of us should change).'

We then recalled that even this amended conclusion threatens to be astoundingly radical, because there was at least some suggestion in Singer that, amongst the 'alternatives' we should be seeking is using certain human beings instead of animals. We could not find a really clear statement in Singer of where he stood, as a utilitarian and anti-speciesist, on the issue of whether the intellectually disabled could count as justifiable experimental subjects along with cats, pigs, etc. so we turned to a brief study of his position on killing to see if this would prove enlightening.

Remaining issues: Singer on killing

Singer's position on killing requires drawing a distinction between 'persons' – who are rational, self-conscious beings with a grasp of their own future – and 'non-persons' – who are sentient but have no such grasp. Some, but not all, human beings are persons; some, but not all, animals are also persons. He maintains that normally, other things being equal, killing a person is worse than killing a non-person. Foetuses, infants, and the severely intellectually disabled all count as non-persons, according to Singer. Normally, other things being equal, killing one of them would not be as wrong as killing a person such as one of us, or a chimpanzee.

We might well regard this as an absurd, not to say horrific, consequence. However, Singer could escape it by, once again, appealing to indirect utilitarianism. And, returning to the issue of using human 'non-persons' as experimental subjects, we could, perhaps, argue on his behalf that 'at the level of practical moral principles' it would be better to reject this altogether.

However, we saw that this would be an odd move to make on behalf of Singer, the utilitarian anti-speciesist. Would he, as an anti-speciesist, say that we should also totally reject experimenting on animals? But then how can he consistently maintain his utilitarianism, given how beneficial the experiments are?

It looks as though, as a professional philosopher, Singer is committed to what I have called the 'horrific' consequence that unwanted infants and the severely intellectually disabled could be justifiable experimental subjects. And that gives us all, not just those of us who do not want to become vegetarians, a very good reason for trying to identify what is wrong with his philosophical arguments. The horrific consequence emerges from his ethical approach – the combination of his utilitarianism with his version of the principle of equality. So, as with his argument about vegetarianism, it is at least one of those two premises that we need to argue against. We shall be looking at some arguments against utilitarianism and also at one that tackles anti-speciesism in later chapters.

But our conviction that, if Singer's philosophical position has this consequence, there must be something wrong with it that we can argue against, should not blind us to what I called the 'brilliantly simple' argument which we can also attribute to him. Its first premise is that what most of us are being party to is a huge amount of animal suffering which could be substantially reduced if we changed – an empirical premise that it is hard, if not impossible, to refute. Its second premise is that our suffering matters morally but animal suffering matters morally too – and this is a premise we can hardly deny without committing ourselves to absolute dismissal (for example, the view that there is nothing wrong with small boys setting fire to cats). Its conclusion is that most of us should change – not, God forbid, to the point of even contemplating using human beings as experimental subjects, but substantially, and uncomfortably, all the same.

Simple and apparently reasonable as this argument is, many of us still do not accept it. In the next chapter we shall look at some of the historical background to our resistance.

Further reading

There is a long-standing debate, going back over forty years and still unresolved, over whether 'indirect' or 'rule utilitarianism' deserves to be called 'utilitarianism' at all. For a discussion of this issue, and many other criticisms of utilitarianism, the most approachable text is still *Utilitarianism For and Against* by J.J.C. Smart and Bernard Williams, Cambridge University Press, 1973. In this short paperback, Smart defends utilitarianism and Williams argues against it.

Notes

[1] For a discussion of this and other versions of utilitarianism see Reading 3 in Nigel Warburton's *Arguments for Freedom* (A211 Book 1).

[2] Mary Midgley describes a nineteenth-century physiologist, Claude Bernard, who flatly refused to anaesthetize the animals he experimented on, claiming that it was sentimental and unscientific to think they felt pain. She adds that the first anti-vivisection society in Europe 'seems to have been founded by Bernard's own wife and daughters, who had come home to find that he had vivisected the domestic dog' (Midgley (1983), p.28). The eighteenth and nineteenth-century vivisectionists dissected living, conscious, struggling cats and dogs by nailing them to boards. Who would not regret that?

[3] It is this aspect of utilitarianism which leads, for example, Tom Regan, who you will be studying later, to reject it.

Differences between Humans and Animals

OBJECTIVES

By the end of this chapter you should have:

- Appreciated the differences between humans and animals emphasized by past philosophers.
- Acquired a good critical understanding of indirect duty views.
- Understood the contractarian position on justice.
- Had practice in the detailed analysis of short philosophical passages.

All of us, I hope, will agree that it would be wrong to torture cats just for fun, but far from all of us agree with Singer's conclusion that we should radically change our attitudes to our use of animals for food and as experimental subjects. It seems that about 80 per cent of the population believes that we are justified in using animals in much the way we do. Maybe quite a lot of us would like to see a few changes here and there, but we are not calling for radical changes. In this chapter, first we shall look at some of the historical roots of the prevailing idea that we are justified in using animals the way we do because we are, as human beings, special in some way that animals are not; then we shall study some ways of keeping human beings special while providing grounds for saying that wanton cruelty to animals is wrong.

Human beings as special

Why might it seem to many of us just absurd of Singer to claim that any preference for our own species is nothing but a prejudice comparable to racism? The natural response (from any non-racist) is to say that racial differences are largely imaginary and, insofar as they exist, insignificant. Moreover they are not hard and fast; over the millennia, we have intermarried and interbred and, as genetics is now revealing to us, a surprising number of us who thought we were all one race have an ancestor from another race somewhere in our inheritance. In many cases, being of one race rather than another is not a hard and fast distinction, but a matter of degree.

But, it is commonly thought, the differences between human beings and the other animals are real, hard and fast, and very significant – significant enough to justify our eating them, using them in experiments and perhaps also hunting them for sport and to supply fashion items. Such thoughts about the differences between human beings and the other animals have a long tradition in Western thought and it is worth looking at very brief extracts from some of the past writings that have, whether we are conscious of it or not, shaped our present views.

Rather than merely taking you on a Cook's tour of some past philosophers' views and arguments, we shall take the opportunity while reading extracts from them to do a series of exercises which will develop your ability to analyse arguments in short passages.

Past philosophers on animals

The idea that it is all right for us to use animals, that indeed they are there for us to use, is at least as old as *Genesis*.

EXERCISE 12
Genesis

What is the key word in this passage, as far as our relation to animals is concerned?

> Be fruitful, and multiply, and replenish the earth, and subdue it: and have dominion over the fish of the sea, and over the fowl of the air, and over every living thing that moveth upon the earth.
>
> (*Genesis*, 1.28)

Check your answer against that at the back of the book before reading on.

Although some Christian defenders of animals have argued that this passage means that God made Adam and Eve custodians, so to speak, of the rest of His animate creation, imposing a special duty on them to take good care of 'every living thing that moveth', it has standardly been interpreted as God's giving Adam and Eve, and thereby all human beings, sovereignty, lordship or ownership over all the animals, to use as they chose.

Human beings are the only rational animals

The Old Testament does not lay much stress on human beings as rational animals; the idea that we are rational and all the other animals non-rational, and that we are rational insofar as we are made in the image of God, came into

Christian thought via the ancient Greek philosophers Plato (427–347BC) and Aristotle (384–322BC). Indeed, Aristotle is our source of the idea that there is a natural hierarchy of sorts of things – a ladder or scale of nature. Inanimate matter (stones, earth, etc.) are at the bottom; next come plants which are at least alive; then come animals which are also sentient; and then comes Man, blessed with rationality. On Aristotle's ladder, beyond Man there is Mind or God who/which is perfect Reason. In virtue of their rationality, human beings have 'a divine element' within them, according to him.

One can see Genesis combining with this Aristotelian idea in the following extract from the influential Christian writer, St Augustine (AD354–430).

EXERCISE 13

Augustine on animals

Answer the following questions when you have read the passage from Augustine.

1 What does Augustine conclude it is all right for us to do to animals?

2 What reason(s) does he give for this?

> ...in the commandment 'Thou shalt not kill,' there is no limitation added...[5]
>
> And so some attempt to extend this command even to beasts and cattle, as if it forbade us to take life from any creature. But if so, why not extend it also to the plants, and all that is rooted in and nourished by the earth? For though this class of creatures have no sensation, yet they also are said to live, and consequently they can die; and therefore, if violence be done them, can be killed. So, too, the apostle, when speaking of the seeds of such things as these, says, 'That which thou sowest is not quickened except it die'; and in the Psalm it is said, 'He killed their vines with hail'. Must we therefore reckon it a breaking of this commandment, 'Thou shalt not kill,' to pull a flower? Are we thus insanely to countenance the foolish error of the Manichaeans? Putting aside, then, these ravings, if, when we say, Thou shalt not kill, we do not understand this of the plants, since they have no sensation, nor of the irrational animals that fly, swim, walk, or creep, since they are dissociated from us by their want [lack] of reason, and are therefore by the just appointment of the Creator subjected to us to kill or keep alive for our own uses; if so, then it remains that we understand that commandment simply of man. The commandment is, 'Thou shalt not kill man'.
>
> (Augustine (1877 edn), Book 1, pp.30–2)

Check your answers against those at the back of the book before reading on.

We see this same idea, that the irrational nature of animals makes it right that they should be subject to us, in the next passage. Given the Aristotelian premise that there is a natural hierarchy and the Christian premise that this world was made with foresight and benevolence by God, it is no longer necessary to appeal to Genesis to show that our dominion over the animals is part of His plan. Here is another influential Christian writer, St Thomas Aquinas (1225–74):

> Now all animals are naturally subject to man. This can be proved in three ways. First, from the order observed by nature; for just as in the generation of things we perceive a certain order of procession of the perfect from the imperfect (thus matter is for the sake of form; and the imperfect form, for the sake of the perfect), so also is there order in the use of natural things; thus the imperfect are for the use of the perfect; as the plants make use of the earth for their nourishment, and animals make use of plants, and man makes use of both plants and animals. Therefore it is in keeping with the order of nature, that man should be master over animals. Hence the Philosopher [i.e. Aristotle] says [*Politics,* i. 5] that the hunting of wild animals is just and natural, because man thereby exercises a natural right. Secondly, this is proved from the order of Divine Providence[6] which always governs inferior things by the superior. Wherefore, as man, being made to the image of God, is above other animals, these are rightly subjected to his government.
>
> (Aquinas (1922 edn) *Summa Theologiae,* 7a, Question 96)

The passage from Aristotle's *Politics* to which Aquinas refers comes a few pages after another famous and influential passage.

EXERCISE 14
Aristotle on humans and animals

Answer these questions after reading the passage that follows.

1 Identify a well-known definition of 'man'.

2 Identify at least two premises about the distinguishing marks of human beings.

3 Note one premise about animals which would please Singer.

> But man is obviously a political animal in a sense in which a bee is not, nor any other gregarious creature such as herding cattle. For nature, as we say, does nothing in vain and man alone of the animals possesses speech. Speech is something different from mere voice, which is possessed by other animals also and used by them to express pain or pleasure; for their nature does indeed enable them to have sensations of pain and pleasure and to impart these sensations to others. But speech, further, serves to indicate what is useful and what is harmful to us and so also what is just and what is unjust. For in this particular man differs from other animals, that he alone has perception of good and evil, of just and unjust and so on and it is sharing of a common view in these things that makes a household and a state.
>
> (Aristotle, *Politics*, 1253a7–17)

Check your answers against those at the back of the book before reading on.

What is particularly interesting and significant about this passage is the way in which it links so many features of human beings together. Note how Aristotle insists that our possession of speech is a real, hard and fast difference. He recognizes that some other animals make meaningful noises (expressing pain or pleasure); he even recognizes that these noises serve to communicate, to 'impart these sensations to others'. Well, isn't our speech just meaningful noises we use to communicate? Of course, we communicate a great deal more than sensations of pain and pleasure, but why not allow that some animals are a bit like us because they have speech to *some* degree? Why insist that all they have is something quite different, namely 'voice'?

Part of his reason is given in the passage. Aristotle links our speech to our being (as we would say) moral agents – our capacity to perceive, or recognize, good and evil. Animals, he assumes – and we might well agree – are not moral agents. They cannot be held morally responsible for what they do because they cannot know or perceive that what they do is good or bad, right or wrong.

Although we might agree with that, we might also wonder again whether the distinction is really so hard and fast. Don't at least some animals have a sense of right and wrong to at least some degree? Most pet owners will say that their cats and dogs do. And many 'gregarious' animals such as wolves, apes and elephants, seem to have their own rules about how they ought to behave and 'punish' delinquent members of the group by, for example, ostracizing them. Maybe it is not really punishment, and maybe our cats and dogs do not really feel guilt – but are they so totally different from us as far as knowledge or 'perception' of good and evil is concerned? Why is Aristotle so sure that they are?

The full explanation, although it is not clear from the passage, is as follows. Aristotle, like most of his predecessors, and many of us, is convinced that human beings are the only rational animals – the only animals who possess reason. And he takes it as obvious that no being can have knowledge of good and evil without having reason – because *knowledge* is an exercise of reason. So no other animals have knowledge of good and evil. He also takes it as obvious that no being can have speech without having reason – because speech too, is an exercise of reason. So no other animals can have speech, only 'voice'.

That no being can have speech without having reason is more 'obvious' in ancient Greek than it is in English, for the word Aristotle uses, *logos,* means not only 'reason' but also 'discourse', 'saying' and 'word'. So to say, in ancient Greek, that a creature has *logos* is to say, simultaneously, that it has reason and speech. ('Logos' occurs in the New Testament in St John, which was written in Greek, in the passage that used to be translated 'In the beginning was the Word (*logos*) and the Word was with God and the Word was God'. 'Logos' is now quite often left untranslated in such contexts, so that it can go on carrying its meaning of 'reason'.)

So in this passage, Aristotle explicitly links two features of human beings – our having speech and our capacity to recognize good and evil – and implicitly links those to a third, our having reason. His certainty that we are unique amongst animals in possessing the third feature underpins his certainty that the other two are unique to us too; all three come together in a package, clearly distinguishing us from all the other animals who have none of these features to any degree at all.

Why not deny Aristotle's implicit assumption (common to most of his predecessors and contemporaries) that the possession of reason itself cannot be a matter of degree? After all, is it not obvious that some animals are much more intelligent than others? Well, a few thinkers did deny it, and, post-Darwin, many more have done so. But in the Christian era pre-Darwin, the assumption that humans possessed reason and animals did not possess any at all, was reinforced by another feature thought to be unique to human beings – our possession of a mind, or an immortal soul.

In other books in this course you will be studying in detail what some philosophers have said about our possession of minds or immortal souls. When you do, you will realize that the next paragraph glosses over a number of important distinctions – I am just trying to give you a crude idea of why Christian doctrine reinforced the Aristotelian assumption.

Aristotle thought of reason as 'the divine element' in human beings. In Christian thought, the divine element in us is our immortal, rational, souls – our minds. As in Aristotle, it is because we have this element within us that we can reason, use language, and have knowledge of good and evil. If we misuse the last capacity, our immortal souls will be punished in the after-life. Now although it seems fairly easy to think of being able to reason, speak and recognize good and evil, as a matter of degree, it is much harder to think of possessing a soul or a mind as a matter of degree. How could anything possess a soul or mind to just a small degree? Does it have just a tiny one or a bit of one? But surely souls or minds do not come in sizes, or have parts. Something either has one or it does not – it's an all or nothing matter. We each have one and the other animals do not.

It is possible to draw a distinction between the mind and the soul. Some people believe we have both and that the soul is immortal but the mind perishes when the brain does; some people believe we have only one – the mind. It is also possible not to jib at the thought that whether or not something has a mind *is* a matter of degree. 'Having a mind', we might say, is just a matter of having certain capacities (perhaps, but not necessarily, located in the brain); a creature can possess these capacities to a greater or lesser degree, so it can have a mind to a greater or lesser degree. Some people find that an easy thought to accommodate. But many, even if they do not believe we have immortal souls, find it extremely difficult; they feel convinced that having a mind must be an all or nothing matter. We each have one; a computer, whatever 'intellectual' capacities it might have, simply could not have one, to any degree at all. And they may feel convinced that the same is true of the other animals.

Animals as machines

When we say, as many of us are inclined to, that no computer could possibly 'have a mind', we may be thinking that no computer could be *conscious*. Is being conscious an all or nothing matter, or are there degrees of consciousness? Thinking of computers, we may say 'all or nothing', finding it impossible to think of computers being conscious to any degree. But what if we think of the other animals? Then we may be more willing to say that there can be degrees of consciousness.

We, and perhaps some of the higher animals, are self-conscious. Some other animals are not self-conscious: they are not conscious of themselves, but they still have some degree of consciousness – they are conscious of pleasure and pain. (Remember that self-consciousness is the basis on which Singer draws the distinction between animals that are *persons* and animals that are not.) In the history of Western philosophy, this last fact about animals – that they are conscious of, or can feel, pain and pleasure – has not usually been denied. However, at least one philosopher famously – or infamously – did deny it in some of his writings. This was René Descartes (1596–1650) who you will be studying later in the course. Descartes did not draw a distinction between the mind and the soul; he believed that whether or not a creature had a mind or soul was an all or nothing matter and he argued, in the passage that follows, that animals were just like machines, or 'automata', operating like elaborate clockwork without any consciousness.

EXERCISE 15

Descartes on animals

This exercise will take about thirty minutes including the discussion that follows.

The extract from Descartes that you are about to read, though short, is much harder in style than anything you have yet encountered. It is not only that even an idiomatic translation of Descartes's seventeenth-century French is going to sound a bit odd and stilted, but also that his sentences tend to be long and densely packed. Hence it would be inappropriate for you to begin by skimming this extract. However, you will need to read it all twice, and some bits of it a third time in order to answer the questions below, and it would make sense to follow a procedure at least similar to the one we were using in the first chapter. I would suggest making the first reading rather like a slow skim: aim only for a rough idea of what Descartes is up to, that is, to get rough answers to the *first three* questions below. On a second reading, aim for a better idea of what his arguments are about and look for answers to the remaining questions. (This might involve discarding some of your first answers.) Watch out for useful signposts and argument-indicators – Descartes is quite helpful with these – and remember to use what you already know. Here are the questions to bear in mind as you read.

1 What is the first conclusion Descartes argues for (in fact, tells us he *has* argued for)?
2 How many reasons does he give?
3 What is the second conclusion he argues for? (This can be expressed in a variety of ways.)
4 What reasons does Descartes give for his first conclusion?
5 What reasons does he give for his second?

> 1 I specially dwelt on showing that if there were machines with the organs and appearance of a monkey, or some other irrational animal, we should have no means of telling that they were not altogether of the same nature as those animals; whereas if there were machines resembling our bodies, and imitating our actions as far as is morally (= practically) possible, we should still have two means of telling that, all the same, they were not real men. First, they could never use words or other constructed signs, as we do to declare our thoughts to others. It is quite conceivable that a machine should be so made as to utter words, and even utter them in connection with physical events that cause a change in one of its organs; so that e.g. if it is touched in one part, it asks what you want to say to it, and if touched in another, it cries out that it is hurt; but not that it should be so made as to arrange words variously in response to the meaning of what is said in its presence, as even the dullest men can do.
>
> 2 Secondly, while they might do many things as well as any of us or better, they would infallibly fail in others, revealing that they acted not from knowledge but only from the disposition of their organs. For while reason is a universal tool that may serve in all kinds of circumstances, these organs need a special arrangement for each special action; so it is morally (= in practice) impossible that a machine should contain so many varied arrangements as to act in all the events of life in the way reason enables us to act.

3 Now in just these two ways we can also recognise the difference between men and brutes. For it is a very remarkable thing that there are no men so dull and stupid, not even lunatics, that they cannot arrange various words and form a sentence to make their thoughts (*pensées*) understood; but no other animals, however perfect or well bred, can do the like. This does not come from their lacking the organs; for magpies and parrots can utter words like ourselves, and yet they cannot talk like us, that is, with any sign of being aware of (*qu'ils pensent*) what they say. Whereas men born deaf-mutes, and thus devoid of the organs that others use for speech, as much as brutes are or more so, usually invent for themselves signs by which they make themselves understood to those who are normally with them, and who thus have a chance to learn their language.

4 This is evidence that brutes not only have a smaller degree of reason than men, but are wholly lacking in it. For it may be seen that a very small degree of reason is needed in order to be able to talk; and in view of the inequality that occurs among animals of the same species, as among men, and of the fact that some are easier to train than others, it is incredible that a monkey or parrot who was one of the most perfect members of his species should not be comparable in this regard to one of the stupidest children or at least to a child with a diseased brain, if their souls were not wholly different in nature from ours. And we must not confuse words with natural movements, the expressions of emotion, which can be imitated by machines as well as by animals. Nor must we think, like some of the ancients, that brutes talk but we cannot understand their language; for if that were true, since many of their organs are analogous to ours, they could make themselves understood to us, as well as to their fellows.

5 It is another very remarkable thing that although several brutes exhibit more skill than we in some of their actions, they show none at all in many other circumstances; so their excelling us is no proof that they have a mind (*de l'esprit*), for in that case they would have a better one than any of us and would excel us all round; it rather shows that they have none, and that it is nature that acts in them according to the arrangements of their organs; just as we see how a clock, composed merely of wheels and springs, can reckon the hours and measure time more correctly than we can with all our wisdom.

(Descartes (1966 edn), pp.41–2)

DISCUSSION

1 *What is the first conclusion Descartes argues for?*

If there were a machine that had inside workings like an animal and looked like an animal we shouldn't be able to tell that it wasn't an animal, whereas, if there were a machine that looked like one of us, and had inside workings like ours and behaved like us (as far as is practically possible) we would be able to tell that it wasn't a human being. Or, paraphrasing very briskly, a mechanical animal would be indistinguishable from a real animal, but a mechanical human being would not be indistinguishable from a real one.

2 *How many reasons does he give?*

He gives two reasons for this claim (or, more properly, for its second half), helpfully signposted ('we should still have *two* means of telling... First...' in the first paragraph; 'Secondly...' at the beginning of the second).

3 *What is the second conclusion he argues for?*

I would expect you to refine your initial answer to this. On a slow skim, you might pick his conclusion out of the beginning of the third paragraph and say his second conclusion is that 'We can recognize the difference between men and brutes' or perhaps that 'There is a difference between men and brutes'. But that hardly gives even a rough idea of what Descartes is up to in the passage. What we are looking for is at least a rough idea of what he says the difference *is*. This is where it would be sensible to use what you know already, namely, that Descartes argues that animals are machines. It would be better to go for the beginning of the fourth and/or the end of the fifth paragraph.

Then we would say that Descartes's second conclusion is that animals are 'wholly lacking in reason', that they have no mind at all ('[this] is no proof they have a mind... it rather shows they have none') that they operate as clocks do. Or, paraphrasing briskly, animals are just like machines, human beings are not but have reason or a mind.

4 *What reasons does Descartes give for his first conclusion?*

(i) We could tell that a mechanical man was not a real human being because it would not be able to talk, i.e. use words, *in the way* we do, namely 'in response to the meaning of what is said in its presence'.[7]

(ii) We could tell that a mechanical human being was not a real one because it would infallibly make certain sorts of mistakes. (In modern terminology, we might say that its behaviour would not adapt to circumstances the way our actions do; it would not be intelligent.)

5 *What reasons does he give for his second?*

Descartes then exploits these two tests as reasons for believing that animals are indeed just like machines. First, they lack speech. (Note that 'natural movements' in paragraph 4 plays the same argumentative role as 'voice' in Aristotle – these noises coming from animals as of pain, pleasure, anger, etc. are not *speech* but something else – further denigrated by the point that they can be 'imitated by machines' and hence indicate nothing about what is actually felt.) Secondly, animals' apparently intelligent behaviour is so uneven that it cannot come 'from knowledge' (paragraph (2)) but must come from 'the arrangements of their organs' (paragraphs (5) and cf. (2)). As we would say, it's just 'programmed in'. (Note that, like Aristotle, Descartes is assuming that knowledge is an exercise of reason. Creatures have reason because of the divine element – the rational soul – within them. Hence the importance, for Descartes, of denying that any apparently intelligent animal behaviour comes 'from knowledge'.)

It may not be immediately obvious from this passage that Descartes denied that animals felt pain or pleasure, but he did. 'Why,' we might ask him, 'do animals cry out when they are burnt or beaten if they do not feel pain?' His answer is implicit in this passage; an animal is a machine built in such a way as to utter those sounds 'in connection with physical events that cause a change in one of its organs'. A machine we built, with no consciousness, and hence no consciousness of pain, could be built to behave in just the same way. 'Why', we ask, 'do cats seek out warm places to lie in, but struggle against being pushed into the fire if they do not feel pleasure and pain?' The answer again is implicit in the passage; this is not intelligent purposive action on the cat's part, intended to gain pleasure and avoid pain; it is 'nature acting in them'; mere instinct as we would say.

The Descartes extract has merited such extended attention not because the arguments are particularly good but, on the contrary, because they are rather bad – *and still very common.* Despite the fact that he wrote almost four hundred years ago, Descartes's way of thinking about the mind, as the seat of reason, purposive intelligence, consciousness and understanding (linguistic and otherwise) is still prevalent today. And it is still affecting our thoughts about ourselves, animals and machines.

Descartes's way of thinking was dualistic in two senses. In the first, philosophical sense, he is a dualist insofar as he believed that everything that exists falls into either of two (hence 'dual') classes, either the mental or the material/physical. But his way of thinking also tends to 'dualism' in the sense in which modern feminism uses the term – it is **black-and-white thinking**. He tends to draw hard and fast, all-or-nothing distinctions where a more reasonable, less rigidly 'dichotomous' approach would admit varying degrees along a continuum. For Descartes, a creature either has a mind or it does not. And to have a mind is to have the whole package – reason, purposive intelligence, consciousness, linguistic capacity, etc. – all or nothing. Moreover, those faculties themselves are an all-or-nothing matter; a creature has them totally or not at all. There is no such thing as having a faculty of reason or the

Black-and-white thinking

faculty of speech to some, perhaps modest, degree; a creature either has the faculty or it totally lacks it.

We use language, other animals do not

That this last way of thinking is still prevalent is easily illustrated. Aristotle's, Descartes's and many other thinkers' confident claim that animals – *all* animals – lack the faculty of speech, or language, received a severe knock in 1971, when it was reported that a chimpanzee called Washoe had been taught a sign language called Ameslan (American Sign Language) commonly used by the deaf and consisting of hand gestures, roughly speaking, one to a word. Over a period of five years, she had acquired a vocabulary of about 150 signs she could use correctly and a further 200 which she could understand. Midgley (writing some time ago, and basing her information on a book published in 1974) reports that:

> Since then other chimps have also been taught the language, with much the same degree of success. Four of them have now (1974) been placed with Washoe in a community on an island, watched but not interfered with. They use Ameslan constantly and spontaneously to talk to one another. And their use of it is increasing. Moreover, they talk to themselves, and, without having been taught to, they swear. (The favoured swearword is the Ameslan sign for 'dirty'.)
>
> (Midgley (1980), p.215)

And Singer, writing in the 1990s, reports that:

> Gorillas appear to be as good at learning sign language. Almost twenty years ago Francine Patterson began signing and also speaking English with Koko, a lowland gorilla. Koko now has a working vocabulary of over 500 signs, and she has used about 1000 signs correctly on one or more occasions. She understands an even larger number of spoken English words... when someone remarked of Koko, in her presence, 'She's a goof ball' Koko (perhaps not understanding the term) signed 'No, gorilla'.
>
> (Singer (1993), p.111)

Fascinating as the details are of what these chimps and gorillas can do, what is more relevant to our purposes here are the reactions to the first and subsequent reports of what they can do. One reaction was fascination, enthralment, a desire to know lots more of the details. Another began, with the first report, by sounding proper notes of caution – perhaps Washoe's capacities were being exaggerated or misdescribed – though they were surely over-cautious in trying, as they did, to make out that Washoe's whole performance was best described in terms of her simply having learnt to make certain hand movements in certain conditions to get a reward. But a third reaction (which the second tended to develop into, as further reports came out) was pure Aristotle and Descartes: whatever the chimps (and gorillas, and orang-utans...) were doing it was not *using language.* Using language – having the faculty of 'speech' – these writers had suddenly realized, was being able to do *this*, and then they would describe a condition that what the apes had been reported as doing did not satisfy.

So, for instance, one of the first moves was that Washoe was not *using language,* did not have the faculty of speech, because, it was claimed, whatever you did didn't count as 'using language' unless you could create new units of meaning out of the building block signs that you had been given. But then it turned out that Washoe could do that. It was reported that she had come up with her own term for 'refrigerator', spontaneously combining the two signs she had been taught for 'cold' and 'food'. And, instead of saying 'How fascinating!' some people just moved the goal posts and said that whatever you did didn't count as 'using language' unless you showed that you grasped it as something that could be passed on by teaching it to the next generation. And some others moved the goal posts in a different way, and said that whatever you did didn't count as 'using language' unless you could do something fairly sophisticated with 'word order' – a concept devised by linguists to apply to the common human context in which the 'spoken' and the written signs correspond, but is not true of sign language.

Various other moves have been tried – and many of them have **absurd consequences** which their proponents certainly did not intend. If they were right, it would turn out that children do not 'use language'; that the deaf do not 'use language'; that people afflicted with the many, various, and sometimes extraordinarily specific, failures in linguistic capacity that can follow on from strokes do not 'use language.'

absurd consequences move

So why have so many people – reasonable, intelligent people – made these moves? Why have they bothered to argue at such length, and in such detail, that the apes *cannot* be using language? Why have they been so anxious to establish this conclusion that they have failed to notice that their arguments yield absurd consequences about human beings? Why do they not respond to the reports by saying 'How fascinating! If (of course *if*) these reports are accurate, *some* animals (a very few species) do have *some* degree of linguistic understanding, can use language to *some* degree'? What is so hard about admitting that?

Midgley's – and some other philosophers' – explanation is that it is the influence of the long tradition we have just briefly surveyed, working hand in hand with the prevalent desire to justify the ways in which we exploit animals.

Conclusion

It is worth reflecting on what Bentham said (see pp.212–13) with hindsight. Considering what difference between humans and animals should 'trace the insuperable line' between those beings to whom we extend moral concern and those to whom we do not, Bentham asks, 'Is it the faculty of reason, or perhaps the faculty of discourse?' and insists 'The question is not, Can they *reason*? nor Can they *talk?* but, *Can they suffer*?' We have seen how, from Aristotle to the present day, the faculty of reason and the faculty of discourse have been viewed as inseparable, part of the same package which draws a hard and fast line between us and all the other animals.

We have also seen that the attempts to draw such a hard and fast line do not appear very plausible; indeed, they sometimes seem like special pleading. Surely it is reasonable to accept that a few, albeit very few other animals have 'speech' to some degree. Surely it is reasonable to accept that many animals are conscious to some degree. Everyone who trains domestic animals relies on this fact – and many will have seen television programmes about squirrels figuring out how to get the nuts people are trying to preserve for the birds. The line between the other animals and us is not so hard and fast after all.

Arguing against cruelty

'Indirect duty' views

In this section of the chapter, we are going to look at two more brief extracts. The study of these will continue, but go well beyond, increasing your understanding of the background tradition which supports our current treatment of animals. It will also be preparation for the next chapter on Tom Regan, who, along with Singer, is one of the major – and extreme – campaigners on behalf of the moral claims of animals.

As I said above, Descartes was almost alone in claiming that animals did not feel pain. Most thinkers of the past followed Aristotle (and common sense) in accepting that they do. And despite a continuing insistence on the point that human beings were the only rational animals, unique amongst the animals in being made in the image of God, able to use language, tool users (another favourite), having a grasp of the past and future, having a grasp of good and evil, having a sense of justice, being moral agents – each of which was, at some time, taken to be a mark of our special unique possession of reason – none of them (so far as I know) made an explicit commitment to 'absolute dismissal'.

Many, in fact, explicitly disavowed it. Though far from being equal, in any sense to Man, God's finest creation, animals, they claimed, were not to be treated with wanton cruelty; this was wrong. What did they say was wrong about it?

The two extracts to be studied in this section consist of slightly different, but basically similar, accounts of what is wrong about wanton cruelty to animals, both of which are called 'indirect duty' views.

The first passage is extracted from the article by Tom Regan (Reading 2) that we shall be studying in the next chapter. When you come to read the article, you will discover that the passage does not express Regan's own views; on the contrary, it is a passage in which he (very briefly) outlines an indirect duty view in relation to our treatment of animals only to reject it in a couple of sentences. We are taking it out of its context and simply regarding it as an outline of an indirect duty view which we will then subject to criticism. The point of doing this now, is so that you can come to the full Regan article armed with the philosophical knowledge you need to understand and assess what he says so briefly there.

EXERCISE 16

An 'indirect view'

To continue the development of your analytical skills, now do an extended exercise on the passage, beginning with some straightforward comprehension questions and then moving on to more sophisticated ones. You should allow yourself an hour in which to do this exercise thoroughly.

Answer these questions after reading the passage that follows.

1 According to the passage:

   (i) Do we have any duties *to* animals?

   (ii) Is it ever wrong to hurt an animal?

   (iii) Do we have duties *regarding* animals?

2 What is the main claim of the passage? (Keep as close as possible to the words in it).

> We have no duties directly to animals...we owe nothing to them... [and]... can do nothing that wrongs them. Rather, we can do wrong acts that involve animals, and so we have duties regarding them, though none to them. Such views may be called indirect duty views. By way of illustration: suppose your neighbour kicks your dog. Then your neighbour has done something wrong. But not to your dog. The wrong that has been done is a wrong to you. After all, it is wrong to upset people, and your neighbour's kicking your dog upsets you. So you are the one who is wronged, not your dog. Or again: by kicking your dog your neighbour damages your property. And since it is wrong to damage another person's

> property, your neighbour has done something wrong – to you, of course, not to your dog. Your neighbour no more wrongs your dog than your car would be wronged if the windshield were smashed. Your neighbour's duties involving your dog are indirect duties to you. More generally, all our duties regarding animals are indirect duties to one another – to humanity.
>
> (Regan, Reading 2, paragraph (6))

Check your answers against those at the back of the book before continuing the exercise.

The following questions test your ability to differentiate between unsupported and supported claims and to identify reasons for claims when they are present. Answer them in complete, grammatical sentences which follow as closely as possible the words in the question.

assertion

3 Is any reason given for the claim that we have no duties to animals in the passage or is it an **unsupported claim**?

4 Why, according to the passage, would it be wrong of me to kick your dog?

5 Is any reason given in the passage for the claim that we have duties regarding animals or is it an unsupported claim?

6 If a reason is given, what is it? (Begin your answer with 'The reason given is that...')

Check your answers against those at the back of the book before continuing the exercise.

The following questions test your ability to work out the implications of claims, i.e. what follows from them.

7 According to the passage, would any of the following clearly be wrong? (Just 'yes' or 'no').

(i) I kill your dearly beloved cat.

(ii) I gratuitously wound a farmer's valuable cow.

(iii) I inflict pain on my own cat in the privacy of my own home.

(iv) I steal your dog and give it to my children to torment.

(v) I take in an obvious stray and torment it.

(vi) You and I decide it would be fun to torment your dog and we do so.

absurd consequences move

8 What is an **absurd** (not to say horrible) **consequence** of the claims in this passage? (Begin your answer 'An absurd consequence of the claims in this passage is that...)

Check your answers against those at the back of the book before continuing the exercise.

Finally, a few questions to elicit your own views on the claims in the passage. Try to give a reason for your view in each case, or make it clear that it is, for you, a basic assumption or **premise**.

premise

9 Do you think that the 'indirect duty' view outlined gives an adequate account of what is wrong about wanton cruelty to animals?

10 Do you think that *all* of our duties regarding animals are indirect duties to one another?

11 Do you think that *some* of our duties regarding animals are indirect duties to one another?

12 Do you think we have some duties to animals?

DISCUSSION

My answers are as follows.

9 No, I do not think it gives an adequate account. My reason is that, although it rules out quite a lot of cruel treatment of animals (as in 7 (i), (ii) and (iv), it makes no objection to treatment which is equally cruel (as in 7 (iii), (v) and (vi)).

10 No, I do not think that all of our duties regarding animals are indirect duties to one another (duties not to upset one another or damage each other's property without permission). My reason is that we can do wrong acts involving animals (and hence have duties regarding animals) when all that is at issue is the suffering of the animal (as in 7 (iii), (v) and (vi) again).

11 Yes, I do think that some of our duties regarding animals are *also* indirect duties to one another. My reason is that if I am cruel to your beloved cat, right in front of you, I agree with the passage that I have done something wrong to you. All I want to insist on is that I have done something wrong to the cat *too*.

12 So, in that sense, I think we have some duties to animals, in particular, the duty not to be cruel to them, regardless of whether anyone else is affected. I take it as a basic assumption or premise that animal suffering matters, and hence that we should refrain from inflicting it when possible.

Conclusion

The points you need to note from the detailed study of this passage are the following.

1 The main claim of the passage is given as 'all of our duties regarding animals are indirect duties to one another – to humanity'. We have now seen that this amounts to the claim 'all of our duties regarding animals are indirect duties to other human beings *who are involved*' – people who will be upset, or people whose property is at issue.

2 Hence, as we have seen, the passage has the absurd consequence that, when someone else is not involved, I do not even have a duty regarding animals, i.e. there is nothing wrong with my being as cruel to them as I may wish.

3 There is no reason given in the passage for the claim that 'we have no duties to animals'.

Kant's indirect duty view

Bearing the above points in mind, consider a second extract, from the eighteenth-century German philosopher, Immanuel Kant (1724–1804), which outlines another indirect duty view. This view is subtly different from the one we have just considered in several important ways, and I shall be asking you to compare it with the first.

As before, we will begin with some straightforward comprehension questions and then move on to more sophisticated ones. Although studying the previous passage may well enable you to tackle the questions more easily, the passage itself is longer and its style more difficult, so allow the same amount of time it took you to work through the previous exercise.

EXERCISE 17
On Kant's indirect view

Answer the following questions, after reading the passage below.

1 According to Kant:

(i) Do we have any (direct) duties *to* animals?

(ii) Is it ever wrong to hurt an animal?

(iii) Do we have duties *towards* animals?

2 What is the main claim of the passage as stated?

Baumgarten speaks of duties towards beings which are beneath us and beings which are above us. But so far as animals are concerned, we have no direct duties. Animals are not self-conscious and are there merely as a means to an end. That end is man. We can ask, 'Why do animals exist?' But to ask, 'Why does man exist?' is a meaningless question. Our duties towards animals are merely indirect duties towards humanity. Animal nature has analogies to human nature, and by doing our duties to animals in respect of manifestations which correspond to manifestations of human nature, we indirectly do our duty towards humanity. Thus, if a dog has served his master long and faithfully, his service, on the analogy of human service, deserves regard, and when the dog has grown too old to serve, his master ought to keep him until he dies. Such action helps to support us in our duties towards human beings, where they are bounden duties. If then any acts of animals are analogous to human acts and spring from the same principles, we have duties towards the animals because thus we cultivate the corresponding duties towards human beings. If a man shoots his dog because the animal is no longer capable of service, he does not fail in his duty to the dog, for the dog cannot judge, but his act is inhuman and damages in himself that humanity which it is his duty to show towards mankind. If he is not to stifle his human feelings, he must practise kindness towards animals, for he who is cruel to animals becomes hard also in his dealing with men. We can judge the heart of a man by his treatment of animals. Hogarth depicts this in his engravings. He shows how cruelty grows and develops. He shows the child's cruelty to animals, pinching the tail of a dog or a cat; he then depicts the grown man in his cart running over a child; and lastly, the culmination of cruelty in murder. He thus brings home to us in a terrible fashion the rewards of cruelty, and this should be an impressive lesson to children. The more we come in contact with animals and observe their behaviour, the more we love them, for we see how great is their care for their young. It is then difficult for us to be cruel in thought even to a wolf. Leibniz used a tiny worm for purposes of observation, and then carefully replaced it with its leaf on the tree so that it should not come to harm through any act of his. He would have been sorry – a natural feeling for a humane man – to destroy such a creature for no reason. Tender feelings towards dumb animals develop humane feelings towards mankind. In England butchers and doctors do not sit on a jury because they are accustomed to the sight of death and hardened. Vivisectionists, who use living animals for their experiments, certainly act cruelly, although their aim is praiseworthy, and they can justify their cruelty, since animals must be regarded as man's instruments; but any such cruelty for sport cannot be justified. A master who turns out his ass or his dog because the animal can no longer earn its keep manifests a small mind. The Greeks' ideas in this respect were high-minded, as can be seen from the fable of the ass and the bell of ingratitude. Our duties towards animals, then, are indirect duties towards mankind.

(Kant (1963 edn), pp.239–40)

Check your answers against those at the back of the book before continuing the exercise.

3 Why, according to Kant, would it be wrong of me to shoot my faithful old dog? (Try, at this stage, to give an answer that uses Kant's own words as far as possible.)

4 Would any of the following be wrong, according to Kant? (Just 'yes' or 'no'.)

(i) I kill your dearly beloved cat.

(ii) I gratuitously wound a farmer's valuable cow.

(iii) I inflict pain on my own cat in the privacy of my own home.

(iv) I steal your dog and give it to my children to torment.

(v) I take in an obvious stray and torment it.

(vi) You and I decide it would be fun to torment your dog and we do so.

5 Is Kant open to the same absurd consequences move that we made against the previous passage?

6 Is Kant, in this passage, to be interpreted as making *exactly the same* main claim as the previous passage?

Check your answers against those at the back of the book before reading on.

DISCUSSION

You should now appreciate some of the ways in which Kant's indirect duty view is different from the previous one. True, the main claims of the two passages are stated in almost the same words. But different authors can use even the very same words to mean different things. In the first passage, 'indirect duties to one another – to humanity' meant 'indirect duties to other human beings *who are involved*', as was made clear by the discussion of your neighbour kicking your dog. But as soon as we come to Kant's discussion of the man shooting his faithful dog, we realize that he cannot be interpreted the same way. There is no one else in Kant's example who will be wronged by being upset if the man shoots his dog, and no one else who is being wrongfully deprived of his property – it's the man's own dog. So there is the crucial difference between the first indirect duty view and Kant's indirect duty view. On the first view, some other human being must actually be involved if the cruelty to the animal is to be wrong. On Kant's view, this is not necessary.

Hence Kant is completely immune to the absurd consequences move we were able to bring against the first passage. Far from having no duty to refrain from torturing my own cat, because no one else is involved, I *do* have a duty to refrain. I owe it to mankind, because, if I do not refrain, I am setting off on the path of becoming 'hard in [my] dealings with men' and (if we accept what Kant says about Hogarth's engravings) apparently due to become a murderer later on! Kant's conclusion rules out not just some cases of wanton cruelty, but all of them.

EXERCISE 18

More on Kant's view

Now for some further questions on Kant.

1 Try to say, in your own words, why, according to Kant, treating animals kindly, or not treating them cruelly is a duty we have towards animals.

2 Identify two or three parts of the text which support your answer.

3 Unlike the first, this passage does contain support for the claim that 'We have no duties to animals'. Identify the parts of the text in which such support is given. (It is, I think, unclear whether several reasons are given or just one, expressed in different ways.)

Check your answers against those at the back of the book before continuing the exercise.

Finally, the following questions are to elicit your own views on the claims in the passage. Try to give a reason for your view in each case, or make it clear that it is, for you, a basic assumption or **premise**.

premise

4 Do you think that Kant's indirect duty view gives an adequate account of what is wrong about wanton cruelty to animals?

5 Do you think it is true that how we treat animals affects or determines how we treat other human beings?

6 Are you satisfied by what Kant says about vivisectionists?

7 Do you think we have some duties *to* animals?

DISCUSSION

My answers are as follows:

4 No, I do not think it gives an adequate account. I have several reasons, but the simplest one is that I think it rests on a false premise, namely Kant's **empirical** generalization that how we treat animals affects or determines how we treat other human beings.

empirical

5 I do not think this is true because I can think of obvious counter-examples. For Spaniards, going to the bullfight or watching it on television, plays the same role as watching football does for us. But modern Spaniards are not notably more prone to murder or cruelty to each other than we are.

6 I am not satisfied by what Kant says about vivisectionists for two reasons. One is ***ad hominem***: he seems to undermine his own empirical generalization. (He could hardly claim that their cruelty was justifiable if he thought it 'hardened' them and made it more likely that they would

ad hominem move

commit murder!) The other is that I do not agree with him that 'animals must be regarded as man's instruments'.

Note that this claim of Kant and his similar unsupported claim that 'Animals... are there merely as a means to an end. The end is man', are reminiscent of those from *Genesis,* Augustine and Aquinas that were considered earlier. We do not have duties to things that are 'our instruments'. The point of saying that something is *ours,* that we have 'dominion' over it, that it is there for us to *use* as a means to our ends, is to say that we have a right to do with it whatever we choose.

7 I continue to believe that we have some duties *to* animals. Even if I grant Kant his empirical generalization, I would still want to insist on this. Suppose his premise is true, then indeed I have an indirect duty to mankind not to be cruel to any animal, say my cat. But, as before, I take it as a basic assumption or premise that animal suffering matters. So I think I have a duty to my cat *too.*

Conclusions regarding 'indirect duty' views

Comparing the two versions of the indirect duty view in the two extracts we can see that they differ in one crucial respect, namely that the first allows some wanton cruelty to animals whereas the second does not. This means that the second, Kant's, is more humane, less like absolute dismissal, than the first.

However, both share the view that none of our duties regarding, or towards, animals is a moral claim to be made *on behalf* of animals. They are all moral claims to be made on behalf of human beings. The fact Bentham emphasized, that a tortured animal suffers, turns out, even for Kant, not to be a fact that can form the basis of a moral claim *on behalf* of the animal or a duty to it. Midgley sums up Kant's position as making the claim 'that decent behaviour to the dog is not real decent behaviour, just practice for real decent behaviour to people... we cannot have a duty to the dog itself' (Midgley (1980), p. 222). But are there, we may wonder, no duties of compassion to animals?

The philosopher Arthur Schopenhauer (1788–1860), responding to Kant's indirect duty view, made just this point:

> Genuine morality is outraged by the proposition that beings devoid of reason [hence animals] are *things* and therefore should be treated merely as *means* that are not at the same time an *end*... Thus only for practice are we to have sympathy for animals, and they are, so to speak, the pathological [i.e. emotional] phantom for the purpose of practising sympathy for human beings. In common with the whole of Asia not tainted with Islam (that is, Judaism) I regard such propositions as revolting and abominable.
>
> (Schopenhauer (1965 edn), §8)

In a later section, he says:

> Boundless compassion for all living beings is the firmest and surest guarantee of pure moral conduct, and needs no casuistry [i.e. subtle argument]... If we attempt to say, 'This man is virtuous, but knows no compassion'... the contradiction is obvious. Tastes differ, but I know of no finer prayer than the one which ends old Indian dramas... It runs, 'May all living beings remain free from pain.'
>
> (Ibid., §19)

The straightforward thought to carry over from the preceding exploration of indirect duty views is hence the following: we have duties, direct and perhaps indirect, to human beings or perhaps to humanity at large. But we have (direct) duties to animals *too.* The idea that we have duties to both human beings *and* to animals, of rather different sorts, is to be found in the next position we shall consider.

Contractarianism

'Contractarianism' is another position that Regan summarizes briefly in the article discussed in the next chapter. But, unfortunately, he does not summarize it correctly, so, before reading him, you need to get clear about what it is so that you will not be misled.

You may have noticed that, in both the indirect duty view extracts, there is something a little odd about the 'direct/indirect' distinction. Why is it there? Why not just say, simply, 'All our duties regarding animals come down to, or simply amount to, duties regarding other individuals or humanity' rather than making a point of insisting 'We have no *direct* duties to animals'? The implication is that our duties regarding animals are different from certain other duties ('direct duties') we have to human beings – and, given the context, it seems that 'direct duties' are the most important. But it is possible to share with indirect duty views the idea that our duties regarding animals are different from certain other duties we have to human beings without giving any pre-eminence to the latter, as we shall see.

Rather than saying 'We have duties regarding animals but no direct duties to them' some philosophers say such things as the following: 'We have duties regarding, and indeed to, animals but animals are outside the scope of *justice*'; or 'We have duties regarding, and indeed to, animals but nothing we do to them is contrary to *justice*'; or 'We have duties regarding, and indeed to, animals but *justice* does not put any constraints on how we treat them'; or, most significantly, 'We have duties to animals but animals do not have *rights*'. For our present purposes, we may regard all these as equivalent.

Amongst the philosophers who hold this view are Kant's immediate predecessor, David Hume (1711–76) and the influential modern American philosopher John Rawls. Hume and Rawls are both 'contract theorists' or 'contractarians' about justice. This means that they both argue that justice obtains only between creatures who are capable of 'contracting into' society, capable of recognizing that they are equally entitled to, and equally bound to respect, certain rights. Clearly, such 'creatures' are human beings (and speech-using human beings at that) yet again, not animals, but both Hume and Rawls regard the sphere of morality as considerably wider than the sphere of justice.

With respect to animals, Hume says we 'should not [i.e. would not], properly speaking, lie under any restraint of justice with regard to them, nor could they possess any right or property... Our intercourse with them could not be called society, which supposes a degree of equality'. But he does not think that justice (and rights) generate the only moral requirements or duties: immediately before the passage just quoted, he says, 'we should be bound by the laws of humanity[8] to give gentle usage to these creatures' (Hume (1902 edn), p.190).

EXERCISE 19
Contractarian views on animals

Towards the end of his monumental *A Theory of Justice* (1971) John Rawls expresses the same view. In the following passage, from near the end of his book, he is looking back over the whole work, adding a few last thoughts, and it is not surprising that it is not easy to discern much in the way of detailed argument here. Try to find two premises which support the conclusion he shares with Hume, state that conclusion and do not worry about any further details.

> Last of all, we should recall here the limits of a theory of justice. Not only are many aspects of morality left aside, but no account is given of right conduct in regard to animals and the rest of nature. A conception of justice is but one part of a moral view. While I have not maintained that the capacity for a sense of justice is necessary in order to be owed the duties of justice, it does seem that we are not required to give strict justice anyway to creatures lacking this capacity. But it does not follow that there are no requirements at all in regard to them, nor in our relations with the natural order. Certainly it is wrong to be cruel to animals and the destruction of a whole species can be a great evil. The capacity for feelings of pleasure and pain and for the forms of life of which animals are capable clearly imposes duties of compassion and humanity in their case. I shall not attempt to explain these considered beliefs. They are outside the scope of the theory of justice, and it does not seem possible to extend the contract doctrine so as to include them in a natural way.
>
> (Rawls (1971), p.512)

Check your answers against those at the back of the book before reading on.

EXERCISE 20
Hume, Kant and Rawls

Complete the following two sentences.

1 Hume, Kant and Rawls share the view that our duties regarding animals are...

2 They differ in that Kant thinks that our duties regarding animals are... whereas Hume and Rawls do not. They think that...

Check your answers against those at the back of the book before reading on.

Despite Rawls's disclaimer here, many people have taken *A Theory of Justice* as offering, if not a complete moral view, at least a nearly complete one – and many, particularly in the United States, have welcomed it as such. One philosopher who has overlooked the disclaimer but not welcomed *A Theory of Justice* as a comprehensive theory of morality is Tom Regan, to whom we turn in the next chapter.

Chapter summary

Human beings as special

A long tradition in Western thought emphasizes differences between human beings and the other animals as real, hard and fast, and very significant – significant enough to justify our using them for food and in experiments. Many philosophers, amongst them the most influential, claimed that human beings were unique in possessing reason, or being rational and were, moreover, certain that no other animals possess reason to any degree at all. Rationality was, according to them, an all-or-nothing matter. Our possession of reason was linked inseparably to various other features we have, such as being moral agents, having speech, and, with Christianity, having an immortal soul. These too were thought to be all-or-nothing matters, and we see the tradition persisting to this day in the attempts some people have made to deny that the chimpanzee Washoe and other primates are using language.

Descartes, in some of his writings, went so far as to claim that animals did not have minds and hence were not even conscious of pleasure and pain. He was, however, almost alone in this view. Most philosophers agreed that animals could suffer, and maintained, further, that some infliction of suffering on animals was wrong.

Arguing against cruelty

According to the first indirect duty view that we looked at, it is wrong to inflict suffering on an animal when this would upset someone else or damage their property. According to the second, Kant's, all wanton infliction of suffering is wrong because it hardens the perpetrator. We should, indeed, be kind to animals – but not because we owe it to them or have a direct duty to them to do so. We should be kind to them because it is good practice for being kind to human beings, those who can judge. We have no direct duties to animals, not even duties of compassion or sympathy.

Contractarianism about justice preserves the traditional idea that there is something special about human beings, with their rationality and discourse. Only they can 'contract into' society and recognize that they are entitled to, and bound to respect, certain rights. So nothing we do to animals is contrary to justice, nor could it violate their rights, because they do not have rights. However, this does *not* mean that we have no duties to them. There are, as well as duties of justice, also duties of compassion (or sympathy or humanity) and these are duties we have to animals. It makes perfectly good sense to make moral claims on their behalf, because they can suffer.

Further reading

Richard Sorabji's *Animal Minds and Human Morals,* Duckworth, 1993, traces the origins of the current debate on our treatment of animals, concentrating on the influential ideas of Aristotle. Immensely scholarly, this book is fascinating for advanced readers, particularly in its discussion of Porphyry (c.232–c.305), who foreshadowed most twentieth-century arguments in defence of animals. More accessible is *Political Theory and Animal Rights* edited by Paul A.B. Clarke and Andrew Linzey, Pluto Press, 1990; a collection of over sixty short extracts from philosophical writings, from Plato to the present day.

Notes

[1] Augustine has just drawn a contrast between this commandment and 'Thou shalt not bear false witness *against thy neighbour*' where the italicized phrase adds 'a limitation'.

[2] 'Divine Providence' is a difficult term for those not brought up using it. Roughly, it is a way of referring to the God of Christianity, but like 'the Creator' it refers to Him under a particular aspect. As Creator, God is the one who created the heaven and the earth, etc. – the God of Genesis. God as Providence is particularly foreknowing and beneficent.

[3] Later, you will be studying a fascinating modern version of Descartes's test here, called the 'Turing test' for intelligence. This involves two humans and a super-computer. One of the humans is the assessor, alone in a room with a more ordinary computer. She types in questions addressed to A or B, and their answers appear on her screen. A and B are the other human and the super-computer, and, at the beginning, the assessor has no idea which is which. Her goal is to see if she can find out which is which on the basis of their answers. If she can't tell, then the computer passes the Turing test and counts as intelligent. Descartes's assumption about machines amounts to the prediction that *of course* she will be able to tell – a prediction that is looking increasingly shaky. But he can hardly be blamed for this; he shows quite remarkable prescience in imagining that a machine might be built that could say 'What do you want to say to me?' or 'Ouch, that hurt' in response to a certain physical input.

[4] 'Laws of humanity' for Hume does not mean anything like 'indirect duties to humanity' in Kant. Rather it means 'the requirements of the virtue of benevolence or sympathy' which, in Hume, figures as a more important virtue than that of justice.

The Rights-based Defence of Animals

OBJECTIVES

By the end of this chapter you should have:

- Acquired a good knowledge of Regan's position on animal rights.
- Understood his objection to utilitarianism.
- Appreciated the reasons that may be given for denying that animals have rights (the 'contractarian' position).
- Extended your ability to follow detailed arguments back and forth.
- Extended your ability to apply the basic reading method.

In the first part of this chapter, we shall be studying Tom Regan's rights-based defence of animals and doing a 'full reading' of his most well-known article. In the second part we shall be exploring arguments against the view that animals have rights.

In favour of animal rights

In the preceding chapter we have been looking at the long Western tradition which draws a hard and fast line between human beings and animals. We noted that, with the exception of Descartes, philosophers who drew such a line accepted the fact that human beings did have one thing in common with many animals – both they, and we, are capable of pleasure and pain. We also looked at two different reactions to that fact. First, indirect duty views recognize the fact that animals can suffer and, at least in the case of Kant, recognize that we have a duty to refrain from wanton cruelty to animals. But in indirect duty views, oddly enough, the fact that an animal suffers if you torture it is not the basis of our duty not to torture it. What matters is not the suffering of the animal but, for Kant, the likelihood that anyone who tortures an animal will go on to behave badly to other human beings – those superior creatures who possess rationality. We have duties to human beings, but not to animals.

The second reaction contained in the contractarianism of Hume and Rawls, unlike the indirect duty views, takes the fact that animals can suffer as the basis of our duty not to treat them with wanton cruelty. Contractarians agree with Kant that it is only rational human beings who have rights, and nothing we do to the animals can be contrary to justice. But justice is not the whole of morality. We have duties to respect the rights of those who have rights, but we *also* have duties of compassion or humanity – and we have these latter duties to all animals capable of pleasure and pain.

Contractarianism, in Hume and Rawls, allows for two sorts of duties – those that are requirements of justice and those that are requirements of compassion (and/or sympathy, humanity and benevolence.) We might say that, according to contractarianism, there are at least two considerations that matter a great deal in morality, two things we need to consider when we are deciding what we ought to do: one is rights and the other is suffering (and perhaps pleasure).

Looking back to the first two chapters on utilitarianism, we can see that Singer is putting all the emphasis on this second consideration. What matters in utilitarianism is not, fundamentally, whether an action will violate a rational creature's rights, but whether it will maximize the interests of those creatures capable of pleasure and pain.

So there is a third way of reacting to the fact that both we and many other animals can suffer; one can say, with Bentham, that it is the only thing that matters ('The question is not, Can they *reason*? nor Can they *talk*? but, *Can they suffer*?').

Tom Regan occupies a position quite different from any we have so far considered. Like Singer, he emphasizes just one of the two considerations that Hume and Rawls allow. But unlike Singer, he emphasizes *rights* not suffering, although his view of rights is very unlike Hume's and Rawls's. He does not think that the only creatures who have rights are those who are capable of entering into contracts, for he argues that most animals have rights too.

The Regan article which we will be studying in this chapter is his own summary of his book on animal rights.[9] The book is dauntingly long, the article attractively short, but the inevitable consequence is that the article has both to condense and also leave a lot unsaid. It contains several misrepresentations of, in particular, indirect duty views and contractarianism. But the most minimal application of the principle of charity requires that we assume that this is the result of the condensation.

Regan and Singer disagree in a way typical of philosophers. They both argue to, basically, the same conclusion: much of our treatment of animals is wrong, especially the ways in which we use animals for food and in scientific experiments. Both seek to change our views and hence, ultimately, the way our societies are organized. They are colleagues: they have edited books together, and, as you will see from the endnote to the reading, Regan wrote this article especially for a collection edited by Singer. *But* they disagree about which moral theory should provide one of the basic premises of the argument to their shared conclusion. For Singer, as we have seen, it is utilitarianism. For Regan, it is 'the rights view'. So, in fact, they object to each other's argument, each thinking that the other has a false or implausible premise, while agreeing with each other's conclusion.

In the Singer Reading, there was hardly any mention of non-utilitarian moral theories, but in Regan's article he not only outlines his argument to the shared conclusion but first devotes almost half the article to outlining and criticizing rival moral approaches. I shall not discuss what he says about the indirect duty view and contractarianism – part of the point of the earlier exercises was to ensure that you understood these better than you would from the article's account of them – but I will discuss the argument against utilitarianism. Indeed, as with the Singer Reading, I am breaking the 'full reading' of the Regan article into two parts. When we have gone through both, we will proceed to the critical evaluation.

READING
'The Case for Animal Rights', paragraphs 1–22

Remember that you should first skim (about five minutes), and then read slowly, doing a reading outline. You should look for ways to complete the following sentences:

Regan is defending/arguing for (the view that) ...

He argues against ...

He also argues against ...

Please do a full reading of Regan's article (Reading 2, paragraphs 1–22) now.

DISCUSSION
Skimming, paragraphs 1–22

By skimming and using what you already know, you should have seen that Regan is arguing that much of our treatment of animals is wrong or, more precisely, he is arguing for the total abolition of the use of animals in science, the total dissolution of commercial agriculture, etc. (from the helpful opening bullet points).

You should also have seen that Regan argues against utilitarianism: he introduces the topic at the beginning of paragraph 14, and is obviously still pursuing it through paragraphs 15–22, where he concludes that utilitarianism fails in some respect or other.

Good skimming identifies something else going on in paragraphs 6–13, and the last two sentences of paragraph 6 should appear familiar. The previous sentences in the paragraph reveal it to be Exercise 16 in Chapter 3, about the indirect duty view. This sets you up to notice the mention of indirect duty views at the beginning of paragraphs 8 and 13 and hence to be able to note that

Regan also argues against indirect duty views.

Brilliant skimming would pick up the end of paragraph 8 and note the word 'contractarianism' (or 'contracts') at the beginning of paragraphs 9–12 which would allow you to say more:

Regan also argues against indirect duty views, amongst which he includes contractarianism.

If you got this far you will doubtless also have realized that this is a mistake, or misrepresentation, on Regan's part; we saw in Chapter 3 that contractarianism is not an indirect duty view.

DISCUSSION
Reading outline

Here I shall add some reminders about what you learned in the last chapter but they do not have to form part of your reading outline.

1–5 Introduction. Using what you know, you should have noted the statement of Regan's general position, his main claims, namely, that the way we treat animals is wrong (agreeing with Singer) but 'what is (fundamentally) wrong isn't the suffering' (anti-Singer), and perhaps have added that what is wrong is that we violate animals' rights.

6 Outline of a basic indirect duty view.

7 Objection to this view – the dog's pain is morally relevant as well as the humans' interests. (Remember the discussion in Chapter 3: that a major criticism of this argument was that it just assumed the premise that no wrong was done to the dog? But why not say a wrong is done to the dog *as well as* people? The dog's suffering counts – is morally relevant – *too.*)

8–9 Outline of another indirect duty view – contractarianism. 'Morality is a set of rules' that we contract with each other to abide by. Parties to the moral contract 'have rights created and recognized by, and protected in, the contract'. Those such as young children who cannot understand contracts 'lack rights' and are only protected by our duties to rights-holders such as their parents. (Note that, unlike the 'contractarianism' of Hume and Rawls that we looked at, Regan's version (a **straw man**?) does take justice, or rights, to be the whole of morality. Hume and Rawls would say that '*Justice* is a set of rules that we contract with each other to abide by' not that all of *morality* is.)

straw man

10 Consequences of contractarianism for animals. Animals 'cannot understand contracts'. So, as before, they lack rights. All duties regarding them are indirect duties to people who care about them. So if no one cares whether they suffer or die, 'the pain and death they endure... are not wrong'.

11 Objection to (crude) contractarianism – it is inadequate even as an 'approach to the moral status of human beings' because it 'could sanction the most blatant forms of social, economic, moral and political injustice'.

12 Outline of a much less crude version of contractarianism (John Rawls's) – this is an 'improvement' – and an objection. 'It remains deficient' because it still denies rights to children and 'many mentally retarded humans'. (You might have noted that at this point Regan introduces what is, in fact a new premise: if torturing a young child wrongs them (i.e. is something we have a direct duty not to do) then 'we cannot rationally deny the same in the case of animals'. This is clearly shaping up to the anti-speciesism view he shares with Singer.)

13 Conclusion from the arguments in 6–12. Indirect duty views fail. (You might add the explicit denial of what indirect duty views assert: so 'we have some duties directly to animals'.)

14–16 Outline of utilitarianism. 'A utilitarian accepts two moral principles.' A utilitarian 'must ask who will be affected'. 'The great appeal of utilitarianism is its egalitarianism.' (Remember this was discussed at some length with respect to Singer.)

17 Objection to utilitarianism. Utilitarianism has no room for the inherent value or worth of individuals; only their interests or feelings have any value.

18 Clarification of the objection. For the utilitarian, you and I are like a valueless cup containing liquids ('our feelings') which have positive or negative value.

19 More objections ('serious problems arise'). The act which leads to the best consequences, all added up, might not be the one that leads to what is best for each individual.

20–2 This is 'the key objection to this theory', as is shown by the counter-example of Aunt Bea. According to utilitarianism, in killing Aunt Bea in the case described, 'I did what duty required'. But this is false – 'It *is* wrong to kill my Aunt Bea in the name of bringing about the best results for others'. Utilitarianism cannot explain why this is so. Conclusion: utilitarianism is not an adequate moral theory.

DISCUSSION
Paragraphs 13–22

As I said above (p.104), I am not going to discuss paragraphs 6–12, but concentrate on Regan's disagreement with Singer over utilitarianism. As with my initial discussion of the Singer reading, this is your substitute for Windt's 'third stage' of the reading method. Remember that, mostly, I am just summarizing and elaborating on what Regan says, emphasizing charitable interpretations. I am not necessarily endorsing a single sentence of it.

The conclusion of Regan's discussion of the indirect duty view and contractarianism was that 'we have some duties directly to animals, just as we have some duties directly to each other' (paragraph 13), which is something he can now rely on as a **premise**. What moral theories allow for that? Not, he thinks, indirect duty views (and he is right about that). And not contractarianism (about which he is mistaken, as we have seen – Hume and Rawls both allow (direct) duties of compassion to animals). This, he thinks, leaves only utilitarianism and the rights view. So, having cleared indirect duty views (and thereby, he thinks, contractarianism) out of the way, he is now going to clear utilitarianism out of the way, leaving the field clear (so he believes) for the rights view. premise

14–15 He begins, very properly, by specifying what he takes utilitarianism to be. 'A utilitarian accepts two moral principles', and then stating them. In the next paragraph he helpfully elaborates on how a utilitarian decides what she ought to do – what her moral duty is.

It is worth being struck by the fact that he says a utilitarian accepts two moral principles because, as you know, utilitarians are usually described as accepting just one – known as 'the principle of utility' or 'the greatest happiness principle'. Why might he be doing that?

One answer, using what you know, would be that he is particularly concerned to argue against Singer – Singer is by far the most famous utilitarian who writes in defence of animals. Regan is on his side as far as defending animals is concerned – that's why they edit books together – but has a philosophical disagreement with him. He thinks Singer is defending animals on the wrong grounds – on the basis of utilitarianism instead of on the basis of animals' rights (see p.104). And Singer has made a point of bringing out a principle of equality, rather than leaving it implicit as Bentham and Mill did (see p.25).

Another answer (both could be true) might be that he himself accepts one of the two principles and thinks that what is wrong with utilitarianism stems from its other principle. Which of the two is it likely that a non-utilitarian as well as a utilitarian would accept?

16 Clearly, the principle of equality; and in this paragraph, having outlined and elaborated on utilitarianism in the previous two, Regan points out what can be said in favour of utilitarianism. What is good about it is that it is egalitarian – 'odious discrimination' based on race, sex or species membership 'seems disallowed in principle by utilitarianism'.

So far so good. Utilitarians (Singer) and anti-utilitarians (Regan) and probably most of us, are going to accept some sort of principle of equality; none of us wants to defend 'odious discrimination'. But why does he say the discrimination '*seems*' to be disallowed by the utilitarian's principle of equality, rather than just saying that it is disallowed?

17 Well, we can see from the beginning of this paragraph, where he goes on the attack, that he thinks there is something not quite right about 'the equality we find in utilitarianism' – it is 'not the sort an advocate of animal or human rights should have in mind'. Such an advocate wants to say that individuals have 'equal moral rights' and, moreover, that this is *because* they have 'equal inherent value or worth'. But utilitarianism does not accept that individuals have equal inherent value, because it has 'no room' for the *inherent* value of individuals at all. No individual human or animal has any value in themselves according to utilitarianism; only their feelings do – the feelings of satisfaction and enjoyment, or of frustration and pain.

This is a truly difficult paragraph in Regan – not because it is obscurely expressed but because it is so condensed. Fortunately, however, the work you did in Book 1 can be used to give you an understanding of it.

EXERCISE 21

Utilitarians, rights and equality

You may recall Jonathan Wolff on Mill on the right to liberty (Book 1, Reading 3, pp.180–2) discussing how a utilitarian would argue that we have such a right and have it equally.

1 Which of the following sketches is utilitarian?

2 Which could be a sketch of the sort of argument Regan would favour?

A says:

> Sane adults have equal inherent value as rational autonomous beings; therefore they have an equal right to freedom from coercion.

B says:

> God gave man free will that he might exercise it; therefore, it is God's will that men be free to make their own choices of good and evil; therefore all men have an equal right to freedom from coercion.

C says:

> Satisfaction of interests ought to be maximized and frustration of them minimised. The most effective way of bringing this about is by all sane adults enjoying equal freedom from coercion. Therefore they all ought to have it. Therefore they have an equal right to it.

Check your answers with those at the back of the book before reading on.

There is an awkward upshot for utilitarianism because the point that C makes in the second sentence is an **empirical** claim. It claims that, as a matter of empirical fact, the most effective way of maximizing satisfaction and minimizing frustration is to give sane adults equal freedom. But what if C has got her facts wrong?

empirical

EXERCISE 22

False empirical claims

Suppose the claim made by C in that second sentence is false; suppose, for instance, that we had established, fairly conclusively, that the most effective way of maximizing satisfaction and minimizing frustration was through a totalitarian regime that exerted considerable coercion over all but a few exceptionally gifted people.

1 What would C say?

2 What would A definitely *not* say?

DISCUSSION

1 If C is a thoroughgoing utilitarian, she certainly should say that, in that case, the coercion ought to be exercised over the many, that they ought not to have freedom and that, therefore, they have no right to it. The exceptionally gifted few ought to have freedom, and therefore they do have a right to it. So C, as a thoroughgoing utilitarian, would say that, if such a totalitarian regime really did have the beneficial consequences outlined, most people would not have the right to freedom, but a few would.

2 We are not in a position to know what A would say, but the one thing A will definitely not say is what C has said – that most people do not have the right to freedom but a few do. A might say that, in this case, unfortunately, every sane adult's equal right to freedom from coercion cannot – morally cannot – be recognized. Or they might say that, in this case, every sane adult's equal right must be recognized and we just have to live with the consequences and do the best with them that we can. Or they might say that, in this case, the equal right to freedom from coercion conflicts with the equal right to happiness [and so...?]. But the one thing they will *not* do is give up the claim about the equal right – because it was based on a claim about equal inherent value which remains quite unaffected by the empirical supposition.

So why does Regan claim that 'utilitarianism has no room for the equal moral rights of different individuals because it has no room for their equal inherent value or worth'? Because, *insofar* as utilitarianism recognizes equal individual rights, it does not base them on equal individual value or worth. It does not base them on *individual* value at all, but only on the value of maximizing satisfaction of interests and minimizing frustration of them. Speaker A begins with a claim about individuals' value; but speaker C begins with a claim about the aggregate satisfaction of interests.

18 Hence Regan's analogy. What inherent value does utilitarianism attach to *me* and *you* as distinct individuals? None, Regan thinks. It attaches value to the satisfaction of interests and 'disvalue' to their frustration. You and I, from the utilitarian point of view, are just receptacles for, or particular groupings of, positive and negative values, with no value 'as individuals' or 'in (y)our own right'.

absurd consequences move

19–21 Now we can see the example about Aunt Bea, intended as an **absurd consequences move** against utilitarianism, as a development of the above objection. If a utilitarian is treating my interests or feelings of satisfaction as having value, trying to ensure that, so to speak, my cup is full to the brim with feelings of satisfaction, why should I complain that he is not treating me as though I have value? Won't he treat me as well as Regan? What difference does it make? In these three paragraphs Regan argues that the fact that utilitarianism treats us as though we were merely valueless containers for what is valuable does make an important difference.

With Aunt Bea we encounter the disconcerting feature of utilitarianism we have noted before. According to utilitarianism, it is not merely lying that is wrong in some circumstances, right in others, according to the consequences, but also killing. Note that the example is carefully constructed to rule out various replies a utilitarian could make to a less carefully constructed case.

EXERCISE 23
Utilitarianism and evil means

1 What could an indirect utilitarian say if there were more chance of the nephew getting caught?

2 What could a utilitarian such as Singer say if the nephew did not have a once-in-a-lifetime opportunity to make a fortune?

3 Suppose a utilitarian criticizes Regan for failing to take account of the misery Aunt Bea's friends and family will undergo as a consequence of his killing her. Is this a good criticism or a weak one?

Check your answers against those at the back of the book before reading on.

---

22 Producing only one, very specific, counter-example, is a rather weak objection to a theory. But Regan does not think that there is anything special about the Aunt Bea example – the 'same kind of argument can be repeated in

all sorts of cases'. The general point is that 'a good end does not justify an evil means', but, according to utilitarianism, it does. (For a particularly unambiguous statement of this, look again at Singer's paragraph 27, where he explicitly contrasts utilitarianism's willingness to sacrifice an individual to the aggregate interests of others with the view of 'those who believe in absolute rights'.) Utilitarianism has absurd consequences, so utilitarianism is not the theory we want.

This general objection to utilitarianism – that it justifies evil means and thereby has absurd or morally horrific consequences – is the standard objection, one that has been made again and again in anti-utilitarian philosophical literature. You might then wonder why anyone sane is a utilitarian. Are there really people who think there is nothing wrong with killing Aunt Bea, in the circumstances described?

It is important to remember (principle of charity) that many utilitarians are not only sane but also clever. Over the many years during which particular examples illustrating 'the standard objection' have been produced, utilitarians have devised a number of strategies for dealing with them. One is indirect utilitarianism. Another is 'government house utilitarianism' (see Book 1, Reading 3, p.193). Another is insistence on the point that the end of the greatest happiness principle does not justify any means. Why doesn't the man in Regan's example borrow on his expectations, or make a real push to convince Aunt Bea that she should seize the opportunity to make the fortune on the stock market – these would be much better means than killing her. Or the strategy might be insistence on realism, which leads back to indirect utilitarianism; where we cannot be sure, we should stick to the useful general rules such as 'Do not murder', for, in real life, we do not have the certainty written into Regan's imaginary example.

In short, for any such 'absurd consequence' that anti-utilitarians bring up, utilitarians can, to their own satisfaction at least, find a way of denying that it really is a consequence of their position. Anti-utilitarians find these answers unsatisfactory; one major complaint, for instance, is that anyone who seriously follows (so-called) indirect utilitarianism should not describe themselves as a utilitarian at all, for it is just an ordinary commonsense morality that relies on a collection of simple rules (cf. Singer's comment, quoted on p.25 above, that utilitarianism was a big improvement on this). Utilitarians deny this. And so the debate continues, with no resolution in sight. Whole books have been written on it, and all we need to note here, rather mundanely, is that many people would agree with Regan that, for the reasons he gives, utilitarianism is not an adequate moral theory, and that many, along with Singer, would disagree.

No doubt we would all agree that Regan's killing Aunt Bea would be wrong – an evil means – and this is clearly a premise of Regan. What is not yet clear is what he would say was wrong or evil about it. That Aunt Bea has a right to life which would be violated? That she has inherent value or worth (and what does that mean)? Both? Anything else? These are points we hope to get clearer about in the second part of the article.

READING

Paragraphs 23–34: the argument for animal rights

You should now do a full reading of the remaining paragraphs 23–34 of the Regan article (but I suggest re-reading paragraph 22 before you start). Having skimmed (about 3–4 minutes), you should be able to write down at least one complete sentence that begins something like this:

Regan is defending/arguing for (the view that)...

and at least one that begins perhaps as vaguely as this:

His argument also involves something about...

though it would be good to get it as precise as:

His argument is based on...

Brilliant skimming might allow you to complete:

His argument involves arguing that...

DISCUSSION

Skimming paragraphs 23–34

The point of re-reading paragraph 22 was to help you, using what you already know, to get into the right, expectant, frame of mind. You should have reflected back on the earlier paragraphs and asked yourself 'How do I expect him to go on now?'

Paragraph 23 begins 'What to do? Where to begin anew?' and it should be fairly obvious from what you have just read, and using what you know, how he is going to go on. He began by clearing indirect duty views (and thereby, he thinks, contractarianism) out of the way. Now he has cleared utilitarianism out of the way, so (he assumes) the field is clear for the rights view. (It really is a very elegantly constructed article.) So you can expect that now he is going to introduce it.

By skimming, and using what you know, you should have picked up that Regan is arguing that animals have rights, for there is 'the rights view' mentioned at the beginning and end of paragraph 24, the beginning of 25, the end of 29, and the beginning of 30, 31 and 32.

Given that we are hoping to get clearer about inherent value, you should have noticed that, as well as the frequent mention of rights and the rights view, paragraphs 27 (end), 28 and 29 (both beginning and end) all look (at a quick skim) as if they are about inherent value (whatever that may be). So good skimming should produce:

> Regan's argument also involves *something* about inherent value.

But even better, noting the beginning of paragraph 23, would be:

> Regan's argument is based on the premise that we have inherent value

and brilliant skimming – remembering that Regan has endorsed a principle of equality (in paragraph 16) and spotting the end of 28 and of 29 – would produce:

> Regan's argument involves arguing that humans and animals have *equal* inherent value and hence an *equal* right to be treated with respect (whatever that means).

Finally, a cunning skimmer would have read the opening and closing sentences of 30, and then not have spent more than a few seconds on the four final paragraphs, mentally classifying them as giving 'four final points' which can wait for the careful reading.

DISCUSSION

Reading outline

22 (Conclusion of the discussion in the previous paragraphs: utilitarianism is not an adequate moral theory.)
23 There is a lot packed into this paragraph; minimally we need the following: outline of the rights view;'we [human beings]... all have inherent value, [we] all possess it equally, and [we] all have an equal right to be treated with respect'. We could add further: to 'fail to show respect for [another's] independent value is to act immorally, to violate the individual's rights'.
24 Two claims in favour of the rights view (and against some other theories).
25 Conclusion: 'The rights view... is... the most satisfactory moral theory'.
26 Argument for not limiting the scope of the rights view to humans. (Or: argument to the conclusion that animals have inherent value too.) The reading outline needs at least one more sentence, say, 'The... crucial similarity' between animals and us is that we are all 'the experiencing subjects of a life'.
27 Three condensed arguments for and against the view that 'only humans' have inherent value, all familiar (using what we know). Or I might also just sum it up as: Objection – 'only humans have inherent value' and three replies.
28 Objection – 'animals have some inherent value but less than we have'; two similar replies. Conclusion: '*all* who have inherent value have it *equally*' human or not.
29 Conclusion (putting 26, 27 and 28 together): 'Inherent value... belongs equally to those who are the experiencing subjects of a life'.

Premise: 'billions and billions' of the animals that 'are routinely eaten, hunted and used in our laboratories are like us in being subjects of a life'. Putting those two together we get the further conclusion: we must 'recognize the equal inherent value of these animals and, with this, their equal right to be treated with respect'.

30 Summing up the above: 'That *very* roughly... is the case for animal rights'.

31–4 Four final claims: (i) 'The animal rights movement is a part of... the human rights movement'; (ii) 'In the case of the use of animals in science, the rights view is categorically abolitionist'; (iii) and (iv) – not important.

By now, your reading outlines should be coming close to mine, emphasizing conclusions, major claims, arguments, objections, and replies to them.

DISCUSSION

Paragraphs 23–34: inherent value and rights

23 Regan's first premise is that *we* – you and I and Regan at least – have inherent value. Do we agree? Some people think the claim is obviously true and must hence think they have a fair understanding of what it means. But some of us might say more cautiously, or confusedly, that we are not sure whether or not we agree, because we do not know what Regan means by 'inherent value'. The principle of charity then requires us to try to work out what, plausibly, he might mean.

Regan immediately tells us something about what he means: to say we have inherent value is to say that it would be wrong to treat any of us the way utilitarianism would have us treat Aunt Bea. Insofar as we have inherent value we matter morally, as individuals, in some way. So that tells us something, but still not much.

Let's try the second premise – 'all who have inherent value have it equally, regardless of their sex, race, religion, birthplace... talents or skills, intelligence and wealth, personality or pathology, whether [they are] loved and admired or despised and loathed'. This gives us more of an idea of what is involved. Our equal *inherent value* is what makes it wrong to treat us unequally. Do we think it is wrong to treat people unequally? If we are happy to say 'yes', then maybe that is all we need to agree with Regan that we all have inherent value and have it equally.

But although most of us would probably agree with Regan that, roughly speaking, unequal treatment based on sex, race, religion and birthplace is wrong, his further list might give us pause for thought. Consider these more extreme versions of two of his contrasts.

1 The genius and the baby who will never develop a mental age of more than two.

2 Mother Teresa – or, let's say instead, Mandela – and Hitler.

If all who have inherent value have it equally, then having inherent value is an all-or-nothing matter, with no room for degrees. But, insofar as I am beginning to catch on to what Regan means by 'inherent value', I do not think I do agree that all who have it have it equally; I think there are degrees. So, for example I think (a) the morally very good, like Mandela, have more inherent value than most of us and that (b) the wicked, like Hitler, have less. Far from thinking it would be wrong to give Mandela, someone like Hitler, and most of us unequal treatment, I am all for it; Mandela deserves the best we could do for him, someone like Hitler not as much as the rest of us. (I'm not sure what to say about the very severely intellectually disabled in this context.)

But the principle of charity requires that we do not interpret Regan as making implausible claims if we can avoid it. So let's try again. Isn't there *some* sense in which we do all have the same inherent value, even Mandela and the most wicked? This is not, after all, an unfamiliar thought; people do say 'all men [meaning 'human beings'] are equal' in full knowledge of the fact that a few are exceptionally good and a few extremely wicked.

Let us try the following. Suppose we have a truly wicked person in our power. Is it, morally speaking, all right to do anything at all to him, say, torture him, or anaesthetize him and take out his heart and lungs and other useful parts for others' use and then kill him? Most of us think not – even if we are strongly in favour of capital punishment for some crimes. Moreover, most of us would be horrified by the suggestion that people gaoled for certain crimes should be used as experimental subjects without their consent. This suggests that we believe that anyone, however wicked, shares with all the rest of us *a certain core* of rights, for example:

(i) the right not to be killed just because one's body would be useful to others;

(ii) the right not to be tortured;

(iii) the right not to be used as an experimental subject without one's consent, i.e. as a 'guinea pig'.

And I am sure most of us would agree that anyone, no matter how mentally incapacitated has at least those three rights too. Moreover, it seems plausible to say that everyone possess at least these three rights equally. Torturing the wicked is not less wrong than torturing one of us. In both cases it is just horribly wrong, and that's all there is to it. So we could say that, to have inherent value is to have a *certain core* of rights – roughly those three. And then it is very plausible to say 'all who have inherent value have it equally'.

That this, or something very like it, is what Regan is after is strongly suggested by the way he continues: 'all have inherent value, all possess it equally, and all have an equal right to be treated... in ways that do not reduce them to the status of things, as if they existed as resources for others'. When we remember that the torturer uses his victim, either as a source of perverse sadistic pleasure, or as a source of information or some other means to an end of his, we can see all three rights above as instances of the general right not to be *used* in certain ways, not treated as if one were merely 'a resource' for others. So, to have inherent value, in the sense intended by Regan, is to have the general right not to be used in certain ways, as a mere resource for others – a general right that embodies a number of more particular rights such as the three above.[10]

24 A more of less equivalent way of putting the same claim would be to say that to have inherent value is to have the right not to be treated merely as a means. Hence the rights view denies what utilitarianism, wrongly, asserts – that Aunt Bea may justifiably be killed to harvest beneficial consequences to others. So it is a better moral theory than utilitarianism – in that respect at least. Moreover, like utilitarianism, it is egalitarian. The utilitarian's principle of equality insisted that everyone's interests count, regardless of their sex, race, social class, etc. This was a good aspect of it, but Regan argued that it was a mistake to place value on the satisfaction of interests rather than the individual. His principle of equality insists that everyone's inherent value and hence their right not to be used as a means or a resource counts, regardless of their sex, race, etc.

25 We must take this paragraph as calling on many arguments given in the book but not in the article; it would be uncharitable to suppose that Regan thinks it follows just from what we have here. So we will suppose that the book has made out a fairly good case. Now we come to the exciting part – does the rights view apply only to humans, or can it be extended to animals?

26 His argument for the view that not only human beings but also certain (but note, not all) animals have inherent value is very condensed, but discernible. Look at the first premise – *we* have inherent value. Why? What is it about us that gives us this value and thereby the right not to be used as a resource (i.e. 'treated with respect')? Not our sex, race or birth and so on; nor our particular talents, because amongst us all, some of these are bound to be different. No, it is (and this is a crucial premise) a 'basic similarity' we all share – that we are each of us 'the experiencing subject of a life'. *That* is why we all have inherent value – have that general right. But certain animals – those that concern us – they too are experiencing subjects of a life (note that this is an **empirical** premise). They share this basic similarity with us. So they have inherent value, like us.

empirical

Among the parts of the book that Regan has had to omit here are his long discussions of 'those animals that concern us' and the sense in which they are 'experiencing subjects of a life'. But even without them, we have enough to make sense of what he is saying. He is not saying that *all* animals (1.5 million species of them, including thousands of different species of insect, hookworms, spirochetes, etc.) have inherent value. He is talking about those animals that are involved in the three goals he laid out in the first paragraph – these are the ones that are his concern here – and, by and large, these are mammals and birds of which it is indeed plausible to say that they are experiencing subjects of a life.

27 He then considers, and rapidly discards, a number of rival answers that people might give to the question 'What is it about *us* that gives us inherent value? What is the crucial basic similarity we share?' These are all answers that would ensure that the animals that are his concern did not share the basic similarity, and are all familiar.

EXERCISE 24
What gives us inherent value?

State three different answers to the question 'What is it about us (Regan and you and me, at least) that gives us inherent value?' derived from this paragraph, and Regan's responses, in your own words.

Check your answers against those at the back of the book before reading on.

---

28 Thus these attempts to deny that (certain) animals have inherent value fail. What about the attempt to deny that their inherent value is equal to that of humans? Why not deny Regan's principle of equality and allow that inherent value is a matter of degree? Justifications for denying it could be given – indeed just the same two uncontroversial justifications that were given in the answer to the exercise above for denying that animals have inherent value at all. But to these Regan would make the same two responses. Arguing that animals have less inherent value than us simply because we are human beings and they are not is speciesism. And arguing that they have less inherent value than us because of some less blatantly speciesist characteristic we have and they lack – such as our intelligence, autonomy, use of speech, tool making, knowledge of good and evil, etc. – falls foul of what, by now, is a familiar problem. In trying to keep the animals somewhat less inherently valuable than ourselves, we thus downgrade various helpless human beings as well.

It is important to remember what, in the context of Regan's argument, this means. If A's having inherent value means that it would be wrong to use A as a resource for others then, if A has less inherent value than B, it would still be wrong to use them as a resource – but not *as* wrong. So there might be occasions when, faced with a choice between two evils – a moral dilemma – we would say 'This is a terrible situation and there is only one solution; we must, with great regret, go for the lesser evil'. So, for example, if we thought that certain experiments *had* to be done – to avert or find a cure for a terrible new disease – we would, albeit with reluctance, look to those who had less inherent value. And amongst them would be the various helpless human beings the above argument had downgraded.

So most of us are going to want to say, when we are thinking about human beings, all who have inherent value have it *equally* – and nothing but outright speciesiesm, can block the same claim applying to animals who are experiencing subjects of a life.

29 So Regan concludes, inherent value belongs equally to us and all those animals that are experiencing subjects of a life. So we have the same fundamental duty to them as we have to each other – to respect their right not to be used as a mere resource for others. But using them as a resource for us is just what we do when we use them for food, for fur, for the excitement of the hunt or the spectacle, and in our laboratories. So we must stop doing any of these things.

We can now understand the full weight of Regan's opening claims. '...what is wrong isn't the pain, isn't the suffering, isn't the deprivation. These compound what's wrong. Sometimes – often – they make it much, much worse. But they are not the fundamental wrong. The fundamental wrong is the system that allows us to view animals as *our resources,* here for *us*...' (paragraphs 2–3).

32 Hence Regan is much more uncompromising than Singer. Singer must allow that making animals suffer, or killing them, to serve our purposes, though frequently wrong, may, like anything else, sometimes be right – depending on the consequences. But Regan will have none of this. It is using them for our purposes at all which is the fundamental wrong, and no amount of ingenuity devoted to humane framing, painless killing, replacement of stocks, and securing pleasant lives for laboratory animals – no amount of 'tidying up the system' – can escape this wrong. Hence his opening claims – his goal is the *total* abolition of the use of animals in science, etc.

Criticizing Regan's position

Regan's article is so condensed that it is hard to see precisely what his argument is, but it looks as though, roughly, it goes like this.

Premise 1 We all have inherent value, and thereby a right to be 'treated with respect', not to be used as a resource for others.

Premise 2	All who have inherent value have it equally and thereby have an equal right to be 'treated with respect'.
Premise 3	We have inherent value because we are experiencing subjects of a life.
Premise 4	All the animals that concern us are experiencing subjects of a life.
Conclusion 1	All the animals that concern us have inherent value. (From Premises 3 and 4.)
Conclusion 2	All who have inherent value have it equally, whether they be human animals or not and thereby an equal right to be treated with respect. (From Conclusion 1 and Premise 2.)
Premise 5	Using animals in science, in commercial animal agriculture, in commercial and sport hunting and trapping is using them as a resource for others.
Conclusion 3	Using them in these ways is violating their right to be treated with respect (i.e. their right not to be used as a resource for others). (From Conclusion 2 and Premise 5.)
Conclusion 4	Using animals in these ways is wrong – as wrong as it would be to use human beings in these ways. (From Conclusion 3 and Premise 1.)

I would not claim that this is the only way to outline the argument. One could, for instance, view Premise 2 not as an unsupported premise, but as a subsidiary conclusion derived from Premise 3 and another unmentioned premise – that we are all equally experiencing subjects of a life (though not equally rational or autonomous or good). But such variants do not weaken the argument; if anything, they strengthen it.

So there, roughly, is Regan's argument, leading to his very strong conclusion. If using animals in these ways is as wrong as it would be to use human beings in these ways, no wonder he goes beyond Singer and calls uncompromisingly for a *total* ban on them all. Few of us will be willing to accept this conclusion. How do we set about arguing against Regan's argument for it?

EXERCISE 25
Arguing against Regan

1 State the two ways of criticizing Regan we should begin by considering. (You may need to look back at p.51 for help.)

2 Choose the more promising one. (I.e. which one do you think you could pursue.)

Check your answers against those at the back of the book before reading on.

EXERCISE 26
Regan's weakest premise

Which of Regan's premises should we try to attack?

Check your answer against the one at the back of the book before reading on.

DISCUSSION

Both Premises 1 and 2 can be criticized for being vague, but such criticism is not only, in this case, uncharitable, but also rather weak. It is not much of an *argument* against someone's premise to say 'This is vague'. It is a critical *comment,* and in many cases no doubt, a justified one, but if we want to engage in argument we should try to do better. Similar comments apply to criticizing Premise 4 for being vague. Moreover, I did point out that Premise 4 in Regan is an **empirical** claim and hence it is the sort of premise that one should only attack as a last resort. And we do not need to resort to it because, as with Singer, it is Regan's anti-speciesism that is our obvious target – and this is embodied in Premise 3.

empirical

Premise 3 is the claim that we – you and I – have inherent value, and thereby a right to be treated with respect not because we are rational, or human, but because we are experiencing subjects of a life. How does this embody Regan's anti-speciesism?

Well, let us compare it with Singer's anti-speciesism. Why, according to Singer, should our – yours and my – interests be considered when ethical decisions are being made? Not because we are rational or human, but because we are sentient – capable of feeling pleasure and pain. Just as, in Singer, it is sentience (the capacity for suffering and/or enjoyment or happiness) that 'entitles a being to equal consideration' (Reading 1, paragraph 5), so, in Regan, it is being the experiencing subject of a life that gives a creature inherent value and thereby the right to be treated with respect. Just as, in Singer, sentience is a characteristic we share with the animals that concern him, so, in Regan, being the experiencing subject of a life is a characteristic we share with the animals that concern him.

So let us consider this premise of Regan. What we need to concentrate on is not the obscure claim that we have 'inherent value' because we are experiencing subjects of a life, but what that claim amounts to in the context of Regan's rights-based approach. He has made it clear that when he says that we, and the animals he is concerned with, have 'inherent value' he means that we, and they, have a *right* to be treated with respect and/or *a right* not to be used as a mere resource for others. And he has made it clear that this, or these, general rights embody more specific ones, such as a *right* not to be used in scientific experiments. So what we need to consider is the claim that we (and hence the animals) have such rights *because* we are experiencing subjects of a life.

In the next section we shall see that there is a plausible rival position. It can be argued that we do not have rights *because* we are experiencing subjects of a life but *because* we can understand and make contracts.

Against animal rights

In Chapter 3, we looked at the 'contractarian' position of Hume and Rawls – a position that, as we have seen, Regan overlooked in his article. One way of stating Hume's and Rawls's position was 'We have duties to animals but animals do not have *rights*'. So they would disagree with Regan's view that all animals that are experiencing subjects of a life have rights. Our brief study of Hume's and Rawls's position did not make it clear what reasons someone might have for saying 'animals do not have rights' and hence whether it is a reasonable claim to make, contrary to Regan. In this section I aim to show that it is a reasonable claim – as long as it is understood in the right way, not as absolute dismissal. We shall then be able to see how one can argue against Regan's claim that we have rights *because* we are experiencing subjects of a life.

To many people, even those who agree with Regan (and Singer) that the amount of suffering we inflict on animals is a moral outrage, the idea that animals have *rights* seems simply absurd. But producing that claim, unsupported, as an **absurd consequences move** against Regan simply results in a stand-off. It is an exceptionally clear case of the awkward fact that 'one person's absurdity is another's common sense' (Warburton (1996), p.2). Regan does not find it absurd at all; on the contrary, he sees it as the only way of escaping the 'absurdities' of utilitarianism and the viciousness of speciesism. So how could we set about supporting (arguing for) the claim that it is absurd to say that animals have rights?

absurd consequences move

This may leave us floundering. How could we argue against someone who said that inanimate things have rights – say paintings which are great works of art? Someone might well say that great works of art 'command our respect' and they might say that it would be wrong to destroy great works of art, that we ought not to do such things. That makes sense. But what if they said that destroying a great work of art was wrong because it violated the art work's *rights?* The idea is so unintelligible that it renders us speechless. But, in fact, the very unintelligibility of that idea gives us a clue. Maybe we find the idea that animals have rights absurd, without immediately being able to come up with a reason, because we find the idea unintelligible. And, if that is correct, it suggests where we should look for our argument. Can we argue that it is unintelligible to claim that animals have rights – that the concept of 'a right' does not apply to animals and hence that anyone, like Regan, who assumes that it does, is misusing the concept, and/or has got into a muddle?

This is, indeed, how several philosophers have argued. Their arguments make explicit some rather vague intuitions most of us have about what is wrong with ascribing rights to animals. 'Animals haven't got a concept of rights' we may protest; 'They may know that they are suffering, but they can't know that their rights are being violated'; 'You couldn't expect them to respect our rights, or each others'; 'They are not making any claims about their rights and so on'. Such intuitions may reflect the unconscious knowledge that the concept of *a right* is a rather special one, not merely a forceful way of talking about what we ought and ought not to do. A contemporary philosopher (not engaged in the debate about our treatment of animals) says:

> in the full language of rights – by which I mean our ordinary use of 'a right' as signifying something which one can exercise, earn, enjoy, give, claim, demand, assert, insist on, secure, waive, or surrender, and which can be compared and contrasted with a duty, privilege, liberty, power, etc. – only those who can intelligibly be said to be logically capable of having these relations to rights and to duties, obligations, powers, etc., even if circumstances render them practically incapable, can possess rights.
>
> (White (1984), p.171)

Consider some rights I have. Let's start with the right to vote. This is a right I can exercise or not, as I choose. I 'enjoy' it in the old sense of 'having the use of it' (a sense now almost entirely restricted to rights and possessions); I was given it by the government, which secures it to me. I cannot waive or surrender it – it is an 'inalienable' right, at least while I remain resident in Britain.[11] Mercifully, I do not need to claim or demand it – this was done for me by campaigners in earlier times; nor, living under a stable democratic government, do I need to assert or insist on it.

I did nothing to earn this particular right. Contrast my right to call myself, and to be called, 'Dr Hursthouse', a right I earned by years of postgraduate study and given me by the University of Oxford. It is a right I exercise, enjoy in both senses, assert, claim and insist on and frequently waive. It is a right I would be compelled to surrender if it were shown that my doctoral thesis was plagiarism.

The books in my house I own; thereby I have a right to do with them as I choose. If I do not want to lend one of them to you, I have a right not to. But here is an obvious case where it would often be wrong of me – deplorably selfish or mean – to exercise my right, just as it would often be wrong, because rude and small-minded, of me to exercise, insist on, demand, my right to call myself, and be called by my title. How did I acquire this right concerning my books? Well, in some cases, people gave me the books and thereby gave me the right – exercising and surrendering their own. In many cases I bought them. Suppose one I bought in good faith was stolen. Well, then things are unclear; in British law it sometimes turns out that I do not own it after all, and hence do not have a right concerning it (though I may have a right to compensation).

Do I really have a right to do *anything* with them I choose? Suppose one is a First Folio Shakespeare – part of 'English heritage'. Do I have a right to destroy it if I so choose? Here again, things are unclear. Perhaps one's ownership of such things is partial – one holds them 'in trust for the nation' – and this restricts one's right over them. Or perhaps I *do* have an unrestricted right; but this, again, would be a case where it would be very wrong of me to exercise it in that particular way.

It can be seen from these few examples, that, despite obscurities here and there, much of our talk about rights is clear cut, and is used in relation to the list of words – exercise, earn, enjoy, waive, etc. that White gives. It can also be seen that, thereby, *rights* are closely related to laws, institutions and conventions. However, the concept of a *right* is not, thereby, a purely legalistic, institutional or conventional concept. In certain contexts, we want to distinguish legal from moral rights – but those contexts are usually the ones in which the two do not coincide. When women did not have a legal right to vote, they claimed or insisted on their moral (or 'natural') right to it as a ground for their being given the legal right. But now I simply have '*the* right to vote'; we do not make a point of saying I have two rights, both a legal and a moral one.

That the concept of *a right* – or at least, the concept we see at work in the above examples – is, though legalistic, not purely legalistic but also moral, has been true of it ever since it first came into our vocabulary and thoughts. The history of the concept of *a right* is recognized to be extremely complicated, but from the beginning it was strongly welded to a legal context. And, as we see from the way it relates to laws, institutions and conventions above, it still preserves this strongly legalistic aspect.

But laws, institutions and conventions are all unique features of human societies. Only creatures who can devise, and agree to abide by, laws, conventions and the rules and regulations involved in the setting up of institutions, can have such things, and we are the only such creatures who can. The concept of rights applies against a background of such laws, conventions and institutions; without such a background, it has no application, makes no sense.

So why, according to this line of thought, do *we* have rights? Generally, because we are creatures who can devise, and agree to abide by, laws, conventions and the rules and regulations involved in the setting up of institutions. We can understand rules governing the acquisition and transfer of rights and their corresponding duties. We can understand the surrender or waiving of rights and the corresponding change in our duties. And here is the disagreement with Regan. We do *not* have rights because we are experiencing subjects of a life. We have rights because we can devise and agree to abide by laws, conventions, etc., which establish and protect them.

So the intuition that Regan's conclusion that animals have rights is absurd can be supported. What is absurd about saying that animals have rights, according to this line of thought, is that, implicitly, it absurdly attributes all these capacities to them. But animals cannot devise and agree to abide by laws and conventions with us; they cannot understand rules governing the acquisition, transfer, surrendering and waiving of rights. Animals no more have rights than they have duties and obligations.

In response to discussion of his book *Animal Rights and Wrongs* (1996a), the fox-hunting philosopher Roger Scruton makes the above point in a newspaper article (itself a comment on an earlier article (Scruton (1996b), p.17)

> The concept of a right makes sense only when applied to the members of a moral community – a community whose members have sovereignty over their individual lives and who settle their disputes by negotiation. The concept of a right takes its meaning from this context, as do the concepts of duty and responsibility. To attribute rights to a creature, therefore, is to view it as a member of the moral community – as the kind of thing that has, or can have, duties or responsibilities too.
>
> ... if you see rights as I have suggested, it becomes absurd to act as though animals had them. For you would then be forced to treat animals as members of the moral community, with the responsibilities and duties that stem from that. You would be forced to take towards them attitudes – such as accusation, punishment, judicial prosecution – which are the price exacted for the gift of sovereignty...
>
> It is not just that dogs and bears do not belong to the moral community. They have no potential for membership; they are not the kind of thing that can settle disputes by dialogue, that can exert sovereignty over its life and respect the sovereignty of others, that can respond to the call of duty or take responsibility in a matter of trust.
>
> (Scruton (1996c), 30 August, p.17)

The non fox-hunting philosopher David Wiggins endorsed Scruton's claim.

> If the notion of a right is to have any content then it is best for 'X has a right not to be treated thus and so' to count as conveying a special and distinctive ground for its being wrong to treat X in that way. Compare the way in which Mary's ownership of that book grounds or explains the claim that it would be wrong to deprive her of it. Ownership, being the earliest kind of right, is still a useful abstract model of what is so special about the general concept. It is also a model of that which it presupposes, namely a community of persons who can recognize one another as owing to one another, and being owed by one another, various, however minimal, things, not least a duty to negotiate conflicts of interest.
>
> What would it be like for animals to have full membership of such a community? In the National Gallery in London, one plausible answer to this question is vividly illustrated in a panel by the fifteenth-century painter Sassetta [which has been used as the cover image to this book]. A wolf terrorized the inhabitants of Gubbio. By the intervention of St Francis, an agreement is drawn up with the wolf and ratified in the presence of a notary. The inhabitants provide the wolf with food and the wolf ceases to molest the inhabitants.
>
> (Wiggins (1996), p.22)

I find Wiggins's endorsement helpful both in its avoidance of the obscure word 'sovereignty' and in its illustration of what it would be like for an animal to be a member of 'the moral community' in Scruton's sense. In the making of the agreement, the inhabitants and the wolf establish their related rights and obligations (or duties): the wolf has a right to food; the inhabitants an obligation to provide it; the inhabitants have a right to freedom from molestation; the wolf an obligation to honour it. All parties to the contract recognize what is involved. But this recognition involves an understanding of all the legalistic background of rights. What will happen if the inhabitants run short of food? If an individual inhabitant tries to beat the wolf off its food and take it himself and the wolf molests him? If the inhabitant is a small child? The recognition of what is involved in the possession of rights involves a recognition of the fact that they can conflict and that when they do, right-holders have a duty to negotiate, not just exercise their own right while violating someone else's.

It may well be that we could train a wolf to eat proffered food rather than attack human beings. But we would not thereby have entered into an agreement with it. If we failed to give it food it might then attack us – but it could not be doing so in the belief that it was morally justified in doing so because we have failed to honour our obligation. Or the training might have gone deeper, so that, if we fail to give it food, it just sits and howls, or goes hunting for other prey. But it is not refraining from attacking human beings in the belief that it should show us mercy rather than demand justice. Animals are not, in Scruton's phrase, the *kind of thing* that can have such beliefs. And, thereby, not the kind of thing that can recognize rights or have them.

Conclusion

So there is the support for the claim that animals do not have rights. It is, I think, a reasonable position. It accords with many of our intuitions. It can make out a case explaining and justifying those intuitions, solidly grounded in the history of the concept of *a right* and the linguistic facts which reveal that this concept is still one we commonly employ.

However, we must remember the point I stressed at the outset, that it is a reasonable position as long as it is understood in the right way, not as tantamount to absolute dismissal. Hume and Rawls, Scruton and Wiggins all say that animals do not have rights (nor duties). But they do *not* deny that we have duties to them. Remember that both Hume and Rawls say that we *do* have duties to animals. Note too a key phrase in the first sentence of the quotation from Wiggins, '...it is best for "X has a right not to be treated thus and so" to count as conveying a *special and distinctive ground* for its being wrong to treat X in that way' (my italics). Wiggins's point is that there can be different grounds for its being wrong to treat creatures – even things – in certain ways. One ground, or reason, in the case of a person, might be that that person has a right not to be treated that way. A different ground or reason, in the case of an animal, might be that it was cruel or inhumane to treat that animal that way. Yet another ground or reason, in the case of a work of art, might be that it was irresponsible, or violated other people's rights, to treat it that way. (The latter – that it violated other people's rights – would be a sort of indirect duty view applied to works of art. 'We have duties *regarding* works of art, for example, to preserve them, but no duties *to* them; all our duties regarding works of art are indirect duties to people'.) Just because something does not have rights does not mean we can do anything to it we like. And Scruton (see p.124) also believes that there is more to morality than rights.

It is worth stressing the point that being a contractarian about justice and hence denying that animals have rights does *not* rule out being an 'animal liberationist'. True, Rawls himself seems to think that rights are so important that only a forced choice between violating them can justify doing so, for example, when there just is a clash between my right to liberty and yours and someone's right has to be violated. So he might well think that if the forced choice lies between violating a (human being's) right and saving an animal from great suffering, we were morally required to let the animal suffer. But someone can be a contractarian about justice without believing this. I can be a contractarian about justice; I can agree that in forcibly removing from you an animal you are tormenting I am violating your right to liberty yet consistently maintain that I am morally justified in doing so. Yes, in general, I have a duty not to interfere when you are doing nothing that harms other human beings; I also have a duty of compassion to animals and in this case, I say, the duty to the animal is more stringent than my duty to respect your rights. So there is nothing inherently speciesist about the contractarian position.

We could sum up the position on rights and duties with two phrases:

1 It *is* true that if a being has a right, we have a corresponding duty to that being. (We have duties to rights-bearers; or, wherever there is a right there is a duty.)

2 It is *not* true that if we have a duty to some being, that being has a corresponding right. (We have duties to non rights-bearers *too*; or, it is *not* true that wherever there is a duty there is a right.)

An objection to the position against animal rights

Although I claim this is a reasonable position, I would not claim it is the correct one. Regan is not so easily defeated. It is now time to play author's advocate on his behalf.

So, we are going to embark on a sustained debate, arguing first on Regan's behalf, then against him, then on his behalf again, then against him again. Doing this will show how much you have extended your ability to follow detailed arguments back and forth; but if you don't feel confident, you should turn to p.129 and read the 'bulleted' summary, on where we have been and where we have got to. Then do the following exercises.

EXERCISE 27
Regan's advocate

What absurd consequences move could Regan make to the position against animal rights we have just considered? Try to write two or three sentences, spelling the move out in full.

DISCUSSION

Regan can surely pinpoint what by now should be a familiar difficulty about the position we have just considered. Animals do not have rights because they are not 'members of a moral community'. They are not members of a moral community because they cannot enter into agreements, exercise, transfer, enjoy, waive, etc., rights, they cannot recognize rights and corresponding duties. We – you and I, Scruton and Wiggins – have rights because we can do all these things.

But if that is why animals do not have rights and we do, who, apart from the animals, also lacks them? The 'absurd' not to say shocking consequence is that, as so often, the mentally incapacitated, infants, the senile, many of the insane and so on are in the same category as animals – it does not, according to the position against animal rights, make sense to say they have rights either.

So those of us who want to reject Regan's conclusion are still in difficulties. It looked as though the position against animal rights would provide an escape route – but the route looks like one we will not want to take if it involves denying that infants and the mentally incapacitated have rights. Well, maybe we can take the argument further.

EXERCISE 28

White's, Scruton's and Wiggins's advocate

Play author's advocate on behalf of White, Scruton and Wiggins and respond to this absurd consequences move.

Try to think of a response they might make to it which involves **biting the bullet**, that is, accepting that infants, the mentally incapacitated and so on do not have rights.[12]

biting the bullet

Write about three or four sentences on this response.

DISCUSSION

One standard response to the absurd consequence move is to accept it – and to deny it is absurd. Far from its being absurd, we might argue on the authors' behalf that it is basically what we all believe, and is reflected in the law of most countries whose legal system we are familiar with. True, in law, we accord infants and the deranged some rights, but nothing like the same range as we accord to normal adults. We accept Mill's restrictions on the Harm Principle (Mill (1985 edn), p.68), for instance, agreeing with him that only rational adults have the general right to freedom from interference. This general right brings with it many specific rights, none of which we ascribe to infants, the senile and so on. Human beings who are not rational adults do, in law, have the right to possess property – but they are not allowed to 'enjoy' this right; parents dictate what a child may do with its toys; trustees administer the estates of children and the mentally incapacitated. And finally, the laws we have prohibiting the killing of such human beings, and the use of them in experiments, need not be interpreted as conferring on them the right to life or the right not to be thus used. After all, we have laws prohibiting organized dog-fights and bear-baiting and these do not confer rights on the dogs and bears. They are all laws we have to prohibit particularly callous and inhumane behaviour.

Pursuing an argument in this kind of detail is difficult, and it is easy to lose track of it as it moves back and forth, now supporting Regan, now arguing against him, so let us pause to consider where we have been and where we have got to.

- Regan argues that animals have rights, because they are experiencing subjects of a life (pro-Regan).
- Hume, Rawls, Scruton and Wiggins argue that animals do not have rights because rights-bearers must be able to enter into contracts or agreements, accept duties, etc., and animals cannot do this (anti-Regan).
- On Regan's behalf, we argue that this position has the absurd consequence that infants and the mentally incapacitated do not have rights (pro-Regan).
- On Scruton's, Wiggins's and White's behalf we produce a counter to this absurd consequence move – that it is not absurd (anti-Regan).

So now, as Regan's advocate, we must look critically at this last move and consider whether it really works.

Denying rights to animals and other non-persons

Are we really satisfied with the denial that infants and the mentally incapacitated can intelligibly be said to have rights? It undoubtedly makes some of us feel somewhat uneasy. Is it not opening the doors to all sorts of horrors?

We have seen that the answer to that is 'no', or at least 'not necessarily'. We must keep on reminding ourselves that Hume and Rawls, Scruton and Wiggins all deny that justice and rights are all that is involved in morality. 'We have duties to non rights-bearers *too*'.

Hence, as I pointed out (p.105), Regan is simply mistaken when he says, describing contractarianism (paragraph 9), 'Here, very crudely, is the root idea: *morality* consists of a set of rules that individuals voluntarily agree to abide by, as we do when we sign contracts' (my italics), and goes on to describe Rawls as a contractarian. He must have overlooked that important disclaimer Rawls made that I quoted at the end of the previous chapter (p.98).

Scruton and Wiggins are contractarians about justice and rights too. But, like Hume and Rawls, they deny that all moral questions are to be answered and settled in terms of justice and rights. Our moral duties are not all duties or obligations of justice with corresponding rights. The sphere of morality is larger than the sphere of justice and we have duties – perhaps many – to beings other than rights-bearers. Moreover, these duties may be every bit as stringent as the duties that correspond to rights.

How could Regan have made such a mistake about Rawls? Even if he overlooked the disclaimer, why should he think that a book entitled 'A Theory of *Justice*' (my italics) might just as well have been entitled 'A Theory of *Morality*'?

The answer to this, I think, lies in the fact that people in the United States tend to believe that all moral issues *are* to be phrased in terms of rights. I tried out the material in this book as a lecture course in America; I named the course 'The ethics of our treatment of animals', but discovered that the administration had cheerfully rechristened it 'The question of animal rights'. When I told people there I was lecturing on 'the ethics (or morality) of our treatment of animals' or 'our duties concerning animals', they always paraphrased me; 'She told me she's lecturing on animal rights' they said. They thought that (a) all of ethics or morality is about *rights* because, in part, they thought that (b) if I have a moral duty or obligation to some being – to treat it kindly or not to kill it or destroy it or whatever – then that being has a corresponding *right*. I.e. wherever there is a duty, there is a right. Compare (b) with the second phrase I used to sum up the contractarian position on rights and duties (p.127), namely:

> It is *not* true that if we have a duty to some being, that being has a corresponding right. (We have duties to non rights-bearers *too*; or it is *not* true that wherever there is a duty there is a right.)

Another aspect of the 'American thinking' about rights which leads them to think that all moral issues are to be phrased in terms of them is this: they think that if 'I have a right to do so and so' then 'It would be morally all right for me to do so and so'. And so, putting it round the other way, they think that if it *wouldn't* be all right for me to do so and so (e.g. be cruel to my dog, or insist that I be addressed as 'Dr') then I have *no right* to be cruel to my dog or to insist that I be addressed as 'Dr'. And that means that they find it extraordinarily difficult to understand the idea that, in some circumstances, it might be morally wrong of me to exercise some right that I certainly have. To them, this just sounds like an unintelligible contradiction, because they always construe 'it is morally wrong of me to do such and such' as 'I have no right to do such and such'. So it sounds to them as though I am saying that sometimes I have no right to do such and such even though I certainly do have a right to do such and such! If I try saying, explicitly, it might be rude, or small-minded, or selfish or unkind or cruel or unmerciful... though not, of course, unjust, to exercise a right I have, then sometimes they catch on, but they often do not, and fall back on insisting that I have 'no right' to be rude, small-minded, selfish, unkind... and all the rest of it. By which they mean 'it would be morally wrong'.

This 'American thinking' about rights is undoubtedly gaining ground in Britain, and, if you feel uneasy about denying that children and the mentally incapacitated have rights, believing that this would open the door to all sorts of horrors, this may be because you are thinking the American way.

But there is another possible explanation. We may not think that *all* moral issues are to be phrased in terms of rights, but still be inclined to think that most really important ones are. The contractarians about justice say:

> If a being has a right, we have a corresponding duty to that being and some equally stringent duties to non right-bearers too. So it is *not* true that wherever there is an especially strong duty, there is a corresponding right.

But many of us are inclined to believe that only duties with corresponding rights are really stringent, i.e. whenever there is an especially strong duty, there is a corresponding right. Hence, whenever we are convinced that we have a really strong duty to some being – say a duty not to kill it, or use it for experimental purposes – we want to insist on this by saying that that being has a corresponding right. And it may be that this is all Regan intends or needs.

So we have at least three different ways of thinking and talking about rights in connection with duties:

1 The contractarian about justice: we have lots of duties, only some of them have a corresponding right, and duties with no corresponding right can be every bit as strong as duties where there is a corresponding right.

2 'American thinking': wherever there is a duty, there is a corresponding right..

3 Wherever there is an *especially strong* duty, there is a corresponding right.

Now it would be futile to insist that only one of these ways of thinking and talking about rights and duties is *the* correct one, though I think we would do well to avoid (2) for the reasons Wiggins gives (p.125), to preserve the distinctive wrong of violating a right. But probably most of us occasionally use both the first and the third, albeit on different occasions, because they reflect two different aspects of the history of the concept of *a right.*

As Wiggins mentioned, the first use of rights was concerned with ownership. Hence we have all these trivial examples of the rights I have regarding *my* books, *my* title – even *my* pencil. And hence duties corresponding to rights can be either as strong as any duty can be (e.g. duties regarding *my* life) or so trivial that we despise anyone who makes a fuss about them. But, as we shall see in Chapter 5, talk about rights, connected to talk about equality, has long been fighting talk, used by people campaigning for things they regarded as morally tremendously important, and where they thought that especially stringent duties or moral obligations were being ignored. So when we are talking about such trivia as pencils and titles, we tend to think in the first way; when we are talking about important things, such as not being used as a resource for others, we tend to think in the third way.

So, bearing all this in mind, let us return to the question of whether we want to follow contractarianism about justice and 'bite the bullet' by denying that animals *and* other beings who cannot understand contracts, namely infants and the mentally incapacitated, have rights.

In support of Regan

The charitable interpretation of Regan is not that he is thinking of rights in the 'American' way, but simply in the third way. He is campaigning for something he thinks is morally tremendously important – our very stringent duty not to use animals as mere resources. Of course he does not want to talk about rights in the contractarian way – he believes that *our* right not to be used as a mere resource for others is no trivial matter but of the utmost importance. And if we agree with him about that, we cannot follow the contractarian line either. Hence our unwillingness to deny that infants and the mentally incapacitated have rights. Our duty not to kill them or use them in experiments is as stringent as a duty could be – so, we think, they must have the corresponding rights. But (still pro-Regan) that means we cannot bite on the bullet of the absurd consequences move. Accepting a version of the position against animal rights which cheerfully denies rights to infants and the mentally incapacitated too is not a route we can take – the contractarians are no help to us here.

Scruton and speciesism

Is there another move we can make? Yes, for the argument is not over yet. Turn back to page 129 to remind yourself about what has been going on before we take the next step?

We have just tried to:

- bite on the bullet of the absurd consequences move accepting that infants and the mentally incapacitated do not have rights (anti-Regan).

But then we saw that:

- this will not work because we agree with Regan that the duty not to use others as resources is an especially stringent duty with a corresponding right (pro-Regan).

So now we consider an anti-Regan position again.

EXERCISE 29
A second anti-Regan response

Remember the response we made on behalf of White, *et. al* in Exercise 28. There is another possible response to an absurd consequence move: this second response is to deny that the absurd consequence does actually follow. Look at Scruton's use of the phrases 'potential for membership' and 'kind of thing' in his last paragraph (p.124); then look at the last few lines of the quotation from White (p.122). Bearing these in mind, try to construct a second response on their behalf, in two or three sentences. (Your answer should begin, roughly, 'Contractarianism is not committed to the absurd view that infants and the mentally incapacitated do not have rights. According to contractarianism they *do* have rights because...)

DISCUSSION

Contractarianism (at least according to White and Scruton) is not committed to the absurd view that infants and the mentally incapacitated do not have rights. They *do* have rights because, unlike animals, they are the '*kind* of thing [namely, human beings] that can settle disputes by dialogue' (from Scruton), understand contracts, etc. Their age or their mental disability or their brain damage may render them 'practically' incapable of doing such things, but, as human beings rather than animals, they are 'logically' capable of doing them (from White).

If that is the next anti-Regan move, then we need to consider the pro-Regan response – we look critically at the anti-Regan move and play author's advocate on his behalf. What criticism do you think Regan (or, indeed, Singer) would make to it?

It is fairly clear that both Singer and Regan would object by saying that this response was speciesist. Infants and the mentally incapacitated are *not* 'the kind of thing' that is capable of making contracts. Having said that we – you and I – have rights because we are literally and plainly capable of understanding contracts, this contractarian position has now shifted to the position of saying that you and I, and the infants and the mentally incapacitated are all 'potentially' or 'logically' 'capable of making contracts' just because we all are members of a contract-making species – namely human beings. And this is blatant speciesism.

It must, I think, be admitted, that this is a powerful objection that can be made on Regan's behalf. Consider an unfortunate individual who has suffered irreversible brain damage and is in what is called 'a persistent vegetative state'. What could be meant by saying that such an individual was 'the kind of thing' that was *capable* of understanding contracts, exercising rights and so on? It seems that it cannot mean anything but 'this individual is a human being, and human beings are the kind of thing that is capable of understanding contracts'.

I will now quote Scruton's actual response to the absurd consequences move. You will see that Scruton's actual response is a mixture of the two we have considered.[13]

> **Marginal humans**
>
> But this brings me to a vexed question, much emphasized by Regan and Singer, the question of 'marginal humans', as Regan describes them. Even if we grant a distinction between moral beings and other animals, and recognize the importance of rationality, self-consciousness and moral dialogue in defining it, we must admit that many human beings do not lie on the moral side of the dividing line. For example, infants are *not yet* members of the moral community; senile and brain-damaged people are *no longer* members; congenital idiots *never will be* members. Are we to say that they have no rights? Or are we to say that, since they differ in no fundamental respect from animals, that we ought in consistency to treat other animals as we treat these 'marginal' humans? Whichever line we take, the hope of making an absolute moral distinction between human and animal life collapses.
>
> It seems to me that we should clearly distinguish the case of 'pre-moral' infants, from those of the 'post-moral' and 'non-moral' human adults. The former are *potential* moral beings, who will naturally develop, in the conditions of society, into full members of the moral community. Our attitude towards them depends on this fact; and indeed, it is only because we look on them as incipiently rational that we eventually elicit the behaviour that justifies our treatment. Just as an acorn is, by its nature, the seed of an oak tree, so is an infant, by its nature, a potential rational being. And it is only by treating it as such that we enable it to realize this potential and so to become what it essentially is.
>
> The other cases of 'marginal humans' are more problematic. And this is instinctively recognized by all who have to deal with them. Infanticide is an inexcusable crime; but the killing of a human vegetable, however much we shrink from it, may often strike us as understandable, even excusable. Although the law may treat this act as murder, we ourselves, and especially those upon whom the burden falls to protect and nurture this unfortunate creature, will seldom see it in such a light. On the other hand, to imagine that we can simply dispose of mental cripples is to display not only a callousness towards the individual, but also a cold calculating attitude to the human species and the human form. It is part of human virtue to acknowledge human life as sacrosanct, to recoil from treating other humans, however hopeless their life may seem to us, as merely disposable, and to look for the signs of personality wherever the human eye seems able to meet and return our gaze. This is not part of virtue only; it is a sign of piety. And... virtue and piety are cornerstones of moral thinking.
>
> (Scruton (1996a), pp.47–8)

What are we to make of Scruton's response? We shall not be in a position to understand it fully until the next chapter but, for the moment, we should note the following:

1 Scruton accepts (I think, it is not unambiguously clear – but let us apply the principle of charity) that mentally ordinary infants do have rights, because they are *potential* members of the moral community. They are 'capable of understanding contracts' not simply because they are members of a contract-making species, namely human beings, but because they are 'incipiently rational'. We can say that they have the capacity to understand contracts – it is built into their DNA; it is just that that capacity is not yet developed to the point where it can be exercised. And that is a genuine difference between ordinary human infants and animals.

2 However, Scruton does seem willing to accept that the severely mentally incapacitated do not have rights. They are 'no longer' or 'never will be ' members of the moral community. With respect to them, it seems that he holds the same position as those who are willing to bite on the bullet of the absurd consequences move (p.128). It is not absurd to deny that such human beings have rights – it's basically what we all believe. It does not open the door to all sorts of horrors, because 'virtue' and 'piety' – that is, moral considerations other than those based on justice – require that we 'acknowledge human life as sacrosanct'. (But note that is *human* life.)

So Scruton has a fair response to the speciesism objection as far as mentally ordinary infants are concerned. But, as far as the severely mentally incapacitated of any age are concerned, the pro-Regan side of the argument surely wins. The severely mentally incapacitated do not have rights. If it follows that we can treat them the way we treat other creatures who lack rights, i.e. animals, then we have a consequence that is not merely absurd but horrific. But if this horrible consequence is blocked by the considerations drawn from 'virtue' and 'piety', we seem to be back with blatant speciesism. For why do 'virtue' and 'piety' not require acknowledging that the life of *any creature* which is the experiencing subject of a life is sacrosanct? What is so special about *human* life? These are the questions we should press on Regan's behalf.

So speciesism rears its head again. A problem ever since we looked at Singer, it won't go away. We will confront it in the next chapter.

Chapter summary

In favour of animal rights

Regan argues for the view that the animals that concern us – most of the ones we use for food, in scientific experiments and for sport and fashion items – all have inherent value, equal to ours. What he means by this is that they, and we, have an equal general right to be 'treated with respect', i.e. not to be used as mere resources for others. This right that these animals have is violated by our current practices and hence Regan calls for a total abolition of the use of animals in science, in commercial agriculture and in commercial sport hunting and trapping.

He claims that the rights view is the most satisfactory moral theory, basing this claim on his rejection of indirect duty views, contractarianism (about which he is mistaken) and utilitarianism. His basic objection to utilitarianism is that 'a good end does not justify an evil means' illustrated by the example of killing Aunt Bea.

Against animal rights

His view that the animals that concern us have, like us, an equal right not to be used as mere resources for others, is based on his anti-speciesist premise that we have this right *because* we are 'experiencing subjects of a life.' This premise is denied by contractarians about justice such as Hume and Rawls, and others such as Wiggins and Scruton, who maintain that the concept of a *right* is legalistic as well as moral. They all claim that we have rights not because we are 'experiencing subjects of a life' but because we are capable of understanding contracts. According to this view, it makes no sense to attribute rights to animals – they no more have rights than they have duties.

However, if we are seeking to escape Regan's animal liberation conclusions, the contractarian position will not provide us with a secure foundation. For, on Regan's behalf, it can be argued that, if animals do not have rights because they are not capable of understanding contracts, infants and the severely mentally incapacitated do not have rights either, because *they* are not capable of understanding contracts (the absurd consequences move).

One bold response to this move, suggested by Hume, and other contractarians about justice, concedes that infants and the severely mentally incapacitated do not have rights, but insists that other considerations, such as compassion and humanity, impose duties as stringent as those generated by rights. But most of us feel uneasy about denying that such human beings have rights because we think of rights as generating duties that are stronger than any others, and this reaction can be pressed on Regan's behalf.

Another response to the absurd consequences move involves maintaining that *any* human being is, as such, 'capable of understanding contracts'. But this is open to the objection that such a response is blatantly speciesist, which Regan would certainly make.

Scruton's response to the absurd consequences move involves maintaining that mentally ordinary infants have rights but the severely mentally incapacitated do not. Our treatment of the latter is constrained by considerations derived from 'virtue' and 'piety'. As far as the ordinary infants are concerned, his position looks fairly secure, but, as far as the mentally incapacitated are concerned, it looks insecure. On Regan's behalf, we can argue *either* that this position opens the door to terrible treatment of such human beings *or* that the attempt to close the door by appealing to the requirement to 'acknowledge human life as sacrosanct' is speciesist.

Further reading

The book Regan summarizes in the Reading is *The Case for Animal Rights*, University of California Press, 1983, which, helpfully, is 'written for the intelligent lay person' as well as professional philosophers. Without directly confronting Regan's Aunt Bea example, Singer has responded to Regan's attack on utilitarianism and his claim that it does not recognize the inherent value of individuals in, 'Animal Liberation or Human Rights', *Monist*, 70 (1987) pp.3–14, reprinted in *People, Penguins, and Plastic Trees*, Wadsworth Publishing Company, 1995 (2nd edn).

Notes

[1] Regan, T. (1983) *The Case for Animal Rights,* University of California Press.

[2] There is a famous central claim in the moral philosophy of Immanuel Kant (1724–1804) called the 'categorical imperative'. One expression of this, Kant's basic moral principle, is 'Act in such a way that you always treat humanity, whether in your own person or in the person of any other, never simply as a means, but always at the same time as an end' (Kant (1948 edn), p.91). Although Regan could not be further from Kant on the issue of our having direct duties to animals, in other ways his 'rights view' is Kant inspired. It is indeed from Kant that he gets his very odd use of the word 'respect'. 'To show respect for another's independent value' does not mean, as you might think, 'to honour or esteem or be deferential to another's independent value' (which is fine for Mandela but goes against the grain for Hitler – or hens). It just means 'to take into account another's independent value' – i.e. not treat them as though they did not have it (the general right).

[3] That, contrary to what many people believe, is what is meant by 'inalienable right'. It does not mean 'a right no one can justifiably take away from you'; it means a right you cannot get rid of. The point of saying that the rights to life and liberty are 'inalienable' is that you cannot, even if you want to (because, say, you are desperate for money to support your wife and children) sell yourself into slavery and give your 'owner' the right to dispose of your life and restrict your liberty. Few Americans realize that their 'inalienable' right to life rules out even voluntary euthanasia. Voluntary euthanasia is justifiable, if it is, because you waive your right to life and thereby relieve the rest of us of the obligation not to kill you. But if the right to life is 'inalienable' you can't do this; you have the right to life, and we have the corresponding obligation not to kill you, whether you like it or not.

[4] You might recall Mill's limitations on the application of the Harm Principle (Book 1, Chapter 3).

[5] Even with scare quotes, I regard the term 'marginal humans' as deeply objectionable, and do not believe that any human being, even one in a so-called persistent vegetative state, should be referred to as 'a human vegetable'.

Midgley's Approach: For and Against Speciesism

OBJECTIVES

By the end of this chapter you should have:

- Appreciated the ways in which speciesism is both like and unlike racism and sexism.
- Understood Midgley's objection to total anti-speciesism.
- Grasped some important aspects of Midgley's approach.
- Gained an appreciation of Scruton's approach.
- Become familiar with argument by analogy.
- Extended your ability to apply the basic reading method.

In this chapter we will be concentrating on the writings of the more 'moderate' animal liberationist Mary Midgley. Midgley is interesting for several reasons. One is that she is, as far as I know, the only philosopher who has managed to produce a good defence, against Singer and Regan, of a moderate form of speciesism. The second is that her approach to moral problems is, as we shall see, very different from Singer's and Regan's and our study of it, in relation to Scruton, will form a valuable introduction to the final chapter.

In the first part of this chapter, we will study her views on speciesism, which begin, not by attacking but by defending the parallel that Singer and Regan draw between speciesism on the one hand and racism and sexism on the other. Then we will look at the way in which she moderates their extreme views. In the second part of the chapter, we will explore what is novel about her approach and relate it to Scruton's.

Singer and Regan on speciesism

As we have seen:

1 Both Singer and Regan insist on some sort of principle of equality which applies to both humans and most of the animals that concern us. In Singer, the like interests of *all* sentient animals, not just humans, must be given equal weight; in Regan *all* animals that are experiencing subjects of a life, not just humans, have equal inherent value and thereby an equal right not to be used as a resource for others.

2 Both maintain that to deny this equality is speciesism.

3 Both maintain that speciesism is like racism and sexism and thereby wrong.

You may also recall that, according to Singer, although 'all animals (us included) are equal' it turns out that some are more equal than others. Singer argued that taking the life of any animal that is a *person* will normally be worse than taking the life of an animal that is not a person; basically because a *person*, in having desires about their own future, will have those desires frustrated by being killed, whereas a non-person, not having a grasp of its own future, will not have desires about it that will be frustrated (see p.67). In his book, though not in the Reading, Regan makes a similar move; the fundamental right not to be used is developed into a right not to be harmed for the benefit of others, and, like Singer, he argues, that a *person*, i.e. a being with desires about its own future, is harmed more by being killed than a being without such desires.

So, faced with the classic dilemma of 'Which life to save when you can only save one?' ('Which being should I rescue from the burning building?' 'Which being should not be in the foundering lifeboat?'), both of them come down in favour of you and me rather than the hen. Moreover, since, with any luck, you and I will have a lot more desires about our future than any other animal that may be a person, such as a chimpanzee, they both come down in favour of you and me rather than any other animal.

This, you might think, is just a cheat; when the going gets really rough they massage their application of their principles of equality and become speciesists too, just like the rest of us. But they have a reply to this objection. They both defend their massaged applications of their principles of equality as non-speciesist; they point out that they have not appealed to the fact that you and I are *human*, only to 'impartially observed facts' about the rich range of desires concerning our future that bright persons such as you and I have.

We might continue to press the objection. Isn't the upshot of this supposedly impartial observation a bit too good to be true? How handily it ensures that neither Singer nor Regan, nor any of their readers, are going to be required to sacrifice themselves in the lifeboat case! (They clearly will not get many converts if they demand that of us.) Surely it *is* a cheat, comparable to the way in which, in the United States before the civil rights movement, most blacks were effectively denied the right to vote, despite their having American citizenship, by the literacy requirement. 'This isn't racist' the literate white élite said, 'We have not said anywhere that *blacks* can't vote, only the illiterate'.

But although Singer's and Regan's qualifications on their equality principles have saved us and them from having to be absolutely equal to the other animals, they are, I think, justified in saying they are genuinely anti-speciesist – because of the *further* consequences of their views that they are prepared to accept. For, in appealing not to the fact that normal adult human beings such as us and them are human, but to our psychological capacities, they commit themselves, willingly, to:

1 granting that same superior status to non-human animals with those same psychological capacities, and
2 denying that same superior status to humans who lack it.

So they are both prepared to bite the bullet (though, understandably, neither emphasizes this point) of saying that I should save the chimpanzee rather than a severely mentally incapacitated human being from the burning building. And I think that is radical enough to count as being anti-speciesist (indeed, I think it's crazy).

So this is the general form of the problem that avoiding speciesism presents us with. I assume that we do not want to go back to absolute dismissal and simply deny that the other animals have any interests that matter, or that they have inherent value of some sort. What most of us would like to do is acknowledge their interests or inherent value to some extent, but keep humans – *all* humans – as a bit more special. But we are not allowed, Singer and Regan say, to ascribe greater weight to the interests or inherent value of a being just because it is a member of our own species. That is what is like racism. And it is extremely hard – probably impossible, since so many modern philosophers have already tried and failed – to find some other criterion, apart from being human, which will succeed in downgrading the other animals sufficiently to give us what we want *without,* simultaneously, downgrading those unfortunate and particularly helpless and vulnerable human beings that many of us think are most in need of our protective concern. Perhaps some of us would not mind having the dolphin and the chimpanzee upgraded to almost human status; it's the downgrading of the babies and the mentally incapacitated that strikes most of us as so horrific.

Playing authors' advocate for Singer and Regan on speciesism

However, before we jump to condemn Singer and Regan for heartlessness in this regard, we should recall again what they are trying to do and what they could reasonably say in reply to us.

They could point out that they are not arguing for downgrading the mentally incapacitated, but arguing for upgrading animals. *They* are not saying, 'It is morally all right to treat the mentally incapacitated the way we treat animals' (which is what sounds so horrific) because they are arguing that the way we treat animals is a moral outrage. It is only because *we* are still locked in our speciesist outlook, still thinking in terms of treating animals in ways that we would never dream of treating any human being, that we are horrified by their suggestion that what goes for animals goes for some human beings too. Why, they could say, don't we read the suggestion positively instead of negatively? 'Babies, and the mentally incapacitated, in being particularly helpless and vulnerable, are particularly in need of our protective concern; so animals, in being helpless and vulnerable, are particularly in need of our protective concern.' This does not amount to a heartless downgrading of any human beings.

Most of us will, I take it, still be deeply worried about the burning building/lifeboat dilemma, and still think the whole idea of extending particular protective concern to animals is absurd. But before we set about defending speciesism, arguing that it is unlike racism and sexism and hence not wrong, we must make an effort to get ourselves into the right, charitable, frame of mind. We would do well to begin by pondering a remark Regan makes at the very end of his article, and some remarks by Mary Midgley.

Regan says: 'All great movements, it is written, go through three stages: ridicule, discussion, adoption'. He and Singer take themselves to be in the vanguard of a new great movement – the campaign for animal equality. They expect that, like the campaigns for racial equality and sexual equality, this campaign will, inevitably, go through these three stages. The racists found the suggestion that 'inferior' races were not inferior but entitled to equal consideration and respect simply absurd, flying in the face of the obvious facts and commonsense; sexists still find the suggestion that women are not inferior but are entitled to equal consideration and respect absurd.

We now look back with mixed feelings of horror and incomprehension at the extreme racist and sexist views of our forebears, finding the texts of the few enlightened campaigners filled with luminous justice, compassion and commonsense and wondering how their contemporary readers can have been so blind or so wicked. How can we be sure that Singer and Regan are not right, and that our descendants will not look back on them as heroes and those of us who now reject their views as the blind and wicked?

Might we suppose that we are so much better and more enlightened nowadays that this is clearly impossible? It must be admitted that, in one way, it is awfully hard not to. We *are* better and more enlightened, aren't we? We don't have slavery; we don't limit the vote to people with certain ancestry, or land-owners, or people of a certain race, or men. But, on the other hand, it seems a rather over-confident and self-righteous thought. Are we *so* perfect nowadays? Were our forebears nearly all *so* bad, so blind and wicked? Surely most of them must have been just ordinary people like us, and, like us, thought of themselves as enlightened and as having greatly advanced on the moral thinking of *their* forebears?

Midgley on speciesism

In Chapters 6 and 7 of *Animals and Why The Matter,* Midgley encourages us to do two related things: (a) to view the history of human thoughts about equality in a certain way and then (b) to view our present thoughts about equality in relation to animals in the same way.

With respect to (a), she is urging us to try to understand our élitist, racist, sexist forebears who said they believed in equality, not just dismiss them as blind, wicked, self-interested hypocrites but, to a certain extent, to be tolerant towards them. Our forebears had the same intellectual capacities as we have; some indeed were towering geniuses. Rather than just dismissing them as stupidly or deliberately blind to obvious facts, we should try to understand what made the facts invisible to them.

It is implausible to assume that they deliberately made themselves blind or, even worse, recognized the facts perfectly well and just wickedly pretended not to, to preserve their own privileged position. Some of them – the great campaigners – were admirable people in many ways, who made considerable sacrifices defending the equality they did believe in, against ridicule, through discussion, to eventual acceptance and thereby the benefit of us all today.

If we follow Midgley's suggestion, and do not simply dismiss our élitist, racist and sexist forebears as blind and wicked, how should we then think about ourselves? It will no longer do to say '*We* are not blind and wicked; we have progressed a lot' and leave it at that, for we have just acknowledged that our forebears were not simply blind and wicked – and yet, we say now, they were still wrong about equality. So mightn't we be when we deny equality for animals?

The history of our thoughts about equality shows that, so far, *every time* in the past when we thought we had extended these thoughts far enough, we had overlooked the justifiable claims of some under-privileged group. Somewhere in the literature, there were usually a few lone campaigners on that group's behalf, but what they had to say just didn't get through to us at the time. We may well not be stupidly blind; we may well not be wicked and hypocritical, but, by **induction**, the probability is high that we will be wrong if we say 'All humans are equal but that's extending the principle far enough. It's absurd to extend it "across the species-barrier", in Midgley's phrase, to cover animals'.

induction

Correspondingly, it is not impossible that our descendants will look back on Singer, Regan, Midgley and some others as the great campaigners, as the ones that greatly contributed to the brave new world of the, say, twenty-second century, and at us as the diehard, redneck, anti-revolutionaries, trapped in the mind-set of an earlier, less-enlightened age. There they were, pointing out the justifiable claims of animals, and what they had to say just didn't get through to us.

These are the most important thoughts to bear in mind while reading Midgley. I am not going to suggest that you do a 'full reading' of this: the basic reading method can usually, but not always, be helpfully applied and Midgley's writings form one of the exceptions. It is hard, if not impossible, to get anything out of it by skimming, and what you are about to read is drawn from chapters which are not, by and large, argumentative. Midgley is mostly just describing, in an illuminating way, some of the history of various humans' thoughts about equality. (You will find that, in section 1 (pp.237–40), she discusses one 'contractarian writer', Hobbes, who did try to base all of morality on a contract.)

EXERCISE 30

Midgley on equality, women and animals

Bear in mind the questions below as you read Midgley in Reading 3 and then answer them.

1 What does Midgley say is the point of concepts such as equality and rights? (Sections 1.1, 1.2, 2.3 and 2.4)

2 What, historically, has happened when the concept of equality has been employed? (Sections 1.2, 1.6, 2.3 and 2.4)

3 What group did Rousseau exclude? (Sections 1.5, 1.6 and 2.1)

4 What group, do you suppose, currently forms, for most of us, part of 'the unnoticed background' (p.247), in an 'area of outer darkness which we ignore' (p.248), according to Midgley?

DISCUSSION

1. The concepts of equality and rights are 'essentially tools for widening concern' (p.234); 'the notion of equality is a tool for rectifying injustices within a given group...' (p.235); to be 'used for practical reform' (p.246). The concept of equality is 'a tool of reform' (p.247).
2. When the concept of equality has been employed for reform, it has been applied to a particular group the reformers identify with or are concerned about. People outside that group – foreigners, slaves, other races, women – are excluded. Questions about how they should be treated are often simply not considered, and their existence ignored.
3. Rousseau, notoriously, excluded women.
4. According to Midgley, most of us are currently in the position of excluding animals.

Midgley has given us reasons for taking seriously Singer's and Regan's claim that 'all animals are equal' and the corresponding claim that denying this is akin to racism and sexism. But you might say to this, 'Oh come on, what nonsense. Consider the interests of a mouse equally to those of a human! Consider the mouse as having the same inherent value as a human! But look how different they are! And besides, look at what completely unacceptable consequences follow: we'd have to give up doing the research that's going to find us a cure for cancer, or use humans as well! And besides, it's so much pie-in-the-sky and impractical! We must be realistic. Perhaps in a perfect world, we would love and cherish all the other animals, but it's crazy to think human beings could ever recreate the Garden of Eden. Denying equality to animals, unlike denying it to other races or women, is just plain commonsense.'

But this is just the kind of response that the diehard racists and sexists made. They said extending the principle of equality across a particular barrier, in the way the reformers called for, was nonsense. They said 'look at how different the other races or the women are!' They said completely unacceptable consequences would follow; that, for example, they would have to give other races the vote, and allow them to marry their daughters, or that there would be no one to cook or look after the children! (It never occurred to them that they might help.) And, besides, they said, it's so impractical. Perhaps in heaven there would be the 'brotherhood of man', even of man and woman (still 'brotherhood', of course), but it's crazy to think human beings could ever be this spiritual and detached in this world. Denying equality to non-Europeans or women, unlike denying it to Athenian citizens, or Europeans without land or noble blood, or the working class and so on is just plain commonsense.

We know now that the élitists, racists and sexists exaggerated and were sometimes just wrong about 'how different' the groups they excluded were. Some attempts to justify speciesism have done the same (animals are completely non-rational, don't suffer, are not subjects of a life). We can also recognize, with hindsight, that some of the differences they highlighted, though very probably false, would not have justified what they were trying to justify even if they had been true. It was – and to this day is sometimes – standardly claimed that the non-European races and women generally are markedly less intelligent or much more prone to irrational, uncontrolled emotions, and thereby are much less rational than Europeans or men generally. Now suppose there had been a fair amount of truth in these claims.

It still would not have justified the hard-edged discrimination the racists and sexists were trying to justify, for in their attics and asylums and their gaols were mentally retarded European men who were markedly less intelligent and more prone to uncontrolled emotions than many of the people they were refusing to count as equal. But in many cases, these men were still given rights the others were denied, even if they could not exercise those rights, for example to vote, inherit titles, inherit and own land, to marry as they chose, not to be sexually molested or divorced. After all, as white males, they were 'the kind of thing' that was more rational. (Compare the claim that, as human beings, infants and the severely mentally incapacitated are 'the kind of thing' that is capable of understanding contracts.)

We have seen that many attempts to justify speciesism suffer from the same flaw. True, many differences highlighted between us and the other animals to justify speciesism are not even possibly false – that is, indeed, a genuine difference between speciesism and the other two -isms. But they do not justify the hard-edged discrimination they are intended to justify – the speciesism that gets *all* human beings safely under the principle of equality as well as ruling *all* the other animals out. Kidding ourselves that we have produced such a justification, or hastily adding a few extra clauses to patch things up ('Well, they may not be very rational but at least they are "the kind of thing", namely human, that is rational') is arguing in just the same way the racists and sexists did.

Argument by analogy

So that is the argument for the view that speciesism is like racism and sexism and thereby wrong. Is it valid? No – but it cannot be criticized on those grounds without glaring lack of charity. For here we encounter another form of argument which, like **inductive** ones does not even lay claim to being valid. It is an argument by analogy.

induction

An argument by analogy argues from premises about similarities or analogies between two things to the conclusion that the two things are alike or analogous in some further respect. Above we have various premises about the similarities between speciesism and racism-and-sexism (counting that as one 'thing', say, 'vicious discrimination'). The conclusion is that, given these similarities, it is highly probable that the two things are alike in a further respect – that speciesism, like racism-and-sexism, is wrong.

Such arguments are essential; in science or the law or ethics, an argument by analogy is often the only type of argument that can be developed on an important issue. But clearly, it is only too easy to show that any such argument is invalid.

How did people argue to the conclusion that sexism is like racism and thereby wrong, as many campaigners for women's liberation in the 'sixties did? Schematically, as follows:

Premise 1	Racists say such and such and sexists says so and so and they are saying the same sort of thing.
Premise 2	Racists argue in the following sort of way and so do sexists.
Conclusion 1	Racism is like sexism.
Premise 3	Racism is wrong.
Conclusion 2	Sexism is wrong.

It is easy to show that such an argument is invalid, because it is easy to describe a situation in which all those premises were true but the conclusion false. All we have to do is grant the premises but add a bit more about what goes on, for example:

Premise 1	Racists argue that race makes a difference (which it doesn't) but sexists argue that sex makes a difference (which it does).
Premise 2	Racists have to admit that, because of mixed-blood, being of one race rather than another is a matter of degree, not a hard and fast distinction, but sexists say there is a clear cut difference between men and women (which there is except in a few very rare cases).
Conclusion	So racism is *unlike* sexism. And, moreover, racism is wrong, but a reasonable discrimination between the sexes, giving them separate spheres appropriate to their different needs and capacities, is not only justifiable but perfectly proper.

Whenever someone is arguing that two things are *like* each other – but not, of course, identical in every respect – there are bound to be differences between the two things as well as the similarities described in the premises. So it is always, in theory, open to someone to emphasize the differences and claim they support the opposite conclusion. When you are arguing that something is like something else, the best you can do is assemble the most striking similarities that you can in your premises and hope that these will strike other people as more important, more relevant, to the issue at hand, than any dissimilarities might be. (Of course, you could trivially make the argument valid by adding the premise 'These are the only really important features of the two things in question'. But anyone who disagrees with your conclusion will just think that's implausible and find your argument valid but **unsound**.)

sound argument

It seems to me, especially given Midgley's points, that the similarities between speciesism, on the one hand, and racism and sexism on the other, are rather striking – too striking for comfort. For me, her argument by analogy works. We may still want to say 'But it's *absurd* of Singer and Regan to say speciesism is wrong' – especially when we think of some of their conclusions, but another bit of us may be thinking 'They really do have a point. Maybe I am just thinking like a diehard redneck'. And thereby we seem to be in just that state of 'conflict and confusion' that Midgley mentions in section 1.6 (p.241).

So what can we do? Midgley makes a very interesting and challenging move. She tackles 'the principle of equality' itself.

Exploring the principle of equality

Midgley regards talk about equality – of Athenian citizens, slaves, Frenchman, blacks, women – as fighting talk. The concept of equality is a tool for reform. We might even go so far as to say that she regards the use of the words 'equal' and 'equality' in moral contexts (as opposed to, say, mathematical ones) as a form of **emotive language**. The words are, after all, used to express the user's strong feeling of concern for some disadvantaged group and aimed at evoking that same concern in others. And, as she rightly remarks, they are very powerful (section 1.1). However, this is not to say that those who use them are ducking out of rational discussion; Midgley clearly approves of all the reforms this fighting talk has brought about, and believes that each of them has been backed up by rational argument.

emotive language

So what does she think about the fighting claim that 'animals are equal'? Recall section 1.1:

> concepts like equality and natural rights... are essentially tools for widening concern, and concern, though it may attenuate with distance, is certainly possible in principle towards anything which we suppose to feel. Normally

> prejudice restricts it, but these concepts exist to break down prejudice, as they have repeatedly done. They are essentially destructive. Along with notions like liberty and fraternity, they work to dissolve the screens of callous habit and reveal hidden injustice. All these concepts are vague. All must be supplemented, once their work of revelation is done, by other, more detailed and discriminating ideas. But vague though they are, they are very powerful. They melt away the confused excuses given by custom, appealing... to the deeper standards required for change (p.234).

Now read section 1 of Reading 4 'The significance of species'. **READING**

It seems that Midgley believes that, at least to a certain extent, the fight of the reformers on behalf of animals has been won – the prejudice has been broken down, the screens of callous habit dissolved, the confused excuses given by custom melted away. The dust has now cleared and it is time to supplement the vague, reforming, ideas of equality and speciesism by 'more detailed and discriminating ideas'.

Is she a little over-optimistic to think that the fight has been won? We are certainly still far from being a vegetarian society that condemns the use of animals in science. But she may be right to think that, though practice, as so often, is trailing far behind ideals, the *idea* that we should extend our concern 'across the species-barrier' is now fairly well established. In November 1995, the *Independent's* tabloid cover story was 'The 10 best ideas of the decade' and its first example was 'Animals', which opened 'It is 20 years since Peter Singer published his groundbreaking book *Animal Liberation.* But it is in the Nineties that the idea of animal rights has begun to be taken seriously in the mainstream of politics'. As a society, it may be said, we *have* extended our concern across the species-barrier; from now on, it is a question of details – what forms should this extended concern take?

According to Midgley, not some of the extreme forms of 'equal treatment' recommended by Singer and Regan. It is time to refine and supplement their use of principles of equality and their corresponding sweeping condemnation of speciesism. How does she do it?

A 'principle of equality', as we have seen, can take more than one form. Consider Singer's 'equal interests should receive equal consideration'. True or false? 'True' you may feel compelled to admit – but think again. The claim suffers from **some/all confusion** or **ambiguity**. Does it mean:

some/all confusion

ambiguity

1 'equal interests should *always* receive equal consideration'; or

2 'equal interests should *sometimes* receive equal consideration'?

If it means the former, consider the following objection to accepting it is true.

If equal interests should always receive equal consideration – if, that is, *whenever* I am considering what I ought to do, I ought to give equal moral consideration to the interests of everyone – it seems that it would be wrong of me to give special attention to the interests – the needs, desires and futures – of my family and friends, or those with whom I am in special professional relationships. But parents who do not give special attention to their own children are bad parents; people who do not give special attention to their own aged parents are (pending some justification) ungrateful and irresponsible; someone who never gives me any special attention cannot be a true friend to me; doctors and teachers who do not give special attention to their own patients and students are bad doctors and teachers. This *universal* principle of equality, requiring that equal interests *always* receive equal consideration, requires complete impartiality in our dealings with each other. But although, in certain contexts, we may say that morality should be 'impartial', we do not mean that the above sort of partiality is morally wrong. It is *not* wrong to be a good parent, to be a dutiful son or daughter, to be a true friend or a good doctor or teacher; on the contrary they are all what, if relevant, we should all be trying to be.

Let us invent 'familyism'. 'Familyism' involves:

1 drawing a distinction between members of one's own family and others; and

2 sometimes, in some ways, giving preference to the interests of members of one's own family.

EXERCISE 31
'Familyism' and speciesism

1 Describe speciesism in precisely similar terms as (1) and (2) above, and then answer the following questions.

2 Is 'familyism' always wrong? Is 'familyism' always justifiable? If not, give an example of when it is wrong.

3 What answers does the analogy between 'familyism' and speciesism suggest to the same questions about speciesism?

Check your answers against those at the back of the book before reading on.

It is clear that what generates Singer's most radical anti-speciesist conclusions is his assumption that his principle of equality takes the universal form. Equal interests should *always* receive equal consideration – and this requires complete impartiality in our dealings not only with each other but with other species. And, at long last, we have at least the beginnings of a really strong objection to his position. In its universal form, Singer's principle of equality is false. It is falsified by some of our partial, but morally proper, dealings with each other. So, by analogy, it is likely to be false as far as some of our partial dealings with other species are concerned too.

Can we make the same objection to Regan? In one way no. The details of Regan's position, as revealed in the Reading, are much less clear than in Singer, and, in fact, in his book, he does go on to introduce particular rights – such as children's rights to special care from their parents – which sometimes qualify the application of his universal principle of equality. So, unlike Singer, he does not require complete impartiality in our dealings with each other. So we cannot make exactly the same objection to him.

But in another way we *can* use the same objection, exploiting the fact that Regan has already conceded that 'familyism' is not always wrong. If, according to him, it is not always wrong then, by analogy speciesism need not be. Regan's principle of equality is that all humans and all animals that are subjects of a life have equal inherent value. But, despite the premise that all humans have equal inherent value, he does not demand that we always treat them the same way; he justified some 'familyism' in terms of children's rights to special care from their parents. But the way is then open for us to insist that, on his own terms, maybe some speciesism can be justified too, despite the premise that all animals that are subjects of life (not just humans) have equal inherent value.

Justifying some speciesism

If 'familyism' is not only sometimes morally permissible, but positively desirable, and, by analogy, speciesism is too, what shall we say about racism? Are we not in danger of falling, yet again, into Singer's and Regan's trap? Here we must recall again what one can and cannot achieve with argument by analogy. At best, we can emphasize similarities and hope they strike others, as they strike us, as the most important and relevant. So in order to block the argument by analogy from 'familyism' making racism sometimes all right too, we need to argue that 'familyism' and speciesism have at least one further, important similarity that they do not share with racism. And Midgley boldly attempts this, on several fronts:

1. As we have already seen in Reading 4, section 1 she claims that 'race in humans is not a significant grouping at all, but species in animals certainly is'. Elsewhere in *Animals and Why They Matter*, she claims that family membership is also a significant grouping.
2. She claims that preference for one's own family and one's own species is a natural preference, not, like race-prejudice, a product of culture.

What is an obvious objection that Singer could make to (2)? Responding to the objection that it is natural and therefore justifiable for us to eat meat, Singer replied that this not only made a factual mistake, but also relied on the false assumption that 'because this process is natural it is right'. We do not, he said, 'have to assume that the natural way of doing something is incapable of improvement' (p.46 above). So, in this case, he could object that Midgley is assuming that, because our preferences for our own family and own species are natural, they are, unlike racial preferences, right and incapable of improvement.

But Midgley does not leave her claim (2) without further support. She claims further that:

3 Both family and species preferences are an 'absolutely central element in human happiness' without which we could not live a full human life. And no one could claim this about racism.

We must be careful to note what she is *not* claiming about 'familyism' and speciesism.

EXERCISE 32

The morality of species preference

Read the passage below and then answer the question:

Is Midgley claiming that, because 'familyism' and speciesism are both natural and a central element in human happiness, they are always justifiable or right?

> Questions about the morality of species preference must certainly be put in the context of the other preferences which people give to those closest to them. These preferences do indeed cause problems. By limiting human charity, they can produce terrible misery. On the other hand they are also an absolutely central element in human happiness, and it seems unlikely that we could live at all without them. They are the root from which charity grows. Morality shows a constant tension between measures to secure justice and widen sympathy for outsiders. To handle this tension by working out particular priorities is our normal moral business. In handling species conflicts, the notion of simply rejecting all discrimination as *speciesist* looks like a seductively simple guide, an all-purpose formula. I am suggesting that it is not simple, and that we must resist the seduction.
>
> (Midgley (1983), p.103)

DISCUSSION

No, she is not. As we have already noted, giving preference to members of one's own family is sometimes wrong, and, by analogy, so is giving preference to members of one's own species. Both are sometimes right, sometimes wrong, and it is the business of morality to try to sort out when they are which. But this is a complicated issue. It is not to be solved by giving a simple answer –

that they are both always right (tribalism and absolute dismissal) or that they are both always wrong (Singer).

This point turns another objection that Singer could make into a **straw man**. Suppose he objected to (3) in the following way:

straw man

> 'Midgley claims that speciesism is an "absolutely central element in human happiness". But so what? Does that justify it? Only if we say that *human* happiness is all that counts. What about the animals' happiness? Midgley is assuming that this does not count at all.'

But Midgley is assuming no such thing, hence the objection is attacking a straw man. She is one of the 'animal liberationists' after all. Just as morality requires that preferences for one's own family members must sometimes give way to wider claims, so it will require that preference for one's own species does the same. What she is doing, we may say, is highlighting the very questionable nature of Singer's implicit assumption that things would be greatly improved if we gave up family and species preferences altogether.

Her grounds for questioning that assumption are not given clearly in any one passage, and, so, before asking you to read the passage that comes closest to giving them, I will briefly sketch her general objection to Singer.

One reviewer of Singer's *Animal Liberation* objected in a similar vein:

> Partiality for our own species, and within it for much smaller groupings is, like the universe, something we had better accept... The danger in an attempt to eliminate partial affections is that it may remove the source of all affections.
>
> (Benson (1978), pp.529–49)

In *Practical Ethics,* Singer replied, 'This argument ties morality too closely to our affections' and went on to set up a couple of straw men i.e. a couple of cases in which acting on the basis of our partial affections would clearly be wrong. Midgley, I take it, would be on the side of the reviewer. She thinks that morality *is* tied closely to our natural affections. It is our natural affections that prompt us, as social creatures, to live together at all and thereby invent morality as something that we can, rationally, choose to live by and teach to each new generation. We are not, by nature, entirely self-interested egoists who are then driven, by the inexorable force of abstract rational argument, to widen our area of concern beyond ourselves to more and more impartial concern, on pain of inconsistency. We are 'bond-forming creatures, not abstract intellects' (Midgley (1983), p.102). We have natural impulses of, at least, charity or benevolence, and an interest in others which, properly developed and moderated by reason, makes us into good moral agents. Without these natural impulses, all moral reasoning would fall on deaf ears.

Saying that these impulses or affections are 'natural' to us is not saying that they will survive any upbringing intact. Midgley (a female philosopher with children) is rare amongst moral philosophers in never losing sight of the fact that morality has to be taught to each up and coming generation. (We do not start acquiring sound moral views only when we start doing moral philosophy; our upbringing has already convinced us of at least some of the premises the moral philosophers need to rely on to get started.) And she thinks that the hugely complex role that familial and species-bonding and hence partial affections plays in the social and moral education of our young shows that partial affections are, indeed, essential to the possibility of morality.

empirical

Now this is an **empirical** claim and it may, for all we know, be false. Perhaps we could, over a long period of time, educating each successive generation in more and more unimaginable ways, eventually turn ourselves into the sorts of creatures that did not bond to those closest to us, and to our own species. And, perhaps, despite lacking these bonds, we would still, somehow, keep going, not only as a social group but as a social group interested in producing, bringing up and caring for, successive generations. But once Midgley has drawn our attention to just some of the features involved in familial and species-bonding, we may lose any inclination to suppose that getting rid of them would constitute any improvement – even for the other animals – at all.

READING Now read Reading 4 'The Significance of Species', sections 2–5.

Remember that what is at issue is not, simply, justifying familial or species preferences. It is justifying *some* familial and species preferences, contrary to Singer's claim that the universal version of the principle of equality is what we should accept. And the very caution and moderation of Midgley's claim inevitably makes it one that it is very hard for Singer to argue against. What could we say on his behalf?

He can claim that familial and species partiality has lead us, and still leads us, to do unjust, irresponsible, cruel and callous things. But this is no objection to Midgley, who concedes it – sometimes such partiality is wrong. But, she may say, sometimes such partiality leads us to do fine and wonderful things, making great sacrifices or running great risks for the sake of others. Singer might reply that complete impartiality would preserve all those fine and wonderful deeds but rule out the wicked ones. But that is a **supposition**, he has put himself into a position of remote speculation. That *might* conceivably be so. But where are our grounds for believing it? We have no idea what a community – or a collection – of completely impartial human beings would be like. Maybe they would regard all interests and lives, their own included,

supposition

equally but indifferently. They resign themselves to their, and consign every other sentient being to its, own fate, accepting and enduring their own suffering with stoical indifference, and watching others suffer with equal indifference. And that would hardly constitute an improvement, even for the other animals.

But we have a very good idea of what a community of partial human beings is like. We *are* one, and, despite being partial, we are not thereby deaf or indifferent to the claims of impartiality.

Midgley's final important point in the context of speciesism is that the species-bond, though strong, is not exclusive. She says later:

> It is one of the special powers and graces of our species not to ignore others, but to draw in, domesticate and live with a great variety of other creatures. No other animal does so on anything like so large a scale. Perhaps we should take this peculiar human talent more seriously.
>
> (Midgley (1983), p.111)

We can, and do, bond with other species too. In the concluding chapters of *Animals and Why They Matter*, she emphasizes the ways in which human sympathy and curiosity carry us straight through the species-barrier, hardly noticing it is there. Just as devotion to one's family may, but need not, form any impediment to a whole-hearted commitment to a cause of impartial justice (say, anti-racism) so the strong species-bond need form no impediment to a whole-hearted sympathy with animal suffering and a recognition of the inherent value of animals' lives.

What we can learn from Midgley

Midgley has provided us with an interesting argument in favour of *some* speciesism. One thing that is interesting about it is that it clearly connects with several intuitive reactions that many people have to Singer's and Regan's claim that speciesism is always wrong. It is not, that is, an abstract philosophical argument which offers a completely new slant on the question of 'speciesism – right or wrong?' It is, rather, the sort of philosophical argument that relies on reminding us about things we know perfectly well already, which are of crucial relevance to that question, but which somehow, faced with the task of arguing against Singer and Regan on speciesism, we forget about.

So what we realize when we read Midgley is that we believe the following two claims:

1. that speciesism is like racism and sexism in some important respects but unlike in others;
2. that speciesism is sometimes justifiable, sometimes not.

And she can give some reasons to back up those beliefs.

But we do not learn from Midgley that these claims are true. Singer and Regan do not believe the two claims, and their writings have convinced many reasonable people. Midgley has shown that those two claims form a possible, reasonable position (which falls far short of 'absolute dismissal').

Do we learn from Midgley that the principle of equality applies sometimes but not always, and that the ideal of its universal application is, when imagined in any detail, not only unrealistic but quite possibly horrific? No. It is not only Singer and (with some qualifications) Regan, and those they convince who do not believe this, but, arguably, some of the world's great religions. There are ways of interpreting Christian doctrine which rule out moral considerations based on familial-bonding, derived, particularly, from Matthew 10: 37–8:

> He who loves father or mother more than me is not worthy of me and he who loves son or daughter more than me is not worthy of me, and he who does not take up his cross and follow me is not worthy of me.

And many forms of Buddhism regard not only familial but also species partiality as natural desires which, ideally, are to be overcome and transcended. But what we are reminded of or learn from Midgley is that hers is a reasonable position to hold (which falls far short of tribalism or nepotism or 'absolute dismissal').

Can we learn anything from her about when it might be reasonable to claim that speciesism is wrong and when it might be reasonable to claim it is right? Unfortunately, no; her ethical approach does not lend itself to giving specific answers to such questions in a short book which is concerned with many other questions. To see why her ethical approach cannot yield simple answers to the question 'When is speciesism right and when is it wrong?' and how it might be developed, we need to consider that approach.

Complex approaches to moral questions

So far we have looked in detail at two different general approaches to our treatment of animals, utilitarianism and the rights-based approach. We have also looked briefly at two versions of the 'indirect duty view', Regan's and Kant's. Does this exhaust the field? No, despite Regan's assumption that it does. Regan, you may recall, made the mistake of treating all versions of contractarianism as though they were another version of an indirect duty view. According to any indirect duty view:

We have no duties (directly) to animals.

But according to the contractarians Hume and Rawls:

> We have duties to rights-bearers; animals do not have rights because they are not capable of understanding contracts; but we have duties to non-rights-bearers, e.g. animals *too*.

Hume and Rawls can hold this position because they hold that there is more to morality than considerations of justice and rights. They recognize not only duties of justice (to rights-bearers) but also duties of 'compassion and humanity' (Rawls) which can be duties to either rights-bearers or non-rights-bearers. (In fact, Hume recognizes many others too.) They are contractarians about justice, but not, more generally, about morality.

Without knowing anything else about them, we can see that Hume and Rawls introduce more *complexity* into the practical situation than Singer or Regan. When I am considering what I should do, or what I should think about some actual or proposed action, I do not *only* consider what rights, if any, are involved, nor do I concentrate *solely* on whether the action will cause happiness or suffering. I may need to consider both. And, even without understanding the details, we can guess that anyone who uses this approach is sometimes going to find it hard to reach firm, **black-and-white conclusions**, and harder still to justify any that they do reach. How, for example, will they be able to justify their claim that, for instance, in *this* particular case, compassion or humanity is a more important consideration than rights, or vice versa?

black-and-white thinking

Where does Midgley stand? She is hard to categorize – not only on the basis of the Readings here, but, indeed, from the whole book. She has, rightly, been described as 'approaching the issues from a completely non-ideological perspective; that is, she approaches each issue without preconceptions and does not try to develop an analysis in terms of a predetermined set of... principles' (Hargrove (1992), p.xviii). She recognizes the possibility of *many* different sorts of moral claims.

We have already come across one example – her acknowledgement of the claims of both impartiality (or justice) *and* partiality. Another example she gives is that of claims based on 'special need'; the Good Samaritan who stopped to help the wounded stranger by the wayside while others 'passed by on the other side' was someone, she says, who recognized such a claim. And, she adds, anyone who stopped to do something about an injured dog lying writhing in the road after being hit by a car would probably stop for the same reason – the special need of the dog – as they would stop for an injured human being. She also recognizes the claims arising from 'special responsibility' – those 'arising from our own acts and the acts of those with whom we identify'. These could cover such varied examples as the obligation to keep a promise I have made, to look after a cat I have taken on as my pet, and to support legislation intended to rectify the injustices that my colonial ancestors perpetrated on the aboriginals of my country. She mentions, too, gratitude, prudence and (perhaps with a view to her environmental concerns) 'admiration and wonder'.

Recognizing the possibility of many different sorts of moral claims, Midgley is in a position to acknowledge the complexity of moral life and moral decision making. Our grounds – the reasons we give – for thinking we ought to do something cover a very wide range.

Now it is true that what one gains on the swings of complexity, one loses on the roundabouts of simplicity and clear moral decisions. The beauty of direct utilitarianism is that, apart from the occasional cases where it is very unclear what the consequences of one's action are going to be, it gives a cut-and-dried answer to almost every moral decision – this is right, that's wrong. It can do that because, by allowing in only one moral consideration – maximizing the interests of those affected – it eliminates all conflict. As soon as we allow in just one other consideration – say, that which comes from indirect utilitarianism – we get possible conflict and thereby the possibility of 'well, it is right in this way, wrong in that way'. Singer's direct utilitarianism (involving his universal principle of equality) bids the scientist experiment, on some occasions, on the helpless human being. His indirect utilitarianism bids her not to. So what should she do?

But Midgley also emphasizes two points. One is that complexity does not invariably import conflict in every case. Yes, sometimes claims made on behalf of animals will conflict with claims made on behalf of humans, but sometimes not. Concern for the plight of factory-farmed animals and their use in at least some experiments need not militate against concern for the suffering of human beings; it is not always a matter of 'either they suffer or we do'.

Her second point is that conflicts between claims are sometimes easily resolvable. Suppose, she says, that 'the Good Samaritan's efforts make him late for supper at his venerable uncle's, or even make him spend the money which was meant for his uncle's present'. The claims of kinship and of special responsibility conflict with that of special need, but the last clearly overrides. (In *this* case – it might not override them if he was on his way to his father's death bed.) And no doubt she would say (though she does not explicitly discuss it) that *if* my choice lay between killing and eating an animal, or starving, of course it is all right for me to kill the animal – the claim of prudence overrides in this case.

However, as before, this is a particular case. Nothing follows about its being all right for me to be a meat-eater in the ordinary situation in which most of us find ourselves. Nor does anything general follow about human lives being of more inherent value than any animal's life. Animals' claims can be overridingly strong on other, different, occasions.

So Midgley cannot give us any clear answers about when speciesism is right and when it is wrong, for the whole book would have to consist of the detailed examination of particular cases. Still, it would be nice to have a better idea of what sorts of answers she could give – or we could give, playing author's advocate. Perhaps surprisingly, we can develop a better idea by looking at the approach of the fox-hunting Roger Scruton, whose contractarian position on rights was discussed in the preceding chapter.

Scruton's approach

Scruton, like Hume and Rawls, is a contractarian about justice but not about morality. Unlike Regan, he thinks of morality as drawing on more than simply considerations of rights; he regards justice as but one of four parts of morality. In the following passage, drawn from a *Times Higher* article referred to earlier (p.124), he summarizes his position.

EXERCISE 33
Scruton's view of morality

Read the passage below and then answer these questions.

In the passage, can you identify (roughly) (i) one part that corresponds to Singer's view of morality, (ii) one part that corresponds to Regan's view of morality, and (iii) one part that Scruton gives a separate status to, but that Regan regards as already covered by his view?

> Morality has four related but distinguishable roots in the human psyche. First comes the calculus of rights and duties, not always recognized under that name, but exemplified in any durable community. Second comes sympathy and its specific form of benevolence. Sympathy is the motive that draws us into the community and makes it natural and rational for us to think in moral terms. Third is the distinction between vice and virtue – between the motives we despise and those we admire. Finally there is the motive which I call, following the Roman usage, piety – the disposition to recognize our frailty, and to acknowledge that we did not create the world but must receive it as a gift.
>
> Although animals stand outside the moral community, they are nevertheless objects of moral concern. They make claims on our sympathy; we can distinguish virtuous and vicious ways of dealing with them; and piety requires that we abandon any title to deal with them purely as instruments or things.
>
> There are those who believe it is wrong to eat animals. But I can find no grounds for this belief. After all, it is not necessarily wrong to eat human beings, provided they are already dead. Our first duty to the animals we rear for food is to provide them with a fulfilling life. Sympathy and piety both speak

> against the battery farm and the veal crate. On the other hand, pigs, cattle, sheep and poultry reared in the right conditions are legitimate food.
>
> (Scruton (1996b), p.17)

DISCUSSION

(i) Scruton's second part corresponds, roughly, to Singer's utilitarianism. Utilitarianism is sometimes described as 'the ethics of benevolence' since what it emphasizes is the benevolent moral concern for others' happiness and suffering.

(ii) His first part corresponds to Regan's view of morality as being concerned with rights.

(iii) His fourth part, 'piety', does not look as though it corresponds to anything in Regan when he first describes it – 'the disposition to recognize our frailty', etc. But a hint of what he might mean by 'acknowledging that we did not create the world but must receive it as a gift' emerges when he says that 'piety requires that we abandon any title to deal with [animals] purely as *instruments or things*' (my italics). Recall that Regan's view about inherent value was that beings with inherent value were beings that it was wrong to treat 'in ways that reduce them to the status of things, as if they existed as resources' (Reading 2, paragraph 23) – or instruments, we might say – 'here for *us*' (paragraph 3).

So we can view Scruton as recognizing that there is something right in both Singer's and Regan's approaches, but thinking that both have made a mistake in concentrating exclusively on just one moral consideration. There are at least four things we may need to consider when we are deciding what we ought to do. Singer is right that we may need to consider suffering (on the distinctive ground of sympathy); Regan is right that we may need to consider rights (on the distinctive ground of justice). Both are wrong in overlooking the fact that we may need to consider both – and also two further considerations, namely virtue and vice, and piety.

Scruton regards Regan as wrong on one, and right on another count as well. As we saw in the preceding chapter, as a contractarian about justice, he thinks it makes no sense to ascribe rights to animals, so he thinks Regan is wrong about that. However, despite disagreeing with Regan over whether animals have rights, it seems that he does agree with him that our using animals as 'instruments' or 'things' is wrong – not indeed because this violates their rights (for they have none) but because it is contrary to 'piety'.

So, as far as our treatment of animals is concerned, it seems that Scruton has taken a leaf from both Singer's and Regan's books. He agrees with Singer that it is wrong to cause animal suffering, in for example, battery farms and veal crates (on the distinctive ground of sympathy). And he agrees with Regan that it is wrong to deal with animals purely as instruments, to *use* them (on the distinctive ground of piety). So one might expect that he would emerge as a committed 'animal liberationist' after their own hearts. But he is a fox-hunter, and he claims that pigs, cattle, sheep, etc., reared in the right conditions, are legitimate food. How come? We will find out in the next reading.

Scruton's Animal Rights and Wrongs

In his pamphlet, *Animal Rights and Wrongs,* Scruton discusses some of the rights and wrongs of our treatment of animals. The section in which he does this (Reading 5) exemplifies some of the features of Midgley's approach (though not many conclusions she would accept). Rather than approaching the topic of our treatment of animals very generally, he distinguishes a number of particular areas and his discussion illustrates the kind of complexity that is introduced into moral philosophy when one allows a whole range of considerations to count as morally relevant.

The Scruton reading is longer than any other you have read during your study of this book and I shall not be giving it anything like a full treatment (although I shall be discussing further some parts of it in the final chapter). Moreover, it contains a mass of details that would be very difficult to summarize succinctly in the sort of 'reading outlines' I gave for Singer and Regan. However, this does not mean that the basic reading method does not apply; rather, your ability to apply it will be extended; you will need to apply it in a slightly different way.

First, skimming. I hope that, by now, you are beginning to develop a sense of what method of skimming suits you. If you are finding it difficult to skim at length, skim a little under a useful sub-heading and then go back and read that sub-section carefully before skimming the next. Or try just a few sub-sections at a time and so on. Try using what you already know to frame the right questions to bear in mind as you skim for yourself.

Second, the reading outline: given how long and bitty the extract is (because Scruton distinguishes so many different areas), it is difficult to avoid getting bogged down. The way to master the extract is to aim to write down (or perhaps highlight in the text) quite a large number of individual points, particularly about what position Scruton holds about the rights and wrongs of our treatment of animals in the various areas he considers. You could write down (or highlight) a few or quite a lot when you skim, depending on what kind of skimmer you are becoming, and then add to them (and perhaps amend those you have) when you read carefully. To give you an idea of what to aim for, I will tell you that I am going to note twenty-five points rarely involving more than one sentence. Noting even half as many would be very good skimming indeed.

Remember the principle of charity and when it should, and should not, be applied; if you like the sound of Scruton's views, read him critically. If you do not, read him charitably.

READING
The moral status of animals

Now read Scruton on the moral status of animals (Reading 5).

Skimming

I think the right general question to bear in mind while skimming is 'What position does Scruton hold regarding our treatment of animals, in the various areas he considers?' As soon as you start skimming, the sub-headings give you particular versions of that general question: What position does Scruton hold regarding our treatment of our pets? What position does Scruton hold regarding animals for human use and exploitation? What position does Scruton hold regarding our inflicting pain on animals? And so on.

Another good general question to bear in mind is 'Where do sympathy, virtue and vice, and piety come in?'

Reading outline

1 Scruton denies that animals have rights, but accepts that we may have duties towards them (paragraphs 1–4).

2 Scruton holds that our pets are 'honorary members of the human community'(10); we have 'clear duties to look after them' (17).

3 Scruton is against 'the more presumptuous kind of genetic engineering in the case of animals'; piety forbids this (25).

4 Scruton holds that, with respect to sporting animals 'the same moral considerations apply here as in the case of pets' (26).

5 Scruton holds that some sports involving animals 'cannot be dismissed as immoral' (27). Some promote virtue ('courage, self-discipline, and practical wisdom') (22). They also promote the well-being of some of the animals involved (23) and human happiness – a moral consideration drawn from sympathy or benevolence.

6 Scruton holds that 'the deliberate infliction of pain (on animals) for its own sake and in order to enjoy the spectacle of suffering' (28) is morally wrong (29). Sympathy, virtue and piety all condemn it (29).

7 Scruton holds that dog-fights and bear-baiting are morally wrong (31). 'Sympathy, virtue and piety must all condemn such activities' (29).

8 Scruton holds that inflicting pain on dogs and horses to train them may not be wrong. It may not be cruel, but kind (31).

9 Scruton has some argument about bull-fighting – perhaps that it is wrong because it displays 'a deficit of sympathy' (35–6)? (I don't think one can say more about his argument without getting bogged down in details.)

10 Scruton holds that 'zoos make no contribution to the store of human virtue' (39).

11 Scruton holds that it is 'right to eat those animals whose comforts depend upon our doing so' (41).

12 Scruton is against 'factory farming', which is contrary to sympathy and piety (44).

13 Scruton holds that 'farm animals should be given a measure of their natural freedom' (45).

14 Scruton holds that we 'cannot regard the practice of slaughtering young animals as intrinsically immoral' (47).

15 Scruton holds that experimental subjects in medical research 'cannot be human, except in the cases where their consent can reasonably be offered and sought' (51).

16 Scruton holds that we have a duty of care to animals used in medical research (52).

17 Scruton holds that some experiments on animals are wrong, because 'they offend too heavily against sympathy and piety'. Some also involve callousness (a vice) (52).

18 Scruton holds that 'we have no duty of care towards any specific wild animal' (54).

19 Scruton holds that 'our general responsibility towards the environment extends to wild animals' (55).

20 Scruton holds that it is 'right to take [wild animals'] joys and sufferings into account'. 'Not to do so is to fail in sympathy' and be arrogant (which is vicious and/or contrary to piety) (55).

21 Scruton holds that we respond selectively to different sorts of wild 'animals' (58), e.g. insects and others (59).

22 Scruton holds that it is as wrong to take pleasure in the suffering of a wild animal as in the suffering of a domestic animal and that it is wrong to use wild animals in vicious ways (60).

23 Scruton holds that angling is morally permissible (62–6).

24 Scruton argues in defence of fox-hunting (67–70). (He holds that protests against it are not 'really justified' (67); that 'our first principle finds no fault with fox-hunting, and the second principle will apply as readily as in the case of angling' (68); that 'the third principle would also seem to favour the sport' (69).) However,

25 Scruton holds that the morality of fox-hunting is 'controversial' (71); the counter-argument (that 'the pleasure involved is either vicious in itself, or an expression of a vicious nature' (73)) 'should not be dismissed, and the case remains open' (78).

Scruton in relation to Regan

How does Scruton stand in relation to Regan? Well, as a contractarian about justice, he begins by denying outright Regan's claim that animals have rights. However, this initial sweeping claim receives some modifications. For a start, pets are made 'honorary members of the moral community', that is, they *are* accorded certain rights, those that correspond to the 'duties of care', without simultaneously being landed with duties themselves. This is because we have assumed responsibility for them. Moreover, there is a suggestion that sporting animals are also made honorary members for the same reason. (I would not say this was perfectly clear, but it seems to me that that is what he is saying in paragraph 26.) There is also a suggestion (once again, it is not clear) that the same even holds true, in some limited way, of animals used in medical research. It seems that they too, are owed some sort of minimal 'duty of care', a duty the experimenter assumes by singling out this particular animal and making himself responsible for what happens to it, thereby conferring on the animal the right to *some* care.

One point which is unambiguously clear is that 'we have no duty of care towards any specific wild animal'. And, as you will see in Book 3 on our relationship to the environment, trying to maintain that wild animals have the same sorts of rights as domesticated ones does involve one in a number of apparently absurd consequences. It is not implausible to say that my cat has a right to my intervention when I see it threatened by cruel small boys or a fox. But if I try to maintain (as Regan in his book seems inclined to do) that any experiencing subject of a life has a right to be similarly protected from harm, it seems that we ought to be intervening to protect the rabbits from the foxes, and quite generally, all the herbivores from the carnivores! But this would be to interfere with the environment to an extent that even the least 'green' amongst us would be unlikely to accept.

There are two, opposing, ways of looking at Scruton's clear, and less than clear, qualifications on his general claim that animals do not have rights. One is to regard them, uncharitably, as inconsistent and probably hypocritical. First, he denies that animals have rights to escape Regan's conclusions. Then he realizes that this position will have various consequences that he regards as unpalatable or 'absurd', so he puts a number of ***ad hoc* qualifications** on it so that he can have his cake (or his animal!) and eat it too. The second, charitable, way, is to regard them, at least initially, as qualifications for which good reasons are given. They are, perhaps, qualifications that he is led to make not merely because they suit his personal beliefs but because he is acknowledging that, even within the single area of 'rights and duties', things are more complex than the simple contractarian view of justice allows. Although, paradigmatically, it is contracts that generate rights (on the contractarian view), when we think about it, we realize that the voluntary assumption of special responsibility on our part sometimes generates rights too.

***ad hoc* clauses**

Scruton in relation to Singer

Scruton's rejection of utilitarianism is unmistakable. Note, especially, paragraphs 5, 11, 12, 30 and 44. Less obviously, it is also operating in paragraphs 24, 29, 52 and 55. (Paragraph 55 is particularly interesting because it hints at the way in which Singer's utilitarianism, like Regan's rights-based approach, threatens to have absurd consequences in the context of environmental ethics. A huge amount of animal suffering goes on in the wild – shouldn't we, as utilitarians, be doing our utmost to prevent this, interfering wholesale in the balance of nature to improve things?)

However, Scruton shares Singer's view that happiness and suffering are important moral considerations. He does argue against factory-farming and, although he does not come out clearly in favour of city-dwellers becoming either vegetarian or making sure that they always pay extra for free-range products, paragraph 44 comes very close to it. Moreover, he seems to share some of

Singer's difficulties about medical research. Although, unlike Singer, he insists straight off that experimental subjects '*cannot* be human except in cases where their consent can be reasonably offered and sought' (paragraph 51), he finds himself unable to strike any satisfactory balance between the long-term benefits of medical research and the many short-term costs in suffering.

That he shares Singer's view that happiness and suffering are important moral considerations does not mean that he always produces similar conclusions, even when these are the only relevant considerations. On the contrary, on a couple of occasions he produces arguments that Singer, on his own grounds, would need to consider.

In some of Singer's other writings, he argues against our keeping of pets. As you might guess, he emphasizes the ways in which many of us make pets suffer from their domestication, cites the startlingly horrific statistics of the number of cats and dogs abandoned each year in the UK and killed by the RSPCA, notes the animal suffering involved in our over-breeding show pets (persian cats that cannot breathe properly, dogs whose hip joints are constantly dislocating) and, in general, condemns the general practice of keeping pets as inconsistent with equal consideration of interests. Scruton is with him in condemning irresponsibility, selfishness, 'kitschification', and over-breeding. But he argues that a general practice of pet-keeping *in which we fulfilled our obligations* to our pet animals would both contribute to the sum of human happiness *and* to the sum of animal happiness. It is not easy to see how Singer could object to this.

I do not know whether Singer has discussed our treatment of sporting animals anywhere. However, he does imply, at the end of Reading 1, that the application of his ethical principles to 'hunting in all its different forms, circuses, rodeos, zoos' will yield the conclusion that by and large, with a few qualifications perhaps, these should all be given up. The suggestion is that this is perfectly obvious and can be left to the reader. But Scruton's discussion suggests that Singer, as a utilitarian, may have been over-optimistic in supposing that the wrongness, because of the suffering to animals involved, of all these practices is an obvious matter. In fox-hunting, in particular, the fear and suffering of the foxes has to be weighed, in the utilitarian calculation, against not only the enormous happiness of the human hunters, but also, according to Scruton, the 'intense pleasure' of the hounds and the horses. And since, on any particular hunt, there are many more people, horses and hounds than there are foxes involved, is it not inevitable that a utilitarian – for whom no actions, apart from failing to maximize interests, are intrinsically wrong – will have to accept that fox-hunting is a good thing? Once again, it is not easy to see how Singer could object to this.

Scruton in relation to speciesism

Does Scruton think that there is nothing wrong with speciesism, that giving preference to considerations about humans rather than animals is always justifiable? He certainly does not sound like someone who belongs in the 'animal liberationist' camp. But he is willing to discount some human desires, preferences, interests and rights, and give preference instead to animals' concerns. Wherever sympathy, virtue or piety speak against what some or even most humans want or would like, the considerations of what the humans want or would like are put to one side and considerations of animal suffering or life or freedom are the ones that count. As far as keeping a pet is concerned, I am *not* justified in considering only the humans involved – myself and my family; nor am I justified in automatically giving our concerns a greater weight than that of my pet. Scruton would surely condemn (though not in such terms) the speciesism of those who treat their pets as though they were inanimate toys and throw them away when the children become bored with them or when they become expensive to feed or care for. The fact that many of us want to buy cheap factory-farmed food and enjoy taking our children to zoos; the fact that many human beings enjoyed dog-fights and bear-baiting and that many still enjoy bull-fights, the fact that preventing us from doing any of these things would be curtailment of our liberty – none of these considerations is given any preferential weighting.

We could sum up Scruton's position regarding speciesism as follows.

> When giving special weight to considerations involving humans rather than animals is ruled out by sympathy, virtue or piety it is wrong. When giving special weight to considerations involving humans rather than animals is at least compatible with sympathy, virtue or piety it is at least justifiable. When giving special weight to considerations involving humans rather than animals is required by justice, sympathy, virtue or piety, it is right.

Chapter summary

Midgley on speciesism

In this chapter we have been looking particularly at the views of Mary Midgley, a philosopher who is on the animal liberationist side, but less extreme than Singer and Regan. She gives us reasons for taking seriously their claim about animal equality and the corresponding claim that denying it is akin to racism and sexism. Talk about equality and rights, she thinks, is a tool for reform, for widening concern for some particular group. Every past attempt at reform has left some group overlooked, forming part of an unnoticed background, and we have no good reason to suppose that, having reached 'all human beings are equal', we are not, like our racist and sexist forebears, making a mistake in resting content and refusing to push the area of concern beyond the species-barrier. Many 'commonsense' responses to animal liberationists like Singer and Regan are all too similar to those that the racists and sexists made. So she agrees with Singer and Regan that speciesism is like sexism and racism and thereby wrong – to a certain extent.

But she also thinks that speciesism is *un*like racism. Racism as commonly conceived – giving preferential treatment to members of one's own race – is always wrong. But speciesism, like 'familyism', is not always wrong. Sometimes it is right. This plausible claim undermines Singer's universal version of the principle of equality. She argues, contrary to Singer, that we should not *always* be impartial. This would make being a good parent, a good daughter, a good friend, teacher or doctor all wrong. And they are not.

She argues that, unlike racial preferences, preferences for one's own species and family are (a) based on significant groupings, (b) natural, and (c) a central element in human happiness. She does not make the mistake of supposing that, because they are natural they are thereby right. Rather, she emphasizes the complex role that familial and species-bonding plays in the social and moral education of our young, thereby challenging Singer's speculative assumption that things would be improved if we got rid of them.

Complex approaches to moral questions

So, according to Midgley, speciesism is sometimes right, but sometimes wrong, like some other forms of partiality. But her ethical approach, which emphasizes the complexity of moral claims and the number of different moral considerations which may need to be brought to bear on a particular case, does not leave her room, in a short book, to say anything much about when it is right and when it is wrong.

Like Midgley, Scruton holds that, in moral decisions, we may need to draw on a range of moral considerations, not limit the discussion the way Singer and Regan do. He claims that there are four parts to morality – four areas from which considerations may need to be drawn: (a) rights and (corresponding) duties (justice), (b) sympathy or benevolence, (c) virtue and vice, and (d) piety. Given that he is a contractarian about justice, and hence denies that animals have rights, we might expect that when we are considering the morality of our treatment of animals, we can be sure that we have no need to consider their rights. But, when we come to the details, this turns out not to be so. Scruton qualifies his general contractarian stance, and accepts that we confer rights on certain animals – pets, for example – by assuming responsibility for them.

Scruton's views on 'the ethics of our treatment of animals' cannot be neatly summarized because the four areas he draws on yield different results in different cases (e.g. pets and wild animals, factory-farmed animals and free-range animals), and even different results within the same kind of case (e.g. bear-baiting and fox-hunting). Whether something like his kind of detailed, piecemeal approach is to be preferred to the more systematic approaches of Singer and Regan is something you will have to decide for yourself at the end of this book.

Further reading

It would do no harm to read further from the works of Mary Midgley: *Beast and Man,* Methuen, 1980; *Animals and Why They Matter,* Penguin, 1983; and *Utopias, Dolphins and Computers: problems of philosophical plumbing,* Routledge, 1996.

The Virtue Ethics Defence of Animals

OBJECTIVES

By the end of this chapter you should have:

- Acquired a good knowledge and understanding of the virtue ethics approach.
- Appreciated its strengths and weaknesses when applied to our treatment of animals.
- Anticipated some ways in which the three approaches might be applied to environmental ethics.

The virtue ethics approach

In this chapter we shall be looking at the third mainstream approach to moral questions current in contemporary moral philosophy – virtue ethics. As you will see it is not unlike Midgley and Scruton's approaches, though it is a bit more systematic. I will outline the approach, and then use it to explore some of Scruton's views.

The following pages up to page 180, are straightforward exposition, with very little argument in it – I am just going to tell you about the virtue ethics approach. The exposition is quite detailed, so you should not read it with the usual questions about arguments objections and replies in mind. You should aim for a rough idea of what the virtue ethics approach is about, and you should note a number of individual points, particularly about what virtue ethics claims.

Virtue ethics: an exposition

Virtue ethics as new

Up until about thirty years ago, moral philosophy in English-speaking universities was basically centred around just two ethical approaches, utilitarianism and deontology. Utilitarianism derived from the late eighteenth and nineteenth-century philosophers Jeremy Bentham and J.S. Mill.[14] Deontology is also known as 'Kantianism' because it derives from the writings of the eighteenth-century philosopher, Kant (who you have already encountered with respect to the 'indirect duty' view about our treatment of animals (pp.92–7).

The word 'deontology' comes from the ancient Greek word 'deon' ('that which is binding', sometimes translated as 'duty'), and 'duty' is certainly *the* central moral concept for Kant, who rarely speaks about rights. But, as we have seen when we studied Regan, talk about duties tends to go hand in hand nowadays with talk about rights. If you have a stringent duty to me, say, to treat me with respect, or not to inflict gratuitous suffering on me, then, we tend to think, I must have a corresponding right to be treated with respect and a right not to have such suffering inflicted on me. And, conversely, if I have a right, say, to negative freedom, then you have a duty to me not to coerce and constrain me if all I am doing is harming myself; hence Scruton's phrase, 'the calculus of rights *and* duties'. So Regan's rights approach, despite his disagreements with Kant, counts as a form of Kantianism or deontology.

During those thirty years, scores, perhaps hundreds, of books and collections of articles were published, treating utilitarianism and deontology as the only real contenders in the field. In books or collections with titles such as 'Moral Problems' or 'The Rights and Wrongs of Abortion' or 'Principles of Biomedical Ethics', or 'In Defence of Animals', the utilitarian and deontological approaches would be contrasted – but no other approach would be mentioned.

But, gradually, a change was observable; the books and articles started to mention 'virtue ethics' as a third possible approach to moral problems. At first, the mentions were rather dismissive; it was regarded, not as a third approach in its own right, but as emphasizing a few interesting points that utilitarians and deontologists should incorporate into their approaches. Then, as more was written in defence of it, it acquired the status of 'the new kid on the block' – yet to prove its right to run with the big boys, but not to be dismissed. And in the latest collections (as I write in 1998), virtue ethics has acquired full status, recognized as a rival to utilitarian and deontological approaches, as interestingly and challengingly different from either as those approaches are from each other.

Virtue ethics as old

So, in that way, it is new – a recent addition to contemporary moral philosophy. But in another way it is old, for it is derived, not from eighteenth or nineteenth-century philosophers, but from the ancient Greek philosophers, Plato and, more particularly, Aristotle. Now, given how very long ago Aristotle wrote (fourth centuryBC) and also given that he held unacceptable views on both slavery and women, it is important to emphasize the word 'derived'. Those who espouse virtue ethics nowadays do not regard themselves as committed to any of the lamentable, parochial details of Aristotle's moral philosophy, any more than deontologists think they are committed to Kant's views on animals (as we saw with Regan). What each has done has provided Western moral philosophy with a distinctive approach, an approach that, its proponents think, can fruitfully be adapted to reflect contemporary moral thought. (It is worth noting that the modest number of Western philosophers who work on ancient Chinese moral philosophy find many of its schools more akin to virtue ethics than to utilitarianism or deontology.)

The virtue ethics approach did not die out with Aristotle only to be revived 2000 years later; it persists, discernibly, through some later Roman writers, such as Cicero (106–43BC), it is incorporated into Christianity by Aquinas,[15] and it is still going strong in the seventeenth and eighteenth centuries. Hume (1711–76), one of the contractarians about justice, provides an interesting point of departure: Bentham regarded him as having inspired his utilitarianism, but many philosophers now regard him as being the last (until the current revival) virtue ethicist.

What is a virtue?

So what is the virtue ethics approach? It relies on the concept of a *virtue,* and, correspondingly, that of a *vice.* We must pause to consider these, since both are words that do not occur much in common conversation now. A virtue is, first, a good, or admirable, or praiseworthy, *character trait* – the sort of thing that is cited in a character reference, for example.

Conversely, a vice is a bad, or despicable or unpraiseworthy character trait – the sort of thing we condemn or despise people for having. Another way to think of the virtues is as the ways someone aspires to be, or hopes they have become, if they want to be a good person, and as what we try to instil in our children when we are giving them a moral education. Virtue ethics assesses people *and* actions in terms of the virtues and vices.

Although the words 'virtue' and 'vice' are no longer common in ordinary conversation, we still employ a surprisingly large and rich vocabulary of virtue and vice terms, some of which we encountered in Midgley and Scruton. We praise and admire people for being benevolent or altruistic, generous, compassionate, kind, honest, wise, just, honourable, loyal, industrious, conscientious, fair, responsible, caring, brave or courageous, idealistic, public-spirited, for having good will, integrity and self-respect, for being a good sort of person to have as a friend... And we condemn, despise or, more mildly, criticize (if only to ourselves) people for being self-interested, mean, callous, cruel, spiteful, dishonest, silly and thoughtless,[16] unjust, dishonourable, disloyal, lazy, unfair, irresponsible, uncaring, cowardly, materialistic, anti-social, greedy, envious, small-minded, arrogant, for lacking good will or integrity, for being the sort of person who sucks up to others, for being the sort of person who does not make a good friend... Neither list pretends to be complete, nor need you agree with every example – they are just to give you the idea of the sorts of character traits that are called virtues and vices.

Once you have the idea, you can see, looking back, that virtue ethics embraces all Scruton's four parts of morality. Indeed, it regards Scruton's four parts as an arbitrary, if not downright inaccurate, division within the one part he calls 'virtues and vices'. Since Plato and Aristotle, justice has counted as one of the paradigm cases of a virtue; Plato regarded (something we translate as) 'piety' as a virtue (Aristotle does not discuss it) and so did the Romans whose usage of *pietas* Scruton is following. What we now call 'benevolence', which Scruton singles out as the second aspect of morality under the name 'sympathy', used to be called 'charity' and was the virtue Christianity most notably added to ancient Greek thought.

What does virtue ethics tell us to consider before we act?

We can now introduce the idea of 'a virtuous person'. Virtuous people are those who have, and exercise, the virtues, i.e. certain character traits. Such people are, say, benevolent, generous, compassionate, kind, honest, a good friend, etc., and thereby they have a characteristic way of behaving – they act benevolently, generously, compassionately, honestly, justly, the way a good friend does, etc; they do not act self-interestedly, selfishly, callously, cruelly, dishonestly, the way no good friend would, etc. Virtuous people act virtuously, in a word – and virtue ethics tells us we should aim to do likewise, to act in the same way as they do.

In virtue ethics, 'the virtuous person' whether she is ever to be found in this wicked world, or whether she is only an ideal, sets the standard for how we ought to act. This is best understood by contrasting with the other two mainstream approaches what it tells me to consider when I am trying to decide what I ought to do. On the direct utilitarian approach, I concentrate solely on whether the action will maximize interests. On the deontological approach we are familiar with, I consider only what rights and corresponding duties are involved. Virtue ethics tells me that we should act in the way in which the virtuous person would characteristically act in the circumstances – that is, compassionately, or honestly or loyally, etc, and not the way she would *not* act, that is, callously or dishonestly or disloyally, etc. So virtue ethics tells me to consider whether, if I did so and so, I would be acting compassionately or callously, honestly or dishonestly, and so on, in the particular circumstances in which I find myself.

The fact that virtue ethics employs the large vocabulary of the virtues and vices enables it to bring in the great variety of moral considerations that Midgley and Scruton emphasize. Here is a proposed course of action, let us imagine, that would minimize suffering. That is certainly something to be said in its favour. But unfortunately, it would involve violating a right, and that is surely something to be said against it. So is it right or wrong?

Let us imagine an example in which the suffering at issue is very serious and the right in question comparatively trivial, as in something like Midgley's case of the man on the way to his uncle's party who comes across an injured dog. We can add to Midgley's example the supposition that the man had actually promised his uncle to come at a particular time; his uncle thereby has a right to expect him to keep his word. So here is a case in which stopping to help the injured would minimize suffering but violate a right. How does virtue ethics assess this particular action?

It says that what is right about stopping to do what one can for the injured animal is that to do so, in these particular circumstances, is compassionate and that it would be callous and irresponsible not to stop. It thereby takes account of the fact that stopping to help would minimize suffering, for it is benevolence and compassion that require that we be concerned with the relief of suffering. But it does not simply ignore the fact that a right would be violated, for justice requires that we respect people's rights. Instead, it claims that the breaking of one's promise, or the failure to keep one's word is not, in these particular circumstances, either unjust or dishonourable. We do not describe people as unjust, dishonourable, or even unreliable if the only occasions on which they break their promises or fail to keep their word are those sorts of occasions.

Stopping, in these particular circumstances, would be acting compassionately and not unjustly.

But note the emphasis on 'in these particular circumstances'. There could be different circumstances in which minimizing suffering was not compassionate or benevolent – for example, when I must cause a human or animal pain to save its life. And there are many circumstances in which breaking a promise is unjust and dishonourable.

This illustrates another feature of the vocabulary of the virtues and vices. It is not only large, it is subtle (people who do not like the virtue ethics approach say 'hopelessly vague' rather than 'subtle' – I will consider this objection later). The virtues cannot be simply defined as dispositions to follow particular rules such as 'minimize suffering', 'respect the rights of others', 'keep promises', 'tell the truth', 'stick up for your friends'. Quite unconsciously, we tailor them to fit the occasions when we think those largely, but not totally, reliable rules or principles *should* be broken, by any decent, sensible, virtuous person. We are relying on this subtlety when we say it would not be unjust or dishonourable to break the promise about the party in order to help the injured.

Consider, again, compassion and callousness. When we, correctly, describe a benevolent and compassionate person as someone who is concerned about the happiness and suffering of others, as someone who seeks the good or welfare of others and the relief of their suffering, do we mean that they are direct utilitarians, who always follow the rule 'maximize the interests of others'? Obviously not, for 'benevolent' and 'compassionate' is one of the last ways we would describe someone who even contemplated killing or experimenting on a human being simply on the grounds that this would be the most effective way of maximizing the interests of others. As Scruton notes (Reading 5, paragraph 11), 'Even if they are calculating for the long-term good of all sentient creatures, we are critical of them [as callous] precisely for the fact that they are *calculating,* in a situation where some other creature has a direct claim on their compassion'.

The upshot of this subtlety (or, perhaps, vagueness) is that, although virtue ethics does tell us what we ought to consider, it does not thereby make our moral decisions easy or straightforward. Like Midgley, it tells us to look at the particular circumstances. Unlike Midgley, it specifically directs us to use the large vocabulary of the virtues and vices to apply to them. But it leaves it up to us to apply the vocabulary correctly and this is often difficult.

Reasons, motives and emotions

Another respect in which the vocabulary of the virtues and vices is subtle (but not 'hopelessly vague') is that it draws attention to the motives or reasons for an action, and often, the feelings or emotions that accompany it. Suppose someone comes across me carefully preserving the coppices in which foxes live, and chasing people who are trying to shoot them off my land. 'Ah, yes', an animal liberationist may think, 'a fine, pious, compassionate act. That's the way people should behave.' But then they discover that my reason for doing this was not to allow the foxes to live out their natural life-span, nor was my motive concern for the foxes' well-being. I am someone who takes a sadistic pleasure in the sport of fox-hunting. I revel in the ritual of getting dressed up in a pink coat to watch the legitimized rending of the flesh and blood-letting. My reason for protecting the foxes is to ensure that they will be available for me to hunt them down, and my motive is pure self-interest – I want to gratify my sadistic desires. In seeking the gratification of such pleasures, I am acting *in the way* a cruel and sadistic person would act, not virtuously.

My action then appears in a totally different light. Was it right? Was it wrong? Well, we might say that it was right insofar as it was the sort of thing that a virtuous person, someone with the virtues of compassion and piety, would have done. But virtue ethics tells us we should act *in the way,* in the manner, that the virtuous person would, compassionately and piously, not cruelly. Insofar as I have totally failed to do that, I acted wrongly. In order to act compassionately and piously, I must not only do what on the surface appears to be a compassionate and pious act, I must do it for the right reasons and motives – in this case, for the sake of the foxes I am preserving, not for the sake of my own perverse and illegitimate pleasure.

Given that this looks like an anti-Scruton example, it is important to note that he agrees with the general point it is used to illustrate, namely, that motives or reasons are morally relevant. Indeed, he uses 'the distinction between vice and virtue' to bring in motives (p.159 above). Suppose Scruton comes across me protecting the foxes. Rather than being initially inclined to assess this as a pious and compassionate act, he would doubtless condemn it as a foolish and sentimental one. But it is still true of him that my action will appear in a totally different – and worse – light, when he discovers my sadistic motive and reason. He recognizes that *if* 'the pleasure involved (in fox hunting) is either vicious in itself, or an expression of a vicious nature' (Reading 5, paragraph 73) then this would show fox-hunting was wrong.

How do feelings or emotions come in? We have a hint of that already because they are closely connected to motives. To take my cat to the vet and thereby inflict some suffering on it may be kind rather than cruel, if the cat will benefit from the treatment. But if I rather enjoy taking my cat to the vet, because it makes me feel that I am a loving, caring, deeply responsible person; if I rather enjoy his being sick and dependent on me rather than healthy and independent, once again my action appears in a different light. (Vets frequently deplore the selfishness and self-indulgence of pet-owners, complaining that they insist on treatment their pets do not need.) A compassionate cat-owner would take her cat to the vet only when necessary, and regret, not enjoy, the necessity.

That emotions are relevant, in the virtue ethics approach, is a reflection of the fact that the virtues are character traits. To be a certain sort of person (to have a particular set of character traits) – generous, honest, public-spirited, loyal, responsible, compassionate, just and so on – is not only to be disposed to act in particular ways, for particular reasons, but to be disposed to *feel* in certain ways. This is not limited to how you feel when you act, but how you feel when you see how other people act, or when you learn about things that have happened. The just are distressed and angry about the distant violations of rights; the honest uncomfortable in the presence of liars, the benevolent and compassionate delighted by news of benefits that have befallen others, distressed by news of distant suffering.

So when you act 'in the way' that the virtuous agent would act – which is what virtue ethics tells us we should do – you not only do certain things; you also do them for certain reasons or motives and you feel about what you are doing in a certain way.

Applying virtue ethics to Scruton's arguments

The way in which virtue ethics is to be applied to the ethics of our treatment of animals can be helpfully illustrated by considering some of Scruton's arguments. The discussion will display both some of the strengths, and the weaknesses, of the virtue ethics approach.

First, a few questions to test your understanding of the previous section.

EXERCISE 34
Understanding virtue ethics

1 Would virtue ethics give a straightforward answer (i.e. 'right' or 'wrong') to the general question 'Is it right or wrong to keep a pet animal'?

2 Briefly, what answer would virtue ethics give?

3 Would virtue ethics give a straightforward answer to the general question 'Is it right or wrong to treat one's pet *in the way* a cruel, or a selfish, or a callous or a self-indulgent person would characteristically treat them'?

4 Would virtue ethics give a straightforward answer to the question 'Is it right or wrong to treat one's pet *in the way* a compassionate, responsible, caring, unselfish person would characteristically treat them'?

5 In what way do your answers to these questions reveal virtue ethics to be rather like Singer's direct utilitarianism? (No more than two sentences.)

6 In what way or ways, do they reveal virtue ethics to be very unlike Singer's direct utilitarianism? (No more than three sentences.)

To answer (5) and (6), you will need to recall that, according to Singer's direct utilitarianism, (a) no actions are intrinsically right or wrong except maximizing, or failing to maximize, interests, and (b) all other actions can be right or wrong according to the particular circumstances.

Check your answers against those at the back of the book before reading on.

EXERCISE 35

Virtue ethics and pets

Read the questions below. Then re-read paragraphs 10–17 in Scruton's Reading 5 and try to answer them, bearing both Scruton and my outline of virtue ethics in mind. You cannot get all the answers from Scruton, and even when you can get the answer from him, you should try to think of your own. I provide quite long answers; but you should aim for answers of two or three sentences.

1 What, using the virtue ethics approach, would you say was wrong about my letting my pet starve to death in order to feed a number of hungry strays?

2 What, using the virtue ethics approach, would you say was wrong about my acquiring a cat for my small children and letting them ill treat it?

3 What, using the virtue ethics approach, would you say was wrong about my keeping my large dog pent up in a city flat?

DISCUSSION

1 Scruton is helpful here. One thing he would say, using the virtue ethics approach, was wrong about the way I acted is that I am being irresponsible. As we noted in relation to Midgley, when I take on a pet, I acquire a special responsibility to it, just as I acquire special responsibilities when I have children, or take on students if I am a teacher, or patients, if I am a doctor. To ignore such special responsibilities is irresponsible.

Although a utilitarian might claim that, being concerned about suffering, I should calculate that the suffering of my pet is outweighed by the suffering of the many strays, on a virtue ethics approach we might say, following Scruton, that such calculation was itself callous rather than compassionate. It is my own pet who has a direct claim on my compassion.

2 On a virtue ethics approach it might be said, again, that letting my children ill treat the cat was irresponsible. Though I may have given the cat to my

children, it and its welfare are still my responsibility – I am the adult. But wouldn't it be cruel of me to give the cat to my children and then restrict what they can do to it? *They* may well say I am being mean and unkind if I stop them trying to bathe it or tie crackers to its tail. No, it might be said, it wouldn't be being cruel to the children. Being kind to children doesn't require letting them do anything they want to, nor, in particular letting them ill treat animals. Indeed, letting them do anything they want is itself unkind and irresponsible; it is my responsibility to give them a moral education (cf. Scruton, paragraph 13).

Using the virtue ethics approach, you might also look for further details in the circumstances. Did I get the cat for my children in the manner of someone getting them a toy? Am I completely indifferent to its sufferings, thinking of it simply as 'one of the children's toys'? Then virtue ethics might say that my letting them ill treat it is worse than it appears on the surface. I am acting not only irresponsibly but also callously, perhaps even 'impiously', to use Scruton's term.

3 On a virtue ethics approach, it might be said that it was, if not cruel, at least hardly compassionate, very selfish and, once again, irresponsible of me to keep a large dog pent up in a city flat.

Suppose I say that I *am* compassionate, unselfish and responsible, it's just that I have no choice. I deeply regret having to keep the dog pent up, and feel genuinely on its behalf, but I can't do anything about it; I am at work all day and I am too tired in the evenings to give it more than a short walk around the block. Then, on the virtue ethics approach, we might press the question 'Wouldn't a compassionate, unselfish and responsible person be trying to find the dog a better home?' If I am not and have not been trying, then I am not acting in the way I should.

But suppose I now further say (truly) that I have the dog only because it was my mother's and she died recently, and that I have been trying to find a good home in the country for it ever since? Well, if indeed, *those* are the particular circumstances in which I am treating the dog as I am, virtue ethics would presumably say there was nothing wrong with it.

Some objections to the virtue ethics approach

The questions in the last exercise asked for *your* view, *using the virtue ethics approach*, on what was wrong about some actions and you may have noticed that my answers were correspondingly non-committal. This represents a change, for the earlier exercise questions asked you to tell me what someone else's view – say, Singer's, as a utilitarian – would be on the morality of some action. And my answers have been what I consider to be the correct ones. So why did I not ask, 'What would a virtue ethicist say was wrong about these actions?' and answer firmly, 'A virtue ethicist would say it was wrong because...'?

I could not ask, 'What would a virtue ethicist say was wrong about these actions?' and give the correct answer, because there is no knowing what someone using the virtue ethics approach might say. It would all depend on which character traits she took to be the virtues and the vices, how she applied the vocabulary, and what she noticed and took as relevant in the circumstances described. And this fact about virtue ethics brings us to a number of objections that are made to it.

Objection 1　Who is to say which are the virtues and which are the vices?

This is a question you may have been wanting to make ever since I gave the lists of virtue and vice terms in my exposition. Who am I to lay down the law about laziness being a vice? Why should you accept that piety is a virtue just because Plato, the Romans and Scruton think it is? But a rhetorical question is not yet an objection. What is the objection, precisely?

It is probably something like this. 'Whether a particular character trait, such as compassion or callousness, is a virtue or a vice is just a matter of personal opinion. So virtue ethics cannot *establish* that an agent would be acting wrongly if she, for example, acted callously and irresponsibly.' There are two responses to this objection, an abstract theoretical one and a practical one.

The details of the theoretical response would take us well beyond the limits of this book into the arguments for and against the difficult abstract question of whether morality or ethics is *objective.* This question arises not only in relation to virtue ethics but also in relation to the other two mainstream approaches. Isn't it just a matter of personal opinion whether or not maximizing interests is the only thing that matters morally? How could a utilitarian establish that it was wrong to limit one's concern to oneself and one's family? Isn't it just a matter of personal opinion whether or not everyone has an equal right not to be used as a mere resource for others? How could someone who used the rights-based approach establish that it was absolutely wrong to use criminals as experimental subjects, to at least a mild and relatively harmless extent?

There is, currently, an extensive philosophical literature devoted to answering such theoretical questions, because most moral philosophers deny that ethics is just a matter of personal opinion. They think that rational arguments can be given for and against particular views within morality. Some utilitarians and deontologists, for example, argue that the failure to extend a concern for one's own particular selfish interest to an equal concern for the interests or rights of others is a rational failing – a failure of consistency. And, even since Plato and Aristotle, virtue ethicists have had a standard way of giving reasons for and against the view that a particular character trait is a virtue. The virtues, they say, are those character traits that human beings need to acquire and exercise if they are to live well, to live a full, satisfying human life. So, for example, the traditional argument in favour of justice being a virtue is, in brief, that we need justice in order to live together as social beings and reap the benefits that law-governed society brings; without justice, human life is, in Hobbes's famous phrase 'nasty, brutish and short'.

But, as I said earlier, all argument has to start somewhere, with some **premises** that are not argued for, and when philosophers using the different approaches are dealing with practical moral problems, they often leave these theoretical issues aside. On the utilitarian approach, say, they just take it as a premise that maximizing interests is the only thing that matters, and devote their energies to arguing that animals' interests matter too. On the rights-based approach, say, they take it as a premise that we all do have an equal right not to be experimented on, and then devote their energies to arguing that animals do, or do not, have the same right. Similarly, on the virtue ethics approach, they take as premises that, say, compassion is a virtue, and cruelty and callousness vices, and devote their energies to arguing that these character traits can be manifested in our treatment of animals as well as of each other.

premises

When they do so, they rely on our being honest and sincere in our reaction to them. We *could* object, theoretically, to their moral premises and point out that some self-interested mafioso type, or perhaps someone from a different cultural background, might disagree. But do *I* disagree? If I do not, then their arguments are relevant to me, and I should take them seriously.

This brings us to the practical response to the objection. Many, perhaps most, people nowadays think that 'morality is subjective' or 'just a matter of personal opinion'. But, despite believing that, many strive to bring up their children well, are concerned when they seem to be going astray, condemn the actions of some people they read about in newspapers, and worry about their own moral decisions because they want to make the *right* decision. It is as though we wore two hats. Wearing our philosophical hat, engaged in abstract argument, we might say 'Morality is a matter of personal opinion – someone might think that it was virtuous to be cruel, irresponsible, dishonest, mean... and they are entitled to their opinion'. But wearing the hat of someone engaged in the day-to-day business of living, we tell our children it is wrong to be cruel and irresponsible, condemn erring politicians for their dishonesty and greed, and worry about whether we are acting as we should, in the way the people we admire, or aspire to be, would act.

I would be very surprised if you disagreed with many of the terms in my lists of the virtues and vices. Insofar as you agree with the classification, you can give your own answer to 'Who is to say?', namely, 'I say, and thereby agree with Midgley, Scruton and Hursthouse'. So, from now on, we will put this objection to one side, and treat the lists of virtues and vices as premises in our application of the virtue ethics approach.

Objection 2 The virtue and vice terms are vague and tendentious

However, even if we agree that, say, kindness, compassion and even piety are virtues, and cruelty, callousness and impiety are vices (or faults), there is still the objection that I mentioned in the exposition. 'These terms are so vague' it may be objected, 'that there is lots of room for disagreement about their correct application. Singer, Scruton and Hursthouse all say that factory-farming is a cruel and callous practice; Scruton (and Hursthouse) even say it is impious. I don't agree. Which side is correct? Who is to say? Isn't it, once again, just a matter of personal opinion?'

Once again, there is a theoretical and a practical response to this objection, and, once again, the details of the theoretical one would take us too far afield. In brief, virtue ethics maintains that the correct application of the virtue and vice terms is determined by the people with moral or practical wisdom. This sort of wisdom is to be found only in virtuous people who have experience of life, who know 'what's what', as we say. The answer to 'Who is to say?' is 'The morally or practically wise'.

The practical response is to assume, as we all do, that we have some measure of practical wisdom ourselves, and to work out, in each particular case, what *we* would say was the correct application. This does not mean that we can say whatever suits us; 'working it out' means thinking carefully, honestly and conscientiously, trying to make sure we have considered everything relevant in the circumstances. Although it might be said that, in one sense, the virtue and vice terms are rather vague – i.e. that there is a lot of leeway in their application – in another way, they are rather precise. 'Cruel' and 'callous', for instance, are a great deal more precise than 'right' or 'wrong' or 'justifiable'. Look them up in the dictionary and it is immediately obvious that we cannot just choose when to apply them and when to withhold their application in whatever way suits us. When certain facts are drawn to our attention, we may find ourselves compelled to apply the terms, however much we might wish to do otherwise.

This brings us to a third objection.

Objection 3 The application of the virtue and vice terms depends on how you see things

This objection could reasonably be regarded as the same as the second. I distinguish them only in order to discuss separately the issue of straight disagreement about applying the virtue and vice terms from the issue of perception or 'how we see things'.

I said above that working out how to apply the virtue and vice terms means trying to think carefully, honestly and conscientiously, trying to make sure we have considered everything relevant in the circumstances. We can never do more than try to do this, and the extent to which we succeed is going to depend both on how careful, honest and conscientious we are, and on what other people point out to us.

Recall Midgley's discussion of our past thoughts about equality. Suppose, living in some past century, I think about some problem concerning the application of 'just' and 'unjust' as carefully and conscientiously as I can. In the end, I conclude that the present social set-up is correctly to be described as just. But then along comes a new reformer, and draws to my attention the claim of some underprivileged group that I had simply overlooked. What I may immediately recognize is that, in this area at least, the reformer is wiser, more perceptive than I have been; I blush for my previous blindness and immediately change my application of 'just' to 'unjust'.

Or, perhaps, the change is not so quick. I am inclined to resist, to dismiss the arguments of the reformer as cranky. But, thinking about them honestly, my perception of the current set-up begins to change, until I come to agree with the reformer's application of 'unjust'.

In neither case do I think of the change in myself as merely a personal change, like becoming bored with Thai food which I hitherto loved. I think that my eyes have been opened, that I have learnt something, that I have grounds for my new application of the term.

But, as Midgley reminded us, I may not change – many people remained deaf to the arguments of the reformers, and blind to the facts they pointed out, for many generations. They retained their distorted perception of how things were. Hence, our disagreements about the correct applications of the virtue and vice terms may stem from our different perceptions of situations. The differences may be quite simple. The person who is keeping his large dog pent up in the flat may simply have overlooked the possibility of finding it a better home, seeing its present sufferings as something that 'can't be helped'. That is just the sort of mistake that (fairly) thoughtless people make and they may recognize the mistake as soon as someone points it out. But, as Midgley's discussion, and our own experience, of racism and sexism shows us, the differences in perception may be extremely complex and correspondingly difficult to correct.

Those who favour the virtue ethics approach accept this as an inescapable fact about moral life, and willingly acknowledge that personal example, novels and films may do as much as, if not more than, rational argument, to change people's moral views for the better, because they all change the way we see things. The virtue ethics approach continues to hold that rational argument has an important role to play, but, as with arguments by analogy, does not hold that such argument can establish anything conclusively – not, in particular, when it falls on deaf ears. Those who favour either of the other moral approaches regard this as an unacceptable counsel of despair, and point to the great moral progress that has been made in the last century or so precisely because people produced rational arguments based on utilitarianism or the rights-based approach.

Conclusion

These three objections to virtue ethics, as you can see, take us into deep waters about the nature of moral philosophy. Can it be objective? Can our moral disagreements be resolved by rational argument? Can the way we perceive the moral landscape be changed by rational argument? And (a related objection I have not discussed) does moral philosophy have to be as complicated as virtue ethics makes it? Isn't a simpler approach, such as utilitarianism or deontology, better?

It would be premature of you to form firm opinions regarding any of these questions and, since they are currently much disputed amongst moral philosophers, impossible for me to give you authoritative answers to them. The important thing you should have learnt is that they are questions that can be raised, and argued about, and the above discussion should have developed your understanding of why this is so. We will now develop that understanding further by looking at a more complex piece of Scruton's discussion.

Scruton on fox-hunting

I will now ask you to re-read parts of Scruton (Reading 5) and use the virtue ethics approach to object to what he says about fox-hunting.

EXERCISE 36
Virtue ethics, Scruton and fox-hunting

Re-read Scruton on inflicting pain (Reading 5, paragraphs 28–41 and 60), and on fox-hunting (Reading 5, paragraphs 67–78), then answer the questions below, all of which are to be taken as asking 'Could it be argued, *using the virtue ethics approach*, that...?' Elaborate on each answer, i.e. do not just answer 'yes' or 'no'. The whole exercise should take about an hour.

Check your answers against those at the back of the book before reading on.

1 Could it be argued that fox-hunting is wrong because it is unjust?

2 Could it be argued that fox-hunting is wrong because it is cruel and/or callous?

3 Could it be argued that fox-hunting is wrong because it is a failure in sympathy or benevolence?

4 Could it be argued that fox-hunting is wrong because it is impious? (You can remind yourself of what Scruton says about piety by looking at the summary of his position I gave on p.160).

5 Could it be argued that Scruton, the fox-hunter, has failed to address the question 'Am *I*, Scruton, by going in for fox-hunting, acting in the way a virtuous person would act?' and that if he did, he would be compelled to answer 'No'?

6 Could it be argued that...? (See if you can think of any further objections to what Scruton says, using the virtue ethics approach.)

DISCUSSION

1 According to Scruton, fox-hunting cannot be condemned on the grounds that it is unjust, because wild animals do not have rights to be violated – 'we have no duty of care towards any specific wild animal'. Any virtue ethicist who regards justice as but one virtue amongst many is bound to be more inclined to the contractarian view of justice and rights than someone like Regan. They will want to preserve the violation of rights as, in Wiggins's words, 'a *distinctive* ground' for saying that some action is wrong (p.125), leaving callousness, meanness, selfishness, inconsiderateness, cruelty, etc., with some independent work to do. So, taking the virtue ethics approach, this would be an unlikely objection.

2 Scruton concedes that the fox-hunting activities of those who derive a sadistic pleasure from it are an abuse of the sport (paragraph 76), and I take it that he would willingly agree that, in such circumstances, *their* fox-hunting is wrong. (It would be a violation of the principle of charity to ignore the fact that Scruton is *not* defending the activities of each and every fox-hunter.) But he claims that cruelty ('sadism towards the fox') is rarely one of the vices displayed in the hunting field.

It might be thought that Scruton is just making an empirical claim about the psychology of most of those who hunt, a claim that his fellow fox-hunters will endorse and people who are against it reject. If so, the argument gets stuck. But I suspect that the disagreement lies in the application of the vice term 'cruel'.

Scruton accepts that the deliberate infliction of pain for its own sake and in order to enjoy the spectacle of suffering is cruel and thereby wrong (paragraph 29). He denies that fox-hunting (or angling) is like this (paragraph 76), in the case of most hunters, and I am willing to concede him this empirical premise. But it gradually emerges that he is *limiting* his application of the vice term 'cruel' to such cases, and not considering callousness at all.

Consider the deliberate infliction of pain in order to achieve some other purpose, to which pain is a necessary means. He suggests that this is not necessarily cruel or callous (paragraph 31) and with this, any virtue ethicist will agree – it all depends on what the purpose is. (Remember the case of inflicting pain on an animal or child in order to save its life.) But surely there are some cases where it would be cruel or callous because the purpose did not justify the pain inflicted, regardless of whether the agent enjoyed the suffering. Some experimenters on animals have inflicted horrifying suffering on cats. Their purpose is to discover how much pain cats can stand before it kills them; they do not take any pleasure in the cats' suffering, but regard it with what they call 'scientific detachment'. Personally, I would say that such experiments are cruel, notwithstanding the lack of sadistic feelings, and also callous. The knowledge gained is far too insignificant to justify the experiment, and the 'scientific detachment' deplorable rather than praiseworthy. And I would be surprised if Scruton did not agree, given his remarks in paragraph 52.

Similarly, I would say that the purpose of bull-fighting, which, according to Scruton, is entertainment and the enjoyment (and display) of the courage of the matador, is not sufficient to justify the suffering inflicted on the bull (and, I might add, the horses of the picadors). Watching bull-fighting is acting cruelly and callously, notwithstanding the putative fact that the spectators take no pleasure in the animals' suffering. But Scruton insists that it is only if they do take such pleasure that their interest, and hence their watching, can be condemned as cruel. And he does not consider whether it might not still be callous.

In fact, Scruton goes so far as to deny that fox-hunting even counts as the deliberate infliction of pain in order to achieve some other purpose, to which the pain is a necessary means. He maintains that both angling and fox-hunting count as the deliberate embarking on an action of which pain is an inevitable *but unwanted* by-product. We would be justified in questioning this claim. But for the sake of the argument, let us grant it. Other examples of cruel and callous scientific experimentation will fit this description too, such as some testing of totally unnecessary new cosmetic products on animals, where the pain is an inevitable but unwanted by-product.

Now the purpose of fox-hunting, according to Scruton, seems to be fun (paragraph 76). So the question at issue is, is it not cruel to think that one's own fun is sufficient to justify the suffering of the foxes? Is it not callous to be so indifferent to the sufferings of the fox that one's fun is unimpaired? On the question of whether it is cruel, Scruton merely reiterates the claim that it is not cruel because the hunters take no pleasure *in* the suffering of the fox. On the question of whether it is callous, he is silent.

3 This seems to me to be a telling objection, especially in conjunction with 5 and it is noteworthy that Scruton does not address it head on. Suppose we read paragraph 72 as an answer to the question 'Would a sympathetic or compassionate person, concerned about suffering, go in for fox-hunting?' When we look for the answer, we do not find one. Implicitly, he answers a quite different, and very hypothetical question: 'Would a sympathetic person, concerned about suffering, but acknowledging that the fox population must be kept down and that this cannot be done by expert marksmen, make a law banning fox-hunting?' Quite possibly not, but that is not the question at issue.

Indeed, it looks as though Scruton does not take himself to be addressing the question at issue until after paragraph 74. But what then does he say in answer to it? He merely reiterates that, as practised by most people, it is not cruel. But there is a spectrum between vicious cruelty and failure of compassion. It is cruel to kick the wounded man by the roadside; a failure of compassion, though not cruel, to pass by on the other side. Even if, contrary to 2 he could make out a case for saying that fox-hunting (by non-sadistic fox-hunters) is neither cruel nor callous, he would still need to find a defence to the objection that it is a failure of sympathy and compassion.

4 When we first looked at Scruton, we noted that, although he denies Regan's view that animals have rights, he does acknowledge that it is wrong 'to deal with them purely as instruments or things'. So we might expect him to say something in defence of the view that foxes (and fishes) are not used as instruments or things by fox-hunters (or anglers). But he does not. The landowners are praised for their piety, because their renouncing of their claim to their land manifests their 'sense that we are stewards and tenants, not absolute owners, of the world in which we live' (paragraph 77). But could the fox-hunters be said to be manifesting that? Are they not, rather, acting in the way someone who thought he *owned* the foxes, had 'dominion' over them, had

the right to use them as instruments for his purposes, would characteristically act? Like 3, this objection is particularly telling in conjunction with 5.

5 If virtue ethics were to maintain that fox-hunting was absolutely wrong, or even, more specifically, that fox-hunting in Britain, under current conditions, was absolutely wrong, it would have to be on the grounds that no decent person would go in for it. I do not think that I would want to argue that: I just do not know enough about the details. But if, as so often, virtue ethics allows that fox-hunting is sometimes wrong, sometimes all right, according to the particular circumstances, that does not mean that it is barred from pressing objections against a particular fox-hunter. Suppose we conceded to Scruton that fox-hunting may sometimes be all right – when done by certain people, for certain reasons, in certain circumstances, with certain feelings. It does not follow that it is all right for *him* to do it. Does *he* feel compassionate about the fox when the hounds catch it? What does *he* feel when new members of the hunt are 'blooded'? Does *he* have a pious attitude towards foxes? Why does *he* get dressed up in a pink coat? Does *he* think he is displaying courage when he hunts, and encouraging this virtue in himself by doing so? Is he justified in doing so? Is *his* hunting making a 'contribution to the store of human virtue?' If not, then, according to virtue ethics, *he* is acting wrongly. But, in the Reading, he does not address the question 'Am I, Scruton, acting in the way a virtuous person would act?'

***ad hominem* move (in the second sense)**

6 The last three ***ad hominem*** questions bring me to the further objection that I would, using the virtue ethics approach, make to Scruton. There is more than a hint that he would boldly answer 'Yes' to all three, and, using the virtue ethics approach, I would argue that the answer to all three was 'No.'

The kind of hunting that involves danger (as riding to hounds certainly does) is often described as courageous precisely because of the danger involved, and I take it that, in his final paragraph, Scruton is endorsing this view. He also speaks of 'the courage' of the matador (paragraph 35), and says that 'courage, self-discipline and practical wisdom are promoted by careers [and hence, presumably, activities] in which risk is paramount' (paragraph 22).

Is fox-hunting courageous – the sort of thing a person with the virtue of courage would do? If you think the answer is 'obviously yes', do you think that making your motor-bike leap over cars in a car park is courageous – the sort of thing a person with the virtue of courage would do?

For some people, the answer is still, 'obviously yes'. We tend to use the word 'courage' straightforwardly in relation to facing danger, either without fear, or by conquering fear – and that is certainly what it says in the dictionary. But used in the context of virtue ethics, as a virtue term, 'courage' does not mean simply 'facing danger'; it means 'facing danger for a good reason, or for a worthwhile end' and is contrasted with 'daring' and 'recklessness', both of which standardly count as vices or faults. If, in some very peculiar circumstances, leaping one's motor-bike over cars was going to save someone's life, or avert some disaster, it would be courageous. But if it is only done, as reckless teenagers do it, for fun and excitement and to terrify the people in the car park, it is not courageous and not the sort of thing a virtuous person would do. (If you were inclined to say about the motor-bike example 'Well, it depends on why you do it' or 'Well, it could be courageous if you had a good reason' you were picking up on this way of using the term.)

Now it would be foolish to insist, in the teeth of the dictionary definition, that the word 'courage' *really* means 'facing danger for a good reason, or for a worthwhile end'. But it is reasonable to insist that Scruton, talking in terms of the virtues and vices (and well-acquainted with the many philosophical texts in which this restricted meaning is emphasized), should use it in the restricted way, not the standard dictionary one. But if he were to do so, his claim that fox-hunting 'displays and encourages' the virtue of courage, in himself and others, would show, in Mary Midgley's words, 'the glaring faults of confused vainglory and self-deception' (Midgley (1983), p.15).

Midgley uses these words to describe a nineteenth-century big-game hunter, having quoted a passage from his memoirs in which he congratulates himself on having shot an elephant. Midgley accuses him of confused vainglory and self-deception because his self-congratulation

> flows from a false view of one's own achievements, in particular what can be achieved by shooting game. It is not possible to become a ruler, entitled to fantasies of empire and dominion, simply by letting off guns.
>
> (Ibid., p.16)

I would say that similar remarks apply to Scruton, and indeed, most strikingly, to two of the writers he mentions with approval, Trollope and Surtees. Both of them constantly describe the fox as 'a noble adversary' and the hunt as Homeric, a noble battle, 'a contest with the quarry' (Reading 5, paragraph 65), encouraging in themselves, and their readers, the ludicrous fantasy that the contest between one small animal (albeit, as they always say, 'a remarkably cunning one') and a pack of riders, horses and hounds, is comparable to the war between the Greeks and the Trojans. They encourage themselves and their readers to believe that their willingness to risk their necks riding to hounds is a guarantee of their moral courage, their willingness to risk their all for some genuinely worthwhile end such as the defence of justice or truth. But, to paraphrase Midgley, they are not entitled to fantasies about their moral courage, simply because they ride to hounds. It is 'confused vain-glory and self-deception'.

So it can be claimed, against Scruton, and in his own words, that fox-hunting (in most cases) 'makes no contribution to the store of human virtue' (paragraph 39), not even to the virtue of courage.

Conclusion

Using the virtue ethics approach, we can make a number of detailed, plausible objections to Scruton's views on fox-hunting. Moreover, they are all objections that he would be compelled, on his own grounds, to take seriously. Objections based on purely utilitarian grounds, or the Regan premise that the fox has rights, will leave him unmoved, but can still be adapted, as in 2, 3 and 4, and to those we can add objections 5 and 6 – in all, a respectable number of objections.

But, supposing he read them, are they likely to change him? I rather suspect not. Part of the argument in objections 2 and 3 involved pointing to examples of cruel and callous actions which Scruton simply overlooks when he is discussing fox-hunting. I said I would be surprised if he denied that they were cruel and callous, once they were pointed out to him, but I would not be at all surprised if, recognizing them, he continued to deny that they were analogous to fox-hunting. He will, quite sincerely, just see them as very different. And convincing him that he and the writers he admires suffer from confused vain-glory and self-deception, that, far from being a noble sport, fox-hunting is a self-indulgent, foolish, impious, cruel and callous one, would be a task for a close personal friend he admired, or a great novelist – or a psychotherapist. It would require a whole shift in moral vision and the arguments of virtue ethics will not achieve it.

Chapter summary

The virtue ethics approach

In this final chapter we have been studying the virtue ethics approach to the morality of our treatment of animals. This approach relies on the concept of a virtuous agent, and thereby of a virtue (and a vice, or fault). The virtues are standardly taken to be such character traits as sympathy or benevolence, compassion, justice, courage, etc. – if we include piety it can be seen that virtue ethics embraces all Scruton's four parts of morality. Virtue ethics assesses actions as right or wrong in terms of what a virtuous agent would, characteristically, do in the particular circumstances in question. It is right to act in the way a virtuous agent would – compassionately, justly, kindly, etc. – and wrong to act in the way such a person would not act – callously, unjustly, cruelly, etc. What is involved in acting virtuously cannot be summed up in simple rules such as 'Minimize suffering' or 'Do not break promises'; though it is often the case that minimizing suffering is compassionate and breaking promises unjust or dishonourable, this is not always so – it depends on the particular circumstances.

Virtue ethics draws attention to the motives or reasons for an action, and the feelings that accompany it, as well as to what is actually done. Whether someone acted, for example, kindly or cruelly (and hence rightly or wrongly) on a particular occasion depends not only on what they actually did, but on their reasons, and how they felt about doing it. So, for example, taking one's cat to the vets would count as acting kindly only if one did it for the cat's sake, and with regret; to take it to the vet in order to make it suffer, or to enjoy its suffering, would be acting cruelly.

Hence virtue ethics does not usually give a straightforward 'right/wrong' answer to the question 'Is such and such a sort of action right or wrong?' Keeping a pet could be right or wrong, depending on the circumstances, the agent's reasons for keeping it, and the associated feelings the agent has. However, unlike utilitarianism, it claims that many actions are intrinsically right or wrong. Any action described in terms of a virtue or vice term (e.g. acting in the way a compassionate/cruel person would act) is intrinsically right/wrong.

One of the standard objections to virtue ethics is that the virtue and vice terms are vague and tendentious. There is room for much disagreement about their correct application, because they all have borderline cases and, moreover, how one applies them depends on how one perceives particular situations and the general moral landscape. This makes it impossible for virtue ethics to establish moral conclusions by rational argument alone.

Scruton on fox-hunting

This feature of virtue ethics is illustrated by considering what objections could be brought against Scruton's views on fox-hunting. The deliberate infliction of pain for its own sake and in order to enjoy the spectacle is cruel – this is straightforwardly settled by the dictionary meaning of 'cruel'. But whether it is cruel to deliberately inflict pain in order to achieve some other purpose, to which pain is a necessary means, is a tendentious matter – it depends on whether one regards the 'other purpose' as justifying the infliction. Midgley and Hursthouse would probably describe Scruton's fox-hunting activities as displaying confused vain-glory and self-deception; Scruton describes them as displaying the virtue of courage and it seems unlikely that rational argument could settle which side is applying their virtue and vice (or fault) terms correctly.

Philosophers who favour virtue ethics do not regard the likelihood of such breakdowns in rational argument as a flaw in the approach; they regard it as an inescapable feature of moral life. Nor do they believe that the fact that rational argument in morals *may* break down and prove fruitless as a reason for abandoning it – for, although it may prove fruitless, it may also work.

Further reading

Given the comparatively recent reappearance of virtue ethics on the scene, what you have just read is so far (as I write, in 1998) the only available application of virtue ethics to our treatment of animals. However, several excellent collections giving some indication of its scope have recently become available, notably *Virtue Ethics*, Roger Crisp and Michael Slote (eds), Oxford Readings in Philosophy Series, Oxford University Press, 1997 and *Virtue Ethics,* Daniel Statman (ed.), Edinburgh University Press, 1997.

Beyond the books and articles cited in relation to each chapter, a few more should be mentioned. *Against Liberation* by Michael Leahy, Routledge, 1991 and *The Animals Issue* by Peter Carruthers, Cambridge University Press, 1992 both attack the 'animal liberation' position. Andrew Linzey has written several books in defence of animals from a specifically Christian perspective, including *Christianity and the Rights of Animals*,. SPCK, 1987 and *Animal Theology*, SCM Press, 1994. Michael A. Fox defended animal experimentation in *The Case for Animal Experimentation*, University of California Press, 1986, but changed his mind – and heart – in the light of its reviews, a process he describes in 'Animal research reconsidered: a former defender of vivisection struggles with his radical change of heart' in *New Age Journal*, Jan.–Feb., 1988.

Postscript

Looking back

We have come a long way since I suggested that you could monitor your progress over these six weeks by doing the exercise about vegetarianism in the Preface. Go back to that exercise now and, using what you know, answer the questions again. *Only then* compare them with what you wrote when you embarked on this book. Do you think you have made progress?

I would judge that you had made considerable progress if, whatever view you now hold on the morality of vegetarianism, you are in a much better position to argue for it than you were when you started. 'Being in a much better position to argue for it' does not mean 'being able to produce a quick knock-down argument for it and thereby show immediately that anyone who disagrees with you must be wrong'. It means having a deeper, more detailed, understanding of your grounds for your conviction, being aware of what you are taking as basic premises and what is problematic about your view. All this helps you to understand why other people might disagree with you, and the extent to which rational debate with them might continue. Moral debates between people with no philosophical training very often run out of steam almost immediately because neither side knows how to argue beyond the first step. One person says 'I think eating meat is wrong because animals have a right to life', another says 'Animals don't have *rights*' and neither can then progress beyond 'Yes they *do*', 'No they *don't*'.

Now I am not suggesting that, armed with your new philosophical expertise, you should go out looking for people with whom to have lengthy disagreements. I am pointing out that, if the objectives of this book have been achieved, you now understand, in considerable detail, how such debates could be continued. When you read someone in a newspaper expressing a view on our treatment of animals, you can mentally construct how their position might be defended and how it might be argued against – you know how to go on.

I said at the outset that I was not aiming to convert you to vegetarianism but 'to give you a good knowledge of some of the most important philosophical arguments against much of our treatment of animals and objections to those arguments'. Looking back, you can probably see why I did not aim at conversion, as Singer and Regan do. I am an adherent of the virtue ethics approach. According to that approach, rational argument in morals has an important role to play, and is sometimes decisive in changing people's minds – but sometimes what is needed to bring about change is rational argument aided by a shift of moral vision.

This is what happened to me. As I mentioned early on, I was not converted to vegetarianism by Singer's and Regan's arguments, but by reading someone else. It was Stephen R.L. Clark in his book, *The Moral Status of Animals* (1984) in which he argued for 'the immediate rejection of all flesh-foods and most bio-medical research' basically on just the two grounds of the significance of animal suffering and the moral necessity for something very like Scruton's piety. Reading his characterizations of the attitudes embodied in what was, at the time, my own view, and, over quite a long period, absorbing them, gradually changed the way I saw things, in particular, my own actions. I began to see those that related to my conception of flesh-foods as unnecessary, greedy, self-indulgent, childish, my attitude to shopping and cooking in order to produce lavish dinner parties as parochial, gross, even dissolute. I saw my interest and delight in nature programmes about the lives of animals on television, and my enjoyment of meat, side by side and at odds with one another, instead of as totally distinct and having no bearing on each other. Without thinking that animals had rights, I began to see both the wild ones and the ones we usually eat, as having lives of their own, which they should be left to enjoy. And so I changed. My perception of the moral landscape and where I and the other animals were situated in it shifted.[17]

Another way of describing the effect that Clark's book had on me would be to say that it made me take to heart Singer's 'brilliantly simple argument' (p.70). 'What most of us are being party to is a huge amount of animal suffering which could be substantially reduced if we changed. Our suffering matters morally, but animal suffering matters morally too. Therefore, most of us should change'. Singer's professional version of this argument, elaborated in terms of utilitarianism and his anti-speciesist principle of equality left me unmoved – I was so busy objecting to the utilitarianism and the call for complete impartiality that I barely noticed it was there. Only when Clark had changed the way I saw myself and my own actions did it come sharply into focus for me and cease to form part of what Midgley describes as 'the unnoticed background'.

Notes

1 You might recall the introduction on utilitarianism (Book 1, Chapter 3).

2 Remember the way he refers to Aristotle simply as 'The Philosopher' (p.78 above).

3 Some of the so-called vices are character traits we might more naturally call 'faults' or 'defects' or 'failings'. The ancient Greek word we translate as 'vice' covers all of these.

[4] Oddly enough, I still do not see the actions of my meat-eating friends in the same condemnatory terms, and whether this shows that I still lack the courage of my convictions and that I am being inconsistent, or whether I am modestly conscious of the fact that I am far from perfect and that we should not rush to condemn others, particularly those we love and respect, I do not know. I don't know what I think about 'most biomedical research' either, though I have met, and read about, some experimenters whose actions I would unhesitatingly condemn.

Revision Test

This test is intended to help you revise some of the main points covered in this book. Try working through the questions without using your notes or referring back to the text. Then compare your answers with those at the back of the book.

READING As preparation for this test, read the summaries of philosophical positions on animals in Reading 6.

Chapter 1

1 Which of (i) or (ii) is absolute dismissal and which is relative dismissal?

(i) Whether or not animals suffer does not matter at all; it is not a moral issue.

(ii) Animal suffering does matter, but not as much as human suffering.

2 Singer is a utilitarian because (tick one or more):

(i) He believes that lying is bad in some circumstances and good in others, depending on its consequences.

(ii) He believes that equal consideration should be given to the interests of all human beings.

(iii) He believes that pain and suffering are bad.

(iv) He believes that it is right to make one being suffer in order to save thousands.

(v) He believes that when I am trying to decide what I ought to do I must consider what the consequences of my action are likely to be.

3 Which of the following is the best statement of the principle of equality, as interpeted by Singer:

(i) We must not give unequal weight or consideration to the interests of people of different races or different intelligence.

(ii) We must give equal weight or consideration to the interests of all sentient creatures.

(iii) We must not give unequal weight or consideration to the like interest of any sentient creatures.

4 According to Singer (tick one or more):

(i) No one should ever eat meat.

(ii) Those of us who live in cities and/or cannot be sure how the animals whose flesh is available to us have been treated should never eat meat.

(iii) Those of us who live in cities and/or cannot be sure how the animals whose flesh is available to us have been treated are rarely justified in eating meat.

(iv) We should destroy battery farms.

(v) We should eat fish instead of meat.

5 Singer actually says in the Reading that we should use mentally retarded human beings and babies for experimental purposes.

(i) True.

(ii) False.

(iii) Unclear.

6 Singer implies in the Reading that we should use intellectually disabled human beings and babies for experimental purposes.

(i) True.

(ii) False.

(iii) Unclear.

Chapter 2

1 Playing author's advocate on Singer's behalf, we may take his conclusion concerning vegetarianism to be (tick at least one):

(i) Those of us who live in cities and/or cannot be sure how the animals whose flesh is available to us have been treated are rarely justified in eating meat.

(ii) No one should ever eat meat.

(iii) Most of us should aim to cut down on eating meat, favour free-range products, encourage those we know to do the same and eventually become vegetarian.

(iv) Most of us should change our attitude to eating animal flesh.

2 Which, if any, of the following can form the basis of a conclusive objection to Singer's argument for vegetarianism?

(i) Animals do not suffer much as a result of our using them for food.

(ii) Animals do not feel pain the way we do.

(iii) The Darwinian law of natural selection justifies our preying on animals.

(iv) The consequences of our all becoming vegetarian immediately might well be disastrous.

(v) Some people need to eat meat to survive.

(vi) Those of us who live with other people cannot become vegetarian without imposing our views on other people.

(vii) No one who buys meat at a supermarket causes any animal suffering.

3 Singer appeals to

(i) Direct (or 'act' utilitarianism).

(ii) Indirect (or 'rule' utilitarianism).

(iii) Both direct and indirect utilitarianism.

4 Singer believes that (tick at least one):

(i) When I am trying to decide what I ought to do I must consider only what the consequences of my particular action are likely to be for all those affected.

(ii) When I am trying to decide what I ought to do I must sometimes consider whether the effect of a general practice of doing the sort of thing direct utilitarianism would lead me to on this occasion will benefit all those affected.

(iii) When I am trying to decide what I ought to do I must always consider whether the effect of a general practice of doing the sort of thing I am considering would be beneficial or not.

5 Singer's conclusion regarding experiments on animals is clearly stated in the Reading as:

(i) All experiments causing animal suffering are wrong.

(ii) Most experiments causing animal suffering are wrong.

(iii) Many experiments causing animal suffering are wrong.

(iv) Some experiments causing animal suffering are wrong.

(v) None of the above.

6 Singer's indirect utilitarianism commits him to which of the following (tick at least one).

(i) Our current practice of using animals in experiments is justifiable because the general practice of science is beneficial.

(ii) Any particular experiment which causes suffering to an animal in which the benefits to humans are either non-existent or uncertain is wrong.

(iii) Many apparently unnecessary experiments which cause animal suffering are justifiable because the general practice of science is beneficial.

(iv) The end justifies the means.

7 Playing author's advocate on Singer's behalf, we may take his position regarding the experimental use of animals to be (tick at least one):

(i) Many experiments causing animal suffering are wrong.

(ii) Most of us should change our attitude to the use of animals as experimental subjects.

(iii) We should change our current scientific practices.

8 By 'person' Singer means (tick at least one):

(i) Human being.

(ii) Member of the species homo sapiens.

(iii) A rational self-conscious being that is aware of itself as a distinct entity with a past and a future.

(iv) A rational self-conscious human being that is aware of itself as a distinct entity with a past and a future.

9 Which of the following are definitely not persons according to Singer (tick at least one)?

(i) Human foetuses.

(ii) You, me and Singer.

(iii) Snails.

(iv) Babies.

(v) Permanently (very) intellectually disabled human beings.

(vi) Sheep.

(vii) Chickens, ducks.

Chapter 3

1 Aristotle claimed that 'man alone of the animals possesses speech'. Why did he think this (tick one or more)?

(i) Because only human beings possess reason.

(ii) Because only human beings make meaningful noises.

(iii) Because only human beings communicate.

2 Why have some people thought that possessing reason must be an all or nothing matter, not a matter of degree (tick only one)?

(i) Because only human beings possess reason.

(ii) Because only human beings can use language.

(iii) Because only human beings have an immortal rational soul.

(iv) Because only human beings can enter into contracts.

3 According to Regan's version of the indirect duty view (tick one or more):

(i) Moral claims made on behalf of animals are just nonsensical, like moral claims made on behalf of stones or cars.

(ii) Cruelty to animals is never wrong.

(iii) We have duties regarding animals.

(iv) Cruelty to animals is always wrong.

(v) Cruelty to animals is wrong when it wrongs human beings.

4 According to Kant's version of the indirect duty view (tick one or more):

(i) Moral claims made on behalf of animals are just nonsensical, like moral claims made on behalf of stones or cars.

(ii) Cruelty to animals is never wrong.

(iii) Cruelty to animals can be wrong even when no human but its owner is involved.

(iv) Cruelty to animals is always wrong.

5 According to Hume's and Rawls's contractarian view of justice (tick one or more):

(i) Animals, who cannot enter into contracts, do not have rights.

(ii) Moral claims made on behalf of animals are just nonsensical, like moral claims made on behalf of stones or cars.

(iii) Cruelty to animals is wrong.

(iv) Animals have a right not to be treated cruelly.

(v) Cruelty to animals is wrong because it wrongs human beings.

(vi) We have duties of compassion to animals.

6 I see some small boys about to torment my cat and make one of the following objections.

(i) I make a moral claim on my own behalf. a

(ii) I make a moral claim on behalf of my cat. c

(iii) I make a moral claim on behalf of humanity. b

Match each objection with one of the following:

(a) I believe Regan's version of the indirect duty view.

(b) I believe Kant's version of the indirect duty view.

(c) I believe Hume's and Rawls's contractarian view.

Chapter 4

1 The following four positions all take account of the fact that animals, like us, can suffer: (a) Kant's indirect duty view, (b) Contractarianism about justice, (c) Singer's view, and (d) Regan's view. Match a claim from the following with each position (a)–(d).

(i) The suffering of all sentient beings matters.

(ii) The suffering of an animal does not matter because animals do not have rights.

(iii) Animal suffering and humans' rights both matter and both should be considered, if relevant, when deciding what to do.

(iv) The suffering of an animal does not matter in itself; what matters is the likelihood that anyone who behaves badly to an animal will go on to behave badly to other human beings.

(v) Suffering is the only thing that matters.

(vi) Suffering matters, but not as much as rights which are what should fundamentally be taken into consideration when deciding what to do.

2 What is Regan's objection to utilitarianism (tick at least one).

(i) Utilitarianism does not recognize rights.

(ii) Utilitarianism does not recognize the inherent value of individuals.

(iii) Utilitarianism has absurd consequences.

(iv) Utilitarianism is not egalitarian enough.

(v) Utilitarianism allows a good end to justify an evil means.

3 When Regan says that we all have 'inherent value' he means (tick at least one):

(i) We all have an immortal soul.

(ii) We all have a right to be treated with respect.

(iii) We all have a right not to be used as a resource for others.

(iv) We are all equal.

(v) We are all human beings.

(vi) We are all experiencing subjects of a life.

4 Regan considers three defences of the claims that 'Only human beings have inherent value'. Which are they (tick precisely three)?

(i) Only human beings have an immortal soul.

(ii) Only human beings can understand contracts.

(iii) Only human beings are intelligent, autonomous and rational.

(iv) Only human beings *are* human beings.

(v) Only human beings are experiencing subjects of a life.

(vi) Human beings are more intelligent than the other animals.

(vii) Human beings have desires about their future which other animals do not have.

5 Regan gives an objection to each of the three defences. Identify the three objections below and match them to the appropriate defence you identified in (4) above.

(a) All who have inherent value have it equally.

(b) Some human beings are not intelligent, autonomous and rational but we still think they have inherent value.

(c) This is blatant speciesism.

(d) This is an empirical claim.

(e) This claim is too controversial.

(f) Infants and the severely mentally incapacitated are not experiencing subjects of a life.

(g) I am not religious and hence do not believe in immortal souls.

6 There are at least three different ways of thinking about rights: (a) the contractarian, (b) the 'American', and (c) the way we tend to think when we are talking about morally important things. Match one of the following claims to each different way (a)–(c).

(i) Wherever there is a right, there is a corresponding duty.

(ii) Wherever there is a duty, there is a corresponding right.

(iii) Whevever there is an especially strong duty, there is a corresponding right.

(iv) Some duties corresponding to rights can be trivial, some very important.

7 Scruton claims (tick at least one):

(i) Infants and the severely mentally incapacitated have rights because they are the kind of thing that is capable of understanding contracts, namely, human beings.

(ii) Mentally ordinary infants have rights because, being incipiently rational, they are capable of understanding contracts.

(iii) Infants and the severely mentally incapacitated do not have rights because they are not capable of understanding contracts.

(iv) The severely mentally incapacitated do not have rights because they are not capable of understanding contracts.

8 Scruton is open to the charge of speciesism because he claims which of the following (tick at least one):

(i) Infants and the severely mentally incapacitated do not have rights because they are not capable of understanding contracts.

(ii) Infants and the severely mentally incapacitated have rights because they are the kind of thing that is capable of understanding contracts, namely, human beings.

(iii) Virtue and piety require that we acknowledge human life as sacrosanct.

(iv) Since animals do not have rights we can treat them any way we like.

(v) Since animals do not have rights, moral claims on their behalf are always weaker than claims on behalf of any human being.

Chapter 5

1 According to Midgley (tick at least one):

(i) Loosely speaking, we should extend the principle of equality across the species-barrier.

(ii) Our elitist, sexist, forebears were blind and hypocritical.

(iii) If we do not extend the principle of equality across the species-barrier, we are being blind and hypocritical.

(iv) Speciesism is just like racism and sexism.

(v) We should always apply the principle of equality when considering how to treat animals.

2 Mark the following as true or false.

(i) A valid argument by analogy has true premises and a true conclusion.

(ii) A valid argument by analogy argues from true premises about relevant similarities between two things to a true conclusion that the second thing shares a further feature with the first.

(iii) Arguments by analogy are all invalid because what counts as a relevant similarity is a matter of personal opinion.

(iv) All arguments by analogy are, strictly speaking, invalid.

3 According to Singer:

(i) Speciesism is wrong.

(ii) Speciesism is always wrong.

(iii) Speciesism is never wrong.

(iv) Speciesism is sometimes wrong.

4 Which, if any, of the following does Midgley deny?

(i) Speciesism is wrong.

(ii) Speciesism is always wrong.

(iii) Speciesism is never wrong.

(iv) Speciesism is sometimes wrong.

5 According to Midgley:

(i) Family and species partiality are natural and right.

(ii) Family and species partiality are a central element in human happiness.

(iii) Family and species partiality may well be essential to the possibility of morality.

(iv) Family and species partiality are always justifiable.

(v) We only bond with our own species.

6 According to Midgley:

(i) Moral questions are to be settled by considerations drawn from (a) rights, (b) sympathy, (c) virtue, and (d) piety.

(ii) All moral questions are complex and can only be settled by appeal to a wide range of moral considerations.

(iii) Morality consists of a large number of different principles.

(iv) All moral questions can be settled by appeal to the principle of equality or to considerations of partiality and bonds.

7 Scruton:

(i) Agrees with Singer's utilitarianism.

(ii) Agrees with Midgley that species and family bonding is essential to morality.

(iii) Agrees with Kant that we have no duties to animals.

(iv) Agrees with Singer that happiness and suffering are important.

(v) Agrees with Regan that animals have a right not to be used as instruments, as things.

(vi) Agrees with Midgley that speciesism is sometimes right, sometimes wrong.

Chapter 6

1 According to what you have read, are the following claims true or false?

(i) Virtue ethics employs the large vocabulary of the virtues and vices to register the complexity of moral claims that Midgley emphasizes.

(ii) Virtue ethics requires us to minimize suffering because it is compassionate.

(iii) Virtue ethics avoids any appeal to rights.

(iv) Midgley uses the virtue ethics approach.

(v) Scruton uses the virtue ethics approach.

(vi) Virtue ethics tells me to consider whether I would be acting, for example, compassionately or callously, justly or unjustly if I went in for some proposed action.

(vii) According to virtue ethics, no action is intrinsically right or wrong; any action can be right or wrong depending on the particular circumstances.

2 According to what you have read, are the following claims true or false?

(i) When philosophers use the virtue ethics approach to deal with practical moral problems they assume claims that, for example, justice, compassion and honesty are virtues as premises.

(ii) Which character traits are the virtues and which the vices is a matter of personal opinion.

(iii) Whenever philosophers use the utilitarian or rights-based approaches to deal with practical moral problems, they begin by arguing for their claims that, for example, maximizing interests is the only thing that matters, or that we all have an equal moral right not to be used as a mere resource for others.

(iv) All moral philosophy is a matter of personal opinion.

(v) Since the application of the virtue and vice terms depends on how we see things, we can all choose how to apply them.

(vi) We may find rational argument compelling us to change our application of the virtue and vice terms.

3 According to Hursthouse:

(i) Actions are cruel when they involve the deliberate infliction of pain for its own sake and in order to enjoy the suffering involved.

(ii) Actions are cruel only when they involve the deliberate infliction of pain for its own sake and in order to enjoy the suffering inflicted.

(iii) Actions are not cruel when pain is inflicted in order to achieve some other purpose to which pain is a necessary means.

(iv) Actions may be cruel when the purpose for which pain is inflicted does not justify the infliction.

(v) The virtue of courage involves facing danger without fear (or conquering fear).

(vi) 'Courage' means facing danger for a good reason or a worthwhile end.

Readings

'Equality for Animals?'

Peter Singer

In *Practical Ethics,** Singer applies utilitarianism to a range of issues such as abortion, euthanasia, civil disobedience, overseas aid and, most relevant here, to our treatment of animals. In the first two chapters he argues for utilitarianism and then for the principle of equality, establishing his basic approach. In the chapter from which this extract is taken, he argues against our using animals for food and using them in scientific experiments because of the suffering involved. He concentrates particularly on attacking 'speciesism' (a term originally coined, on the model of 'racism', by another crusader in the animal liberation movement, Richard Ryder). A speciesist, according to Singer, is anyone who gives greater weight to the interests of her own species than to the interests of other species, just as a racist is one who gives greater weight to the interests of her own race.

Racism and speciesism

1 In Chapter 2 [not reprinted here], I gave reasons for believing that the fundamental principle of equality, on which the equality of all human beings rests, is the principle of equal consideration of interests. Only a basic moral principle of this kind can allow us to defend a form of equality that embraces all human beings, with all the differences that exist between them. I shall now contend that while this principle does provide an adequate basis for human equality, it provides a basis that cannot be limited to humans. In other words I shall suggest that, having accepted the principle of equality as a sound moral basis for relations with others of our own species, we are also committed to accepting it as a sound moral basis for relations with those outside our own species – the non-human animals.

2 This suggestion may at first seem bizarre. We are used to regarding discrimination against members of racial minorities, or against women, as among the most important moral and political issues facing the world today.

These are serious matters, worthy of the time and energy of any concerned person. But animals? Isn't the welfare of animals in a different category altogether, a matter for people who are dotty about dogs and cats? How can anyone waste their time on equality for animals when so many humans are denied real equality?

3 This attitude reflects a popular prejudice against taking the interests of animals seriously – a prejudice no better founded than the prejudice of white slave owners against taking the interests of their African slaves seriously. It is easy for us to criticize the prejudices of our grandfathers, from which our fathers freed themselves. It is more difficult to distance ourselves from our own views, so that we can dispassionately search for prejudices among the beliefs and values we hold. What is needed now is a willingness to follow the arguments where they lead, without a prior assumption that the issue is not worth our attention.

4 The argument for extending the principle of equality beyond our own species is simple, so simple that it amounts to no more than a clear understanding of the nature of the principle of equal consideration of interests. We have seen that this principle implies that our concern for others ought not to depend on what they are like, or what abilities they possess (although precisely what this concern requires us to do may vary according to the characteristics of those affected by what we do). It is on this basis that we are able to say that the fact that some people are not members of our race does not entitle us to exploit them, and similarly the fact that some people are less intelligent than others does not mean that their interests may be disregarded. But the principle also implies that the fact that beings are not members of our species does not entitle us to exploit them, and similarly the fact that other animals are less intelligent than we are does not mean that their interests may be disregarded.

5 ...[M]any philosophers have advocated equal consideration of interests, in some form or other, as a basic moral principle. Only a few have recognised that the principle has applications beyond our own species, one of the few being Jeremy Bentham, the founding father of modern utilitarianism. In a forward-looking passage, written at a time when African slaves in the British dominions were still being treated much as we now treat non-human animals, Benham wrote:

> The day may come when the rest of the animal creation may acquire those rights which never could have been witholden from them but by the hand of tyranny. The French have already discovered that the blackness of the skin is no reason why a human being should be abandoned without redress to the caprice of a tormentor. It may one day come to be recognized that the number of

> the legs, the villosity of the skin, or the termination of the *os sacrum,* are reasons equally insufficient for abandoning a sensitive being to the same fate. What else is it that should trace the insuperable line? Is it the faculty of reason, or perhaps the faculty of discourse? But a full-grown horse or dog is beyond comparison a more rational, as well as a more conversable animal, than an infant of a day, or a week, or even a month, old. But suppose they were otherwise, what would it avail? The question is not, Can they *reason*? nor Can they *talk*? but, *Can they suffer*?

In this passage Bentham points to the capacity for suffering as the vital characteristic that entitles a being to equal consideration. The capacity for suffering – or more strictly, for suffering and/or enjoyment or happiness – is not just another characteristic like the capacity for language, or for higher mathematics. Bentham is not saying that those who try to mark 'the insuperable line' that determines whether the interests of a being should be considered happen to have selected the wrong characteristic. The capacity for suffering and enjoying things is a prerequisite for having interests at all, a condition that must be satisfied before we can speak of interests in any meaningful way. It would be nonsense to say that it was not in the interests of a stone to be kicked along the road by a schoolboy. A stone does not have interests because it cannot suffer. Nothing that we can do to it could possibly make any difference to its welfare. A mouse, on the other hand, does have an interest in not being tormented, because mice will suffer if they are treated in this way.

6 If a being suffers, there can be no moral justification for refusing to take that suffering into consideration. No matter what the nature of the being, the principle of equality requires that the suffering be counted equally with the like suffering – in so far as rough comparisons can be made – of any other being. If a being is not capable of suffering, or of experiencing enjoyment or happiness, there is nothing to be taken into account. This is why the limit of sentience (using the term as a convenient, if not strictly accurate, shorthand for the capacity to suffer or experience enjoyment or happiness) is the only defensible boundary of concern for the interests of others. To mark this boundary by some characteristic like intelligence or rationality would be to mark it in an arbitrary way. Why not choose some other characteristic, like skin colour?

7 Racists violate the principle of equality by giving greater weight to the interests of members of their own race when there is a clash between their interests and the interests of those of another race. Racists of European descent typically have not accepted that pain matters as much when it is felt by Africans, for example, as when it is felt by Europeans. Similarly those I would call 'speciesists' give greater weight to the interests of members of their own species when there is a clash between their interests and the interests of those

of other species. Human speciesists do not accept that pain is as bad when it is felt by pigs or mice as when it is felt by humans.

8 That, then, is really the whole of the argument for extending the principle of equality to non-human animals; but there may be some doubts about what this equality amounts to in practice. In particular, the last sentence of the previous paragraph may prompt some people to reply: 'Surely pain felt by a mouse just is not as bad as pain felt by a human. Humans have much greater awareness of what is happening to them, and this makes their suffering worse. You can't equate the suffering of, say, a person dying slowly from cancer, and a laboratory mouse undergoing the same fate.'

9 I fully accept that in the case described the human cancer victim normally suffers more than the non-human cancer victim. This in no way undermines the extension of equal consideration of interests to non-humans. It means, rather, that we must take care when we compare the interests of different species. In some situations a member of one species will suffer more than a member of another species. In this case we should still apply the principle of equal consideration of interests but the result of so doing is, of course, to give priority to relieving the greater suffering. A simpler case may help to make this clear.

10 If I give a horse a hard slap across its rump with my open hand, the horse may start, but it presumably feels little pain. Its skin is thick enough to protect it against a mere slap. If I slap a baby in the same way, however, the baby will cry and presumably does feel pain, for the baby's skin is more sensitive. So it is worse to slap a baby than a horse, if both slaps are administered with equal force. But there must be some kind of blow – I don't know exactly what it would be, but perhaps a blow with a heavy stick – that would cause the horse as much pain as we cause a baby by a simple slap. That is what I mean by 'the same amount of pain' and if we consider it wrong to inflict that much pain on a baby for no good reason then we must, unless we are speciesists, consider it equally wrong to inflict the same amount of pain on a horse for no good reason.

11 There are other differences between humans and animals that cause other complications. Normal adult human beings have mental capacities that will, in certain circumstances, lead them to suffer more than animals would in the same circumstances. If, for instance, we decided to perform extremely painful or lethal scientific experiments on normal adult humans, kidnapped at random from public parks for this purpose, adults who entered parks would become fearful that they would be kidnapped. The resultant terror would be a form of suffering additional to the pain of the experiment. The same experiments performed on non-human animals would cause less suffering since the animals would not have the anticipatory dread of being kidnapped

and experimented upon. This does not mean, of course, that it would be *right* to perform the experiment on animals, but only that there is a reason, and one that is not speciesist, for preferring to use animals rather than normal adult humans, if the experiment is to be done at all. Note, however, that this same argument gives us a reason for preferring to use human infants – orphans perhaps – or severely intellectually disabled humans for experiments, rather than adults, since infants and severely intellectually disabled humans would also have no idea of what was going to happen to them. As far as this argument is concerned, non-human animals and infants and severely intellectually disabled humans are in the same category; and if we use this argument to justify experiments on non-human animals we have to ask ourselves whether we are also prepared to allow experiments on human infants and severely intellectually disabled adults. If we make a distinction between animals and these humans, how can we do it, other than on the basis of a morally indefensible preference for members of our own species?

12 There are many areas in which the superior mental powers of normal adult humans make a difference: anticipation, more detailed memory, greater knowledge of what is happening, and so on. These differences explain why a human dying from cancer is likely to suffer more than a mouse. It is the mental anguish that makes the human's position so much harder to bear. Yet these differences do not all point to greater suffering on the part of the normal human being. Sometimes animals may suffer more because of their more limited understanding. If, for instance, we are taking prisoners in wartime we can explain to them that while they must submit to capture, search, and confinement they will not otherwise be harmed and will be set free at the conclusion of hostilities. If we capture wild animals, however, we cannot explain that we are not threatening their lives. A wild animal cannot distinguish an attempt to overpower and confine from an attempt to kill; the one causes as much terror as the other.

13 It may be objected that comparisons of the sufferings of different species are impossible to make, and that for this reason when the interests of animals and humans clash, the principle of equality gives no guidance. It is true that comparisons of suffering between members of different species cannot be made precisely. Nor, for that matter, can comparisons of suffering between different human beings be made precisely. Precision is not essential. As we shall see shortly, even if we were to prevent the infliction of suffering on animals only when the interests of humans will not be affected to anything like the extent that animals are affected, we would be forced to make radical changes in our treatment of animals that would involve our diet, the farming methods we use, experimental procedures in many fields of science, our

approach to wildlife and to hunting, trapping and the wearing of furs, and areas of entertainment like circuses, rodeos, and zoos. As a result, the total quantity of suffering caused would be greatly reduced; so greatly that it is hard to imagine any other change of moral attitude that would cause so great a reduction in the total sum of suffering in the universe.

14 So far I have said a lot about the infliction of suffering on animals, but nothing about killing them. This omission has been deliberate. The application of the principle of equality to the infliction of suffering is, in theory at least, fairly straightforward. Pain and suffering are bad and should be prevented or minimized, irrespective of the race, sex, or species of the being that suffers. How bad a pain is depends on how intense it is and how long it lasts, but pains of the same intensity and duration are equally bad, whether felt by humans or animals. When we come to consider the value of life, we cannot say quite so confidently that a life is a life, and equally valuable, whether it is a human life or an animal life. It would not be speciesist to hold that the life of a self-aware being, capable of abstract thought, of planning for the future, of complex acts of communication, and so on, is more valuable than the life of a being without these capacities. (I am not saying whether this view is justifiable or not; only that it cannot simply be rejected as speciesist, because it is not on the basis of species itself that one life is held to be more valuable than another.) The value of life is a notoriously difficult ethical question, and we can only arrive at a reasoned conclusion about the comparative value of human and animal life after we have discussed the value of life in general. This is a topic for a separate chapter. Meanwhile there are important conclusions to be derived from the extension beyond our own species of the principle of equal consideration of interests, irrespective of our conclusions about the value of life.

Speciesism in practice

Animals as food

15 For most people in modern, urbanized societies, the principal form of contact with non-human animals is at meal times. The use of animals for food is probably the oldest and the most widespread form of animal use. There is also a sense in which it is the most basic form of animal use, the foundation stone on which rests the belief that animals exist for our pleasure and convenience.

16 If animals count in their own right, our use of animals for food becomes questionable – especially when animal flesh is a luxury rather than a necessity. Eskimos living in an environment where they must kill animals for food or starve might be justified in claiming that their interest in surviving overrides that of the animals they kill. Most of us cannot defend our diet in this way. Citizens of industrialized societies can easily obtain an adequate diet without the use of animal flesh. The overwhelming weight of medical evidence indicates that animal flesh is not necessary for good health or longevity. Nor is animal production in industrialized societies an efficient way of producing food, since most of the animals consumed have been fattened on grains and other foods that we could have eaten directly. When we feed these grains to animals, only about 10 per cent of the nutritional value remains as meat for human consumption. So, with the exception of animals raised entirely on grazing land unsuitable for crops, animals are eaten neither for health, nor to increase our food supply. Their flesh is a luxury, consumed because people like its taste.

17 In considering the ethics of the use of animal flesh for human food in industrialized societies, we are considering a situation in which a relatively minor human interest must be balanced against the lives and welfare of the animals involved. The principle of equal consideration of interests does not allow major interests to be sacrificed for minor interests.

18 The case against using animals for food is at its strongest when animals are made to lead miserable lives so that their flesh can be made available to humans at the lowest possible cost. Modern forms of intensive farming apply science and technology to the attitude that animals are objects for us to use. In order to have meat on the table at a price that people can afford, our society tolerates methods of meat production that confine sentient animals in cramped, unsuitable conditions for the entire duration of their lives. Animals are treated like machines that convert fodder into flesh, and any innovation that results in a higher 'conversion ratio' is liable to be adopted. As one authority on the subject has said, 'Cruelty is acknowledged only when profitability ceases.' To avoid speciesism we must stop these practices. Our custom is all the support that factory farmers need. The decision to cease giving them that support may be difficult, but it is less difficult than it would have been for a white Southerner to go against the traditions of his society and free his slaves; if we do not change our dietary habits, how can we censure those slave holders who would not change their own way of living?

19 These arguments apply to animals who have been reared in factory farms – which means that we should not eat chicken, pork, or veal, unless we know that the meat we are eating was not produced by factory farm methods.

The same is true of beef that has come from cattle kept in crowded feedlots (as most beef does in the United States). Eggs will come from hens kept in small wire cages, too small even to allow them to stretch their wings, unless the eggs are specifically sold as 'free range' (or unless one lives in a relatively enlightened country like Switzerland, which has prohibited the cage system of keeping hens).

20 These arguments do not take us all the way to a vegetarian diet, since some animals, for instance sheep, and in some countries cattle, still graze freely outdoors. This could change. The American pattern of fattening cattle in crowded feedlots is spreading to other countries. Meanwhile, the lives of free-ranging animals are undoubtedly better than those of animals reared in factory farms. It is still doubtful if using them for food is compatible with equal consideration of interests. One problem is, of course, that using them as food involves killing them – but this is an issue to which, as I have said, we shall return when we have discussed the value of life in the next chapter. Apart from taking their lives there are also many other things done to animals in order to bring them cheaply to our dinner table. Castration, the separation of mother and young, the breaking up of herds, branding, transporting, and finally the moments of slaughter – all of these are likely to involve suffering and do not take the animals' interests into account. Perhaps animals could be reared on a small scale without suffering in these ways, but it does not seem economical or practical to do so on the scale required for feeding our large urban populations. In any case, the important question is not whether animal flesh *could* be produced without suffering, but whether the flesh we are considering buying was produced without suffering. Unless we can be confident that it was, the principle of equal consideration of interest implies that it was wrong to sacrifice important interests of the animal in order to satisfy less important interests of our own; consequently we should boycott the end result of this process.

21 For those of us living in cities where it is difficult to know how the animals we might eat have lived and died, this conclusion brings us close to a vegetarian way of life. I shall consider some objections to it in the final section of this chapter.

Experimenting on animals

22 Perhaps the area in which speciesism can most clearly be observed is the use of animals in experiments. Here the issue stands out starkly, because experimenters often seek to justify experimenting on animals by claiming that the experiments lead us to discoveries about humans; if this is so, the experimenter must agree that human and non-human animals are similar in

crucial respects. For instance, if forcing a rat to choose between starving to death and crossing an electrified grid to obtain food tells us anything about the reactions of humans to stress, we must assume that the rat feels stress in this kind of situation.

23 People sometimes think that all animal experiments serve vital medical purposes, and can be justified on the grounds that they relieve more suffering than they cause. This comfortable belief is mistaken. Drug companies test new shampoos and cosmetics they are intending to market by dripping concentrated solutions of them into the eyes of rabbits, in a test known as the Draize test. (Pressure from the animal liberation movement has led several cosmetic companies to abandon this practice. An alternative test, not using animals, has now been found. Nevertheless, many companies, including some of the largest, still continue to perform the Draize test.) Food additives, including artificial colourings and preservatives, are tested by what is known as the LD50 – a test designed to find the 'lethal dose', or level of consumption that will make 50 per cent of a sample of animals die. In the process nearly all of the animals are made very sick before some finally die and others pull through. These tests are not necessary to prevent human suffering: even if there were no alternative to the use of animals to test the safety of the products, we already have enough shampoos and food colourings. There is no need to develop new ones that might be dangerous.

24 In many countries, the armed forces perform atrocious experiments on animals that rarely come to light. To give just one example: at the US Armed Forces Radiobiology Institute, in Bethesda, Maryland, rhesus monkeys have been trained to run inside a large wheel. If they slow down too much, the wheel slows down, too, and the monkeys get an electric shock. Once the monkeys are trained to run for long periods, they are given lethal doses of radiation. Then, while sick and vomiting, they are forced to continue to run until they drop. This is supposed to provide information on the capacities of soldiers to continue to fight after a nuclear attack.

25 Nor can all university experiments be defended on the grounds that they relieve more suffering than they inflict. Three experimenters at Princeton University kept 256 young rats without food or water until they died. They concluded that young rats under conditions of fatal thirst and starvation are much more active than normal adult rats given food and water. In a well-known series of experiments that went on for more than fifteen years, H.F. Harlow of the Primate Research Centre, Madison, Wisconsin, reared monkeys under conditions of maternal deprivation and total isolation. He found that in this way he could reduce the monkeys to a state in which, when placed among normal monkeys, they sat huddled in a corner in a condition of persistent

depression and fear. Harlow also produced monkey mothers so neurotic that they smashed their infant's face into the floor and rubbed it back and forth. Although Harlow himself is no longer alive, some of his former students at other US universities continue to perform variations on his experiments.

26 In these cases, and many others like them, the benefits to humans are either non-existent or uncertain, while the losses to members of other species are certain and real. Hence the experiments indicate a failure to give equal consideration to the interests of all beings, irrespective of species.

27 In the past, argument about animal experimentation has often missed this point because it has been put in absolutist terms: would the opponent of experimentation be prepared to let thousands die from a terrible disease that could be cured by experimenting on one animal? This is a purely hypothetical question, since experiments do not have such dramatic results, but as long as its hypothetical nature is clear, I think the question should be answered affirmatively – in other words, if one, or even a dozen animals had to suffer experiments in order to save thousands, I would think it right and in accordance with equal consideration of interests that they should do so. This, at any rate, is the answer a utilitarian must give. Those who believe in absolute rights might hold that it is always wrong to sacrifice one being, whether human or animal, for the benefit of another. In that case the experiment should not be carried out, whatever the consequences.

28 To the hypothetical question about saving thousands of people through a single experiment on an animal, opponents of speciesism can reply with a hypothetical question of their own: would experimenters be prepared to perform their experiments on orphaned humans with severe and irreversible brain damage if that were the only way to save thousands? (I say 'orphaned' in order to avoid the complication of the feelings of the human parents.) If experimenters are not prepared to use orphaned humans with severe and irreversible brain damage, their readiness to use non-human animals seems to discriminate on the basis of species alone, since apes, monkeys, dogs, cats and even mice and rats are more intelligent, more aware of what is happening to them, more sensitive to pain, and so on, than many severely brain damaged humans barely surviving in hospital wards and other institutions. There seems to be no morally relevant characteristic that such humans have that non-human animals lack. Experimenters, then, show bias in favour of their own species whenever they carry out experiments on non-human animals for purposes that they would not think justified them in using human beings at an equal or lower level of sentience, awareness, sensitivity, and so on. If this bias were eliminated, the number of experiments performed on animals would be greatly reduced.

Other forms of speciesism

29 I have concentrated on the use of animals as food and in research, since these are examples of large-scale, systematic speciesism. They are not, of course, the only areas in which the principle of equal consideration of interests, extended beyond the human species, has practical implications. There are many other areas that raise similar issues, including the fur trade, hunting in all its different forms, circuses, rodeos, zoos, and the pet business. Since the philosophical questions raised by these issues are not very different from those raised by the use of animals as food and in research, I shall leave it to the reader to apply the appropriate ethical principles to them.

Notes

* From *Practical Ethics*, 2nd edn, Cambridge University Press, 1993, Chapter 3.

'The Case for Animal Rights'

Tom Regan

This article* is the contemporary philosopher Tom Regan's brisk summary of a large book (425 pages) he published in 1983, *The Case for Animal Rights.* In it he sketches his objections to other theoretical approaches to morality (the indirect duty view, contractarianism, utilitarianism), offers a 'rights view' in their place, and argues, with necessary brevity, that the rights view cannot be limited in its scope to human beings. Like Singer, he employs a principle of equality, and like Singer, he claims that giving special value to human beings because they are members of *Homo sapiens* is speciesism.

1 I regard myself as an advocate of animal rights – as a part of the animal rights movement. That movement, as I conceive it, is committed to a number of goals, including:

- the total abolition of the use of animals in science;
- the total dissolution of commercial animal agriculture;
- the total elimination of commercial and sport hunting and trapping.

There are, I know, people who profess to believe in animal rights but do not avow these goals. Factory farming, they say, is wrong – it violates animals' rights – but traditional animal agriculture is all right. Toxicity tests of cosmetics on animals violates their rights, but important medical research – cancer research, for example – does not. The clubbing of baby seals is abhorrent, but not the harvesting of adult seals. I used to think I understood this reasoning. Not any more. You don't change unjust institutions by tidying them up.

2 What's wrong – fundamentally wrong – with the way animals are treated isn't the details that vary from case to case. It's the whole system. The forlornness of the veal calf is pathetic, heart wrenching; the pulsing pain of the

chimp with electrodes planted deep in her brain is repulsive; the slow, torturous death of the racoon caught in the leg-hold trap is agonizing. But what is wrong isn't the pain, isn't the suffering, isn't the deprivation. These compound what's wrong. Sometimes – often – they make it much, much worse. But they are not the fundamental wrong.

3 The fundamental wrong is the system that allows us to view animals as *our resources,* here for *us* – to be eaten, or surgically manipulated, or exploited for sport or money. Once we accept this view of animals – as our resources – the rest is as predictable as it is regrettable. Why worry about their loneliness, their pain, their death? Since animals exist for us, to benefit us in one way or another, what harms them really doesn't matter – or matters only if it starts to bother us, makes us feel a trifle uneasy...

4 In the case of animals in science, whether and how we abolish their use... are to a large extent political questions. People must change their beliefs before they change their habits. Enough people, especially those elected to public office, must believe in change – must want it – before we will have laws that protect the rights of animals. This process of change is very complicated, very demanding, very exhausting, calling for the efforts of many hands in education, publicity, political organization and activity, down to the licking of envelopes and stamps. As a trained and practising philosopher, the sort of contribution I can make is limited but, I like to think, important. The currency of philosophy is ideas – their meaning and rational foundation – not the nuts and bolts of the legislative process, say, or the mechanics of community organization. That's what I have been exploring over the past ten years or so in my essays and talks and, most recently, in my book, *The Case for Animal Rights.* I believe the major conclusions I reach in the book are true because they are supported by the weight of the best arguments. I believe the idea of animal rights has reason, not just emotion, on its side.

5 In the space I have at my disposal here I can only sketch, in the barest outline, some of the main features of the book. Its main themes – and we should not be surprised by this – involve asking and answering deep, foundational moral questions about what morality is, how it should be understood and what is the best moral theory, all considered. I hope I can convey something of the shape I think this theory takes. The attempt to do this will be (to use a word a friendly critic once used to describe my work) cerebral, perhaps too cerebral. But this is misleading. My feelings about how animals are sometimes treated run just as deep and just as strong as those of my more volatile compatriots. Philosophers do – to use the jargon of the day – have a right side to their brains. If it's the left side we contribute (or mainly should), that's because what talents we have reside there.

6 How to proceed? We begin by asking how the moral status of animals has been understood by thinkers who deny that animals have rights. Then we test the mettle of their ideas by seeing how well they stand up under the heat of fair criticism. If we start our thinking in this way, we soon find that some people believe that we have no duties directly to animals, that we owe nothing to them, that we can do nothing that wrongs them. Rather, we can do wrong acts that involve animals, and so we have duties regarding them, though none to them. Such views may be called indirect duty views. By way of illustration: suppose your neighbour kicks your dog. Then your neighbour has done something wrong. But not to your dog. The wrong that has been done is a wrong to you. After all, it is wrong to upset people, and your neighbour's kicking your dog upsets you. So you are the one who is wronged, not your dog. Or again: by kicking your dog your neighbour damages your property. And since it is wrong to damage another person's property, your neighbour has done something wrong – to you, of course, not to your dog. Your neighbour no more wrongs your dog than your car would be wronged if the windshield were smashed. Your neighbour's duties involving your dog are indirect duties to you. More generally, all of our duties regarding animals are indirect duties to one another – to humanity.

7 How could someone try to justify such a view? Someone might say that your dog doesn't feel anything and so isn't hurt by your neighbour's kick, doesn't care about the pain since none is felt, is as unaware of anything as is your windshield. Someone might say this, but no rational person will, since, among other considerations, such a view will commit anyone who holds it to the position that no human being feels pain either – that human beings also don't care about what happens to them. A second possibility is that though both humans and your dog are hurt when kicked, it is only human pain that matters. But, again, no rational person can believe this. Pain is pain wherever it occurs. If your neighbour's causing you pain is wrong because of the pain that is caused, we cannot rationally ignore or dismiss the moral relevance of the pain that your dog feels.

8 Philosophers who hold indirect duty views – and many still do – have come to understand that they must avoid the two defects just noted: that is, both the view that animals don't feel anything as well as the idea that only human pain can be morally relevant. Among such thinkers the sort of view now favoured is one or other form of what is called *contractarianism.*

9 Here, very crudely, is the root idea: morality consists of a set of rules that individuals voluntarily agree to abide by, as we do when we sign a contract (hence the name contractarianism). Those who understand and accept the terms of the contract are covered directly; they have rights created and

recognized by, and protected in, the contract. And these contractors can also have protection spelled out for others who, though they lack the ability to understand morality and so cannot sign the contract themselves, are loved or cherished by those who can. Thus young children, for example, are unable to sign contracts and lack rights. But they are protected by the contract nonetheless because of the sentimental interests of others, most notably their parents. So we have, then, duties involving these children, duties regarding them, but no duties to them. Our duties in their case are indirect duties to other human beings, usually their parents.

10 As for animals, since they cannot understand contracts, they obviously cannot sign; and since they cannot sign, they have no rights. Like children, however, some animals are the objects of the sentimental interest of others. You, for example, love your dog or cat. So those animals that enough people care about (companion animals, whales, baby seals, the American bald eagle), though they lack rights themselves, will be protected because of the sentimental interests of people. I have, then, according to contractarianism, no duty directly to your dog or any other animal, not even the duty not to cause them pain or suffering; my duty not to hurt them is a duty I have to those people who care about what happens to them. As for other animals, where no or little sentimental interest is present – in the case of farm animals, for example, or laboratory rats – what duties we have grow weaker and weaker, perhaps to vanishing point. The pain and death they endure, though real, are not wrong if no one cares about them.

11 When it comes to the moral status of animals, contractarianism could be a hard view to refute if it were an adequate theoretical approach to the moral status of human beings. It is not adequate in this latter respect, however, which makes the question of its adequacy in the former case, regarding animals, utterly moot. For consider: morality, according to the (crude) contractarian position before us, consists of rules that people agree to abide by. What people? Well, enough to make a difference – enough, that is, *collectively* to have the power to enforce the rules that are drawn up in the contract. That is very well and good for the signatories but not so good for anyone who is not asked to sign. And there is nothing in contractarianism of the sort we are discussing that guarantees or requires that everyone will have a chance to participate equally in framing the rules of morality. The result is that this approach to ethics could sanction the most blatant forms of social, economic, moral and political injustice, ranging from a repressive caste system to systematic racial or sexual discrimination. Might, according to this theory, does make right. Let those who are the victims of injustice suffer as they will. It matters not so long as no one else – no contractor, or too few of them – cares about it. Such a theory

takes one's moral breath away... as if, for example, there would be nothing wrong with apartheid in South Africa if few white South Africans were upset by it. A theory with so little to recommend it at the level of the ethics of our treatment of our fellow humans cannot have anything more to recommend it when it comes to the ethics of how we treat our fellow animals.

12 The version of contractarianism just examined is, as I have noted, a crude variety, and in fairness to those of a contractarian persuasion it must be noted that much more refined, subtle and ingenious varieties are possible. For example, John Rawls, in his *A Theory of Justice,* sets forth a version of contractarianism that forces contractors to ignore the accidental features of being a human being – for example, whether one is white or black, male or female, a genius or of modest intellect. Only by ignoring such features, Rawls believes, can we ensure that the principles of justice that contractors would agree upon are not based on bias or prejudice. Despite the improvement a view such as Rawls's represents over the cruder forms of contractarianism, it remains deficient: it systematically denies that we have direct duties to those human beings who do not have a sense of justice – young children, for instance, and many mentally retarded humans. And yet it seems reasonably certain that, were we to torture a young child or a retarded elder, we would be doing something that wronged him or her, not something that would be wrong if (and only if) other humans with a sense of justice were upset. And since this is true in the case of these humans, we cannot rationally deny the same in the case of animals.

13 Indirect duty views, then, including the best among them, fail to command our rational assent. Whatever ethical theory we should accept rationally, therefore, it must at least recognize that we have some duties directly to animals, just as we have some duties directly to each other...

14 Some people think that the theory we are looking for is utilitarianism. A utilitarian accepts two moral principles. The first is that of equality; everyone's interests count, and similar interests must be counted as having similar weight or importance. White or black, American or Iranian, human or animal – everyone's pain or frustration matter, and matter just as much as the equivalent pain or frustration of anyone else. The second principle a utilitarian accepts is that of utility: do the act that will bring about the best balance between satisfaction and frustration for everyone affected by the outcome.

15 As a utilitarian, then, here is how I am to approach the task of deciding what I morally ought to do: I must ask who will be affected if I choose to do one thing rather than another, how much each individual will be affected, and where the best results are most likely to lie – which option, in other words, is most likely to bring about the best results, the best balance between

satisfaction and frustration. That option, whatever it may be, is the one I ought to choose. That is where my moral duty lies.

16 The great appeal of utilitarianism rests with its uncompromising *egalitarianism:* everyone's interests count and count as much as the like interests of everyone else. The kind of odious discrimination that some forms of contractarianism can justify – discrimination based on race or sex, for example – seems disallowed in principle by utilitarianism, as is speciesism, systematic discrimination based on species membership.

17 The equality we find in utilitarianism, however, is not the sort an advocate of animal or human rights should have in mind. Utilitarianism has no room for the equal moral rights of different individuals because it has no room for their equal inherent value or worth. What has value for the utilitarian is the satisfaction of an individual's interest, not the individual whose interests they are. A universe in which you satisfy your desire for water, food and warmth is, other things being equal, better than a universe in which these desires are frustrated. And the same is true in the case of an animal with similar desires. But neither you nor the animal have any value in your own right. Only your feelings do.

18 Here is an analogy to help make the philosophical point clearer: a cup contains different liquids, sometimes sweet, sometimes bitter, sometimes a mix of the two. What has value are the liquids: the sweeter the better, the bitterer the worse. The cup, the container, has no value. It is what goes into it, not what they go into, that has value. For the utilitarian you and I are like the cup; we have no value as individuals and thus no equal value. What has value is what goes into us, what we serve as receptacles for; our feelings of satisfaction have positive value, our feelings of frustration negative value.

19 Serious problems arise for utilitarianism when we remind ourselves that it enjoins us to bring about the best consequences. What does this mean? It doesn't mean the best consequences for me alone, or for my family or friends, or any other person taken individually. No, what we must do is, roughly, as follows: we must add up (somehow!) the separate satisfactions and frustrations of everyone likely to be affected by our choice, the satisfactions in one column, the frustrations in the other. We must total each column for each of the options before us. That is what it means to say the theory is aggregative. And then we must choose that option which is most likely to bring about the best balance of totalled satisfactions over totalled frustrations. Whatever act would lead to this outcome is the one we ought morally to perform – it is where our moral duty lies. And that act quite clearly might not be the same one that would bring about the best results for me personally, or for my family or

friends, or for a lab animal. The best aggregated consequences for everyone concerned are not necessarily the best for each individual.

20 That utilitarianism is an aggregative theory – different individuals' satisfactions or frustrations are added, or summed, or totalled – is the key objection to this theory. My Aunt Bea is old, inactive, a cranky, sour person, though not physically ill. She prefers to go on living. She is also rather rich. I could make a fortune if I could get my hands on her money, money she intends to give me in any event, after she dies, but which she refuses to give me now. In order to avoid a huge tax bite, I plan to donate a handsome sum of my profits to a local children's hospital. Many, many children will benefit from my generosity, and much joy will be brought to their parents, relatives and friends. If I don't get the money rather soon, all these ambitions will come to naught. The once-in-a-life-time opportunity to make a real killing will be gone. Why, then, not kill my Aunt Bea? Oh, of course I *might* get caught. But I'm no fool and, besides, her doctor can be counted on to co-operate (he has an eye for the same investment and I happen to know a good deal about his shady past). The deed can be done... professionally, shall we say. There is *very* little chance of getting caught. And as for my conscience being guilt-ridden, I am a resourceful sort of fellow and will take more than sufficient comfort – as I lie on the beach at Acapulco – in contemplating the joy and health I have brought to so many others.

21 Suppose Aunt Bea is killed and the rest of the story comes out as told. Would I have done anything wrong? Anything immoral? One would have thought that I had. Not according to utilitarianism. Since what I have done has brought about the best balance between totalled satisfaction and frustration for all those affected by the outcome, my action is not wrong. Indeed, in killing Aunt Bea the physician and I did what duty required.

22 This same kind of argument can be repeated in all sorts of cases, illustrating, time after time, how the utilitarian's position leads to results that impartial people find morally callous. It *is* wrong to kill my Aunt Bea in the name of bringing about the best results for others. A good end does not justify an evil means. Any adequate moral theory will have to explain why this is so. Utilitarianism fails in this respect and so cannot be the theory we seek.

23 What to do? Where to begin anew? The place to begin, I think, is with the utilitarian's view of the value of the individual – or, rather, lack of value. In its place, suppose we consider that you and I, for example, do have value as individuals – what we'll call *inherent value.* To say we have such value is to say that we are something more than, something different from, mere receptacles. Moreover, to ensure that we do not pave the way for such injustices as slavery or sexual discrimination, we must believe that all who have inherent value

have it equally, regardless of their sex, race, religion, birthplace and so on. Similarly to be discarded as irrelevant are one's talents or skills, intelligence and wealth, personality or pathology, whether one is loved and admired or despised and loathed. The genius and the retarded child, the prince and the pauper, the brain surgeon and the fruit vendor, Mother Teresa and the most unscrupulous used-car salesman – all have inherent value, all possess it equally, and all have an equal right to be treated with respect, to be treated in ways that do not reduce them to the status of things, as if they existed as resources for others. My value as an individual is independent of my usefulness to you. Yours is not dependent on your usefulness to me. For either of us to treat the other in ways that fail to show respect for the other's independent value is to act immorally, to violate the individual's rights.

24 Some of the rational virtues of this view – what I call the rights view – should be evident. Unlike (crude) contractarianism, for example, the rights view *in principle* denies the moral tolerability of any and all forms of racial, sexual or social discrimination; and unlike utilitarianism, this view *in principle* denies that we can justify good results by using evil means that violate an individual's rights – denies, for example, that it could be moral to kill my Aunt Bea to harvest beneficial consequences for others. That would be to sanction the disrespectful treatment of the individual in the name of the social good, something the rights view will not – categorically will not – ever allow.

25 The rights view, I believe, is rationally the most satisfactory moral theory. It surpasses all other theories in the degree to which it illuminates and explains the foundation of our duties to one another – the domain of human morality. On this score it has the best reasons, the best arguments, on its side. Of course, if it were possible to show that only human beings are included within its scope, then a person like myself, who believes in animal rights, would be obliged to look elsewhere.

26 But attempts to limit its scope to humans only can be shown to be rationally defective. Animals, it is true, lack many of the abilities humans possess. They can't read, do higher mathematics, build a bookcase or make *baba ghanoush.* Neither can many human beings, however, and yet we don't (and shouldn't) say that they (these humans) therefore have less inherent value, less of a right to be treated with respect, than do others. It is the *similarities* between those human beings who most clearly, most non-controversially have such value (the people reading this, for example), not our differences, that matter most. And the really crucial, the basic similarity is simply this: we are each of us the experiencing subject of a life, a conscious creature having an individual welfare that has importance to us whatever our usefulness to others. We want and prefer things, believe and feel things, recall

and expect things. And all these dimensions of our life, including our pleasure and pain, our enjoyment and suffering, our satisfaction and frustration, our continued existence or our untimely death – all make a difference to the quality of our life as lived, as experienced, by us as individuals. As the same is true of those animals that concern us (those who are eaten and trapped, for example), they too must be viewed as the experiencing subjects of a life, with inherent value of their own.

27 Some there are who resist the idea that animals have inherent value. 'Only humans have such value,' they profess. How might this narrow view be defended? Shall we say that only humans have the requisite intelligence, or autonomy, or reason? But there are many, many humans who fail to meet these standards and yet are reasonably viewed as having value above and beyond their usefulness to others. Shall we claim that only humans belong to the right species, the species *Homo Sapiens?* But this is blatant speciesism. Will it be said, then, that all – and only – humans have immortal souls? Then our opponents have their work cut out for them. I am myself not ill-disposed to the proposition that there are immortal souls. Personally, I profoundly hope I have one. But I would not want to rest my position on a controversial ethical issue on the even more controversial question about who or what has an immortal soul. That is to dig one's hole deeper, not to climb out. Rationally, it is better to resolve moral issues without making more controversial assumptions than are needed. The question of who has inherent value is such a question, one that is resolved more rationally without the introduction of the idea of immortal souls than by its use.

28 Well, perhaps some will say that animals have some inherent value, only less than we have. Once again, however, attempts to defend this view can be shown to lack rational justification. What could be the basis of our having more inherent value than animals? Their lack of reason, or autonomy, or intellect? Only if we are willing to make the same judgement in the case of humans who are similarly deficient. But it is not true that such humans – the retarded child, for example, or the mentally deranged – have less inherent value than you or I. Neither, then, can we rationally sustain the view that animals, like them in being the experiencing subjects of a life, have less inherent value. *All* who have inherent value have it *equally,* whether they be human animals or not.

29 Inherent value, then, belongs equally to those who are the experiencing subjects of a life. Whether it belongs to others – to rocks and rivers, trees and glaciers, for example – we do not know and may never know. But neither do we need to know, if we are to make the case for animal rights. We do not need to know, for example, how many people are eligible to vote in the next

presidential election before we can know whether I am. Similarly, we do not need to know how many individuals have inherent value before we can know that some do. When it comes to the case for animal rights, then, what we need to know is whether the animals that, in our culture, are routinely eaten, hunted and used in our laboratories, for example, are like us in being subjects of a life. And we do know this. We do know that many – literally, billions and billions – of these animals are the subjects of a life in the sense explained and so have inherent value if we do. And since, in order to arrive at the best theory of our duties to one another, we must recognize our equal inherent value as individuals, reason – not sentiment, not emotion – reason compels us to recognize the equal inherent value of these animals and, with this, their equal right to be treated with respect.

30 That, *very* roughly, is the shape and feel of the case for animal rights. Most of the details of the supporting argument are missing. They are to be found in the book to which I alluded earlier. Here, the details go begging, and I must, in closing, limit myself to four final points.

31 The first is how the theory that underlies the case for animal rights shows that the animal rights movement is a part of, not antagonistic to, the human rights movement. The theory that rationally grounds the rights of animals also grounds the rights of humans. Thus those involved in the animal rights movement are partners in the struggle to secure respect for human rights – the rights of women, for example, or minorities, or workers. The animal rights movement is cut from the same moral cloth as these.

32 Second, having set out the broad outlines of the rights view, I can now say why its implications for... science, among other fields, are both clear and uncompromising. In the case of the use of animals in science, the rights view is categorically abolitionist. Lab animals are not our tasters; we are not their kings. Because these animals are treated routinely, systematically as if their value were reducible to their usefulness to others, they are routinely, systematically treated with a lack of respect, and thus are their rights routinely, systematically violated. This is just as true when they are used in studies that hold out real promise of human benefits. We can't justify harming or killing a human being (my Aunt Bea, for example) just for these sorts of reason. Neither can we do so even in the case of so lowly a creature as a laboratory rat. It is not just refinement or reduction that is called for, not just larger, cleaner cages, not just more generous use of anaesthetic or the elimination of multiple surgery, not just tidying up the system. It is complete replacement. The best we can do when it comes to using animals in science is – not to use them. That is where our duty lies, according to the rights view...

33 My last two points are about philosophy, my profession. It is, most obviously, no substitute for political action. The words I have written here and in other places by themselves don't change a thing. It is what we do with the thoughts that the words express – our acts, our deeds – that changes things. All that philosophy can do, and all I have attempted, is to offer a vision of what our deeds should aim at. And the why. But not the how.

34 Finally, I am reminded of my thoughtful critic, the one I mentioned earlier, who chastised me for being too cerebral. Well, cerebral I have been: indirect duty views, utilitarianism, contractarianism – hardly the stuff deep passions are made of. I am also reminded, however, of the image another friend once set before me – the image of the ballerina as expressive of disciplined passion. Long hours of sweat and toil, of loneliness and practice, of doubt and fatigue: those are the discipline of her craft. But the passion is there too, the fierce drive to excel, to speak through her body, to do it right, to pierce our minds. That is the image of philosophy I would leave with you, not 'too cerebral' but *disciplined passion.* Of the discipline enough has been seen. As for the passion: there are times, and these not infrequent, when tears come to my eyes when I see, or read, or hear of the wretched plight of animals in the hands of humans. Their pain, their suffering, their loneliness, their innocence, their death. Anger, Rage. Pity. Sorrow. Disgust. The whole creation groans under the weight of the evil we humans visit upon these mute, powerless creatures. It *is* our hearts, not just our heads, that call for an end to it all, that demand of us that we overcome, for them, the habits and forces behind their systematic oppression. All great movements, it is written, go through three stages: ridicule, discussion, adoption. It is the realization of this third stage, adoption, that requires both our passion and our discipline, our hearts and our heads. The fate of animals is in our hands. God grant we are equal to the task.

Notes

* From *In Defence of Animals*, Peter Singer (ed.) Blackwell, 1985; this slightly abridged version is taken from *Animal Experimentation,* Robert H. Baird and Stuart E. Rosenbaum (eds.), Prometheus Books, 1991.

'Equality, Women and Animals'

Mary Midgley

In *Animals and Why They Matter,* Midgley sets the topic of our moral relations with animals in the wider context of some central themes in the history of political and general philosophy, and biological and evolutionary considerations. In the chapters from which these extracts are taken,* she explores the ways in which speciesism is like racism and sexism in failing to extend the principle of equality 'across the species-barrier'. She surveys some of the history of our thoughts about equality, illustrating the ways in which, in the past, our forebears have always overlooked the justifiable claims of some under-privileged group and claims that we are now making the same mistake regarding animals.

1 Equality and outer darkness

1.1 Can animals be equal?

It is not till the last decade that philosophers have seriously and persistently extended the concept of equality, and that of basic natural rights, to animals. But they have done it now. 'All animals are equal... No matter what the nature of the being, the principle of equality requires that its suffering be counted equally with the like suffering – in so far as rough comparisons can be made – of any other being' (Peter Singer). And on rights, 'Within an absolute context it is difficult to see how any of us, men or beasts, have any rights at all; and we certainly therefore have no rights upon them. In less absolute terms, any principle, or prince, that accords rights to the weak of our own species must also accord them to animals' (Stephen Clark). Again – 'The right not to be tortured, then, is shared by all animals that suffer pain; it is not a distinctively human right at all,' and 'Whatever rationale is provided for granting humans a right to liberty, it seems that a relevantly similar one is available in the case of at least some other species of animals' (James Rachels). Of course not all philosophers agree, but the disagreement has so far focused mainly on the proper use of words like *rights* and *equality* rather than on defending traditional dismissive habits of thought and practice as a whole. Moreover the interesting term *speciesism* has been coined to describe discrimination against non-humans, thereby branding it as an offence against equality, parallel to racism, sexism, ageism and the like. Isolated writers had said these things before, but this is the first large-scale attempt to extend liberal concepts to the borders of sentience.

Historically, this movement was made possible by the other liberation movements of the sixties, converging with the increasing interest in animals... an interest which has for the first time begun to publicize the relevant facts widely. Books and films about wild life have told people something about the complexities of animal existence and its likenesses to human existence, and also about the widespread threats of extinction, which are themselves a new feature of our age, never considered in traditional thought. At the same time, books and films about such things as factory farming have been able, though with much more difficulty, to spread some information about how animals are actually treated within our civilization. And again, many of the practices revealed are themselves new; tradition is dumb on how to regard them. The discrepancy revealed between ideals and practice is bound to bring into play concepts like equality and natural rights. This move, however, is not just a historical accident. Logically, these concepts demand this use as soon as it is open to them, because they have no built-in limit. They are essentially tools for widening concern, and concern, though it may attenuate with distance, is certainly possible in principle towards anything which we suppose to feel. Normally prejudice restricts it, but these concepts exist to break down prejudice, as they have repeatedly done. They are essentially destructive. Along with notions like liberty and fraternity, they work to dissolve the screens of callous habit and reveal hidden injustice. All these concepts are vague. All must be supplemented, once their work of revelation is done, by other, more detailed and discriminating ideas. But vague though they are, they are very powerful. They melt away the confused excuses given by custom, appealing from local laws and usage to the deeper standards required for change. Everybody who wants reform must sometimes use such concepts, but perhaps all those who do so are sometimes appalled at what they reveal, and find themselves retreating in alarm behind some ill-chosen bush. We must shortly glance at the record of these evasions in the case of the cluster of liberal, French-revolutionary concepts which are our present business. Repeatedly, even people who have used them well have set up crude barriers to halt them at various frontiers, notably those of race and sex – barriers which have crumbled scandalously as soon as they were examined. The dialectical road-block so far thrown up at the species-barrier is not less crude than these were, but far more so, because it has received even less attention. Anyone hoping to reinforce it will have to do the job over again from scratch.

This does not mean that there is nothing wrong with the liberal concepts themselves. They are notoriously obscure. It may well be sensible to halt them for interpretation and replacement long before they reach the species-barrier. But if one does not do this – if one puts complete confidence in notions like equality and natural rights – one lies open to Peter Singer's challenge. His opening chapter, indeed, is directed specially to egalitarians; it has the fighting title 'All Animals are Equal, or Why Supporters of Liberation for Blacks and Women Should Support Animal Liberation Too'. This does not mean, however, that conservatives on these matters can ignore the whole business. In our civilization, everyone who thinks at all has an egalitarian element in his thinking. We all need to clear up these concepts.

1.2 The problem of extent

What, firstly, about equality? This is a rather abstract ideal, distinguished from most others by needing a great deal of background before it can be applied. Who is to be made equal to whom, and in what respect? Historically, the answers given have mostly concerned rather narrow groups. The ordinary citizens of a particular state – often a small one, such as Athens or Rome – demand to share certain powers of a still smaller group, such as their nobility, on the ground that they are all already equally *citizens*. The formula needed is something like 'let those who are already equal in respect *x* be, as is fitting, equal also in respect *y*'. Outsiders, such as slaves, foreigners and women, who are currently not equal in respect *x*, cannot benefit from this kind of argument. It requires a limited public.

The notion of equality is a tool for rectifying injustices within a given group, not for widening that group or deciding how it ought to treat those outside it. As is often necessary for reform, it works on a limited scale. Those working for equality take a certain group (such as that of Athenian citizens) for granted, and ask in what ways the nature of that group dictates that its members should be equal. This question is well expressed by social-contract language: what are its members here for? why did they form it? what, merely by belonging to it, do they agree to do? As we shall see, answers to this vary. But this variation does not affect the main point – namely, that the binding principle of the group tends to emerge as the basis of political obligation, and is easily extended to account for *all* obligation. This is no accident, for it is a central purpose of social-contract thinking to demolish a certain set of non-contractual moral principles – namely, those which tell citizens to obey their betters regardless of their own choice and interest. It demolishes these by applying a strong reducing agent – egoism. It asks, 'Why should I obey the government?' and accepts only answers delivered in terms of self-interest. There is much to be said for this. But when the same process is applied to other sorts of moral principle, results are much less satisfactory. Problems concerning the relations of the group to those outside it, and possibilities of widening the group, as well as relations within the group itself which are not considered as part of its egoistic binding principle, become insoluble. The notion of moral agents as equal, standard units within a contractual circle which constitutes the whole of morality is a blind and limited one. Contract has its place in morality, not vice versa.

It may seem strange and paradoxical to suggest that the notion of equality has these self-defeating properties. We will look in a moment at instances which show the paradox in action. It is true, of course, that the snags are not part of the concept itself. They belong to its supporting apparatus. But since some apparatus of this kind seems needed to bring it into operation, it is very hard to avoid them. The concept itself, as I just remarked, is very abstract, and can in principle be extended to any limit. In theory, when slaves or the like are noticed, the 'equal' group can always be extended to include them. But in practice two things make this very hard. One is simply the well-known difficulty about realistic political objectives. It is hard enough already to persuade the nobility to treat all citizens as, in some particular respect, equal. If we try at the same time to include slaves in the argument, we may well destroy our chances. Reforming movements which won't set limited objectives simply fail; they are not serious. So the 'equal' group comes to be defined as, for instance, that of free citizens, and habit perpetuates this restriction even when it is no longer needed. The other trouble, which goes deeper and will occupy us longer, comes from invoking egoism as the bond which is to keep the equal units together. The private self-interest of group members is often best served by keeping the group small. Where, therefore, pooled self-interest replaces hierarchical bonds, things may become worse, not better, for those currently excluded from the group. And if the whole of morality is in some sense reduced to egoism, the objections to this way of thinking become very hard to state.

1.3 Egoism and the social contract

All contract theorists have, of course, seen that there are difficulties about reducing morality to contract, and not all of them want to move far in this direction. The fervour with which they insist on reduction varies according to the violence of the emergency which they see before them. Hobbes, facing the bleak savagery of the seventeenth-century wars of religion, used a simple, sweeping version of contract theory, aimed at getting rid of all those numerous aspects of morality which he thought led to general destruction, and particularly self-destruction. He took the original respect in which people were equal, *x,* to be simply the power to kill. Everybody is strong enough to kill somebody else some time, and without a contract he may always do it. Since death is incomparably the worst possible disaster for each of us, that distressing fact alone is what makes it worth everyone's while to sign the contract, and equal protection of life is what they all gain. This self-preservatory decision is then the source of all obligation. For Hobbes, obligation simply *is* the fear of danger to one's life if a regulation is neglected. To make this doctrine work, the various duties and virtues have to be twisted into some very strange shapes; in particular 'the definition of INJUSTICE is no other than *the not performance of contract*'.

But it is impossible to extract from this tiny hat that large rabbit, morality. People expect and owe to each other much more than life and the means to life – certainly more than not-killing – and also much more than justice, even if justice is given a wider and more natural definition than Hobbes gives it. Human psychology is altogether not what he hopes for. People do not live in the future to this extent. They are (as their conduct constantly shows) much less interested in just surviving than Hobbes suggested, less prudent, less clever, less farsighted, less single-minded, and much more interested in having the sort of life which they think satisfactory while they do survive.

1.4 The importance of freedom

Hobbes, of course, wrote in an age of civil war, and has special reason to dwell on death. ('The Passion to be reckoned upon is Fear.') He therefore stressed above all the value of the state as a life-preserver, and described the outer darkness, the state of nature, as a state of war – a 'war of every man against every man'. Rousseau, in more peaceful times, took the life-preserving job as done and looked past it to other aims. He asked, now that we are surviving, what do we want the state to do for us? He answered that above all we want it to make us free and independent, to preserve us from every form of slavery. We want equality, not as an end in itself, but 'because liberty cannot exist without it'. The degree of equality we want is therefore simply that which will make it impossible for anybody to enslave anybody, whether by violence, rank or commercial pressure. The emphasis has now shifted from viewing everybody as equally a possible threat to viewing them as originally equal in their capacity and wish for independence. (Thus Émile is to be taught 'to live rather than to avoid death' and to live in the present.) That capacity and wish for independence must be explained. Rousseau explains them by an admittedly mythical description of primitive man as originally solitary and speechless, each person being able to maintain him or herself alone, wandering separately in the woods like bears, and hardly ever meeting. He found it a standing paradox and tragedy that civilization had sacrificed this primitive independence to other, less crucial advantages.

In spite of its staggering implausibility, this myth of primal solitude has a solid moral point. It means simply that people – as they are now – are potentially autonomous, capable of free choice, wanting it and needing to have a say in their own destiny. Rousseau's remark that 'man is born free' means that people are not beings like ants, shaped by and for their community and unable to exist without it, but are true individuals who can live alone, and can therefore stand aside from it and criticize it. Émile, once grown up, is directed to travel, to see many societies and put himself in a position to ask 'Which is my country?'

This native capacity and wish for independence is what makes it necessary that the contract shall be so framed that 'all, being born free and equal, alienate their liberty only for their own advantage'. In this way 'each, while uniting himself with all, may still obey himself alone and remain as free as before' so that 'men who may be unequal in strength or intelligence become every one equal by convention and legal right'. Any other kind of contract is a fraud. The contract now ceases to appear as a single area of light and safety, immediately surrounded by outer darkness. It is more like a patch of fertile country, chosen and fenced for improvement, but surrounded by a much larger expanse of very similar terrain, which shares most of the characteristics which make the enclosed land attractive. Social motivation is something far wider than political order.

1.5 The natural need for freedom

Now to conceive the social contract in this way involves certain psychological views about the kind of beings who make it, that is, about human nature. *Nature* is here, as usual, a fruitfully ambiguous word, combining related views about facts and values. Why is independence so important to *Homo Sapiens?* Why is it not better to live under a benevolent despotism on the lines of *Brave New World*? Rousseau's – or anyone's – reasons for rejecting this suggestion are in part factual, involving evidence about people's actual capacities and wishes, and in part moral, involving objections to certain ways of treating these: (1) People are not like ants, and (2) it would therefore be wrong to treat them as if they were. But neither these facts nor these moral judgements are derived from contract. They are the considerations which make this kind of contract necessary. Rousseau was always willing to appeal to distinct psychological and moral principles in order to explain why the contract had to take this special form.

In passing, it must be noticed at this point that bears are not ants either, nor are they cog-wheels. They, like people, are true individuals. The kind of liberty which Rousseau celebrates here is one which all the higher animals can share, and which all desire. It is outward liberty. It is not a rarefied, intellectual brand of free-will, depending on advanced thought and speech. It is a plain matter of not being imprisoned, bullied and oppressed, of having one's own way.

This outward freedom is what the self-governing devices of the contract are designed to secure. (Free-will, notoriously, cannot be produced by institutions and, if present, can survive in gaol.) Outer freedom does indeed give scope for a much wider inner freedom, which different species will use each in their own way, and for people, freedom of thought and speech will follow. But to see this, one must know the facts about the constitution of the various creatures concerned. And adaptation to liberty is a fact about the constitution of bear as well as man.

This appeal to natural facts – indeed to any considerations other than the contract itself – always causes political alarm, because the beauty of contract ethics is its simplicity. The contract myth – which is never regarded as literal history – is essentially a fence against arbitrary tyranny. It exists to make authority depend on the consent of the governed. Its main use is to cut out other, more superficial and biased, supposed sources of political obligation. It appears at its best in the opening chapters of the *Contrat Social,* where Rousseau makes hay of the jumbled religious-cum-historical theories which were used in his day to shore up the remains of feudalism. Rousseau's derision was a proper answer to theorists who derived the obligation of subjects from the right of conquest, implying that conquerors were entitled to perpetual obedience from the descendants of those they enslaved, or from the supposed biblical ancestry of kings. Nothing but the general will of the governed, he said, could relevantly justify government. As a lever for dislodging unwanted rulers, this principle is excellent. But where that is no longer the problem, difficulties crowd in. Now that we are demanding something more than mere survival from the contract, we shall need a different sort of inducement to obey the general will. Is that will infallible in promoting the liberty we now want, or can it make mistakes? If it can, must no other considerations besides actual consent be relevant after all? In disputes, might not the minority be right? What, in that case, binds the non-consentors to obey their fallible government? And – still more puzzlingly – what binds those who were never consulted at all, such as foreigners? What, in particular, binds women? All these questions except the last seemed to Rousseau extremely serious. He admitted the tension between the simplicity of contract and the complexity of morality as real, and he made tremendous efforts to resolve it. He never fell back on Hobbes's simple, reductive solution of eliminating one pole – reducing morality at a stroke to enlightened self-interest, expressed in contract. He saw conflicts about political obligation as real, because he understood that human psychology was complex.

1.6 The difficulty of looking downwards

The last question, however, struck him as merely a joke, and a joke in bad taste. It was perfectly obvious to him that women's consent to the contract was not needed, and he resented questions about the matter which could only tend to parody his own contentions, distracting people from the serious business of reform. Before glancing at the arguments with which Rousseau and others have justified this dismissal, we have to notice here, as a gloomy general feature of revolutions, something which may be called the Paradox of One-Way Equality. Inequalities above one's own level tend to be visible: those below it to be hidden. This is not just a joke; there is a real conceptual difficulty involved. For instance, readers of *Animal Farm,* encountering the principle 'All Animals are Equal' usually take it to mean that all animals are, in fact, equal. They are mistaken. It refers only to farm animals. In the first flush of revolution, these animals do suggest, and uncertainly agree, that rats are comrades. Attempts to act on this idea, however, peter out almost at once, and the only other outside candidates ever named are rabbits. Foxes, badgers, hedgehogs, deer, mice, voles, weasels etc. and the whole tribe of wild birds, as well as everything smaller, are simply forgotten. It is interesting, though depressing, to see the same principle at work throughout the liberation movements of the sixties; each group of oppressed people, on sighting another, tended at once to see it as a distracting competitor, not as a friend and ally. The story is dismal. It is summed up in the reply of Stokely Carmichael, the noted Black Power leader, to black women who offered to work for his cause – 'The only place for women in the SNCC is prone.' Equally and on the other hand, nineteenth-century women, struggling against odds for the right to education and interesting work, took for granted the cheap labour of uneducated female servants. (It was still common, during my own childhood before the war, for professional women to refuse on principle to do even the simplest cookery or housework, in order to protect their status. The group they identified with was defined by class as well as by sex.) It is amazingly hard even to conceive, let alone to fight for, serious widening of one's group at the same time as trying to equalize status within it. This difficulty is a real limitation on the use of the idea of equality itself and those ideas related to it. Another striking instance is the development of democracy at Athens, where, with infinite efforts, they forged and defended that *isonomia* – equality before the law – of which, as Herodotus said, 'the very name is most beautiful'. This they did while their women were all incarcerated in harems and their daily labour done by slaves. The American Declaration of Independence, likewise, proclaims the proud belief that all men are created free and equal, while explicitly excluding women and implicitly (as far as some of the signatories went) non-European slaves as well. We call this kind of thing hypocrisy, and no doubt rightly. But... hypocrisy is not a simple matter. It is rather seldom the full-scale Tartuffe phenomenon of fully conscious deception. In most of us most of the time, it indicates conflict and confusion. To call hypocrisy 'the tribute which vice pays to virtue' is not just to point out that Tartuffe finds dissimulation worth his while. It is also to observe that people cannot all at once become quite good, any more than they can all at once become utterly villainous. Havering and inconsistency are a condition of most human attempts at goodness. They are often best understood by giving them the benefit of the doubt – by viewing them dynamically as real attempts, and trying to see what blocks them. (This is not a defence of inconsistency, it is a suggestion about how to deal with it.)

In the cases just mentioned, the facts so strangely ignored are visible to us today, partly in the way that paint on one's neighbour's face may be visible, because we are not inside them, and partly because others have already pointed them out. The work which used to be done by slaves is done for us by machines, invented and still produced through a good deal of industrial servitude, much of it in distant countries. Hypocrisy is not, as people seem sometimes to think, an exclusive patent of the Victorian age. Nobody sees everything. This patchiness of vision is certainly a fault, often a disastrous one, but it is a different fault from Tartuffery. When a privileged group tries to consider extensions of privilege, quite special difficulties arise about being sharp sighted. The notion that one has already drawn a correct and final line at which such extensions must end cannot be trusted at all. It is not trustworthy over animals.

2 *Women, animals and other awkward cases*

2.1 *The incommensurability of women: Rousseau*

These four distinct problems on which I have touched – the position of women, of slaves, of other races, and of non-human animals – have to be considered briefly together here, not because their logic is necessarily similar, but because their history is so. Inspected calmly and without passion, these four problems might look very different. What unites them is that they scarcely ever are so inspected. Admirable theorists, who have been giving scrupulous and impartial attention to other questions, tend, when one of these topics heaves up its head, to throw the first argument which occurs to them at it and run. This habit accounts for the sheer neglect of the animal question ...it has notoriously affected the other groups as well. On the rare occasions when these theorists do not run, but consider such matters more fully, their discussion often looks as if they had not written it themselves, but had left their paper for the afternoon to some weird secretary who wanted to discredit their doctrines. Aristotle's discussion of slavery in the first book of his *Politics* is not just immoral, but confused and helpless to a degree which is thoroughly out of character. He writes like a typical Athenian gentleman of his day, capable of seeing some difficulties and of expressing his conflicting prejudices clearly, but innocent of the skills of abstract thinking which might help him to resolve them. Hume and Kant, similarly, as soon as they mention 'the fair sex', lose all sense of what their general style of thinking demands, and simply recite clichés.

On this last topic, however, the really staggering example is Rousseau. Far from avoiding it, he discusses it at length, repeatedly and with great interest, but in the tones of exactly that pig-ignorant old pillar of crusted prejudice whose arguments he so rightly exposed in the *Social Contract.* Rousseau had described women in the state of nature as no less able and willing than men to live independently. One would expect, therefore, that they too would be signatories of the contract. But they are not. As soon as society is formed, their liberty simply vanishes without explanation. The fine thought that 'all... alienate their liberty only for their own advantage' does not apply to them. There is no question of their 'still obeying themselves alone and remaining as free as before'. It turns out that 'woman is specially made for man's delight'. This makes it their duty to submit entirely to men – a duty which does not depend, as all men's duties do, on free consent. In its details, this duty of submission is no sinecure. It involves complete, full-time devotion to pleasing their husbands, and when possible complete abstention from all other social activities – an abstention limited only by unavoidable concessions to the mistaken demands of a corrupt society. Complete seclusion on the Greek model is best; in any case 'the genuine mother of a family is no woman of the world. She is almost as much of a recluse as a nun in her convent.' There must be not only complete fidelity, but an unspotted reputation; to allow suspicion to arise is as bad as to justify it, and actual infidelity is treason. Girls 'should early be accustomed to restraint' because 'all their life long they will have to submit to the strictest and most enduring restraints, those of propriety... They have, or ought to have, little freedom... what is most wanted in a woman is gentleness; formed to obey a creature so imperfect as man, a creature often vicious and always faulty, she should early learn to submit to injustice and to suffer the wrongs inflicted on her by her husband without complaint.'

Rousseau defends this endorsement of chronic oppression, so ruinous to his whole libertarian position, with a few remarkably silly arguments, centring on the frightful danger of cuckoldry. These arguments, however, presumably satisfied him. His public, therefore, might reasonably ask next, 'If these arguments are valid, why not educate women to understand them, and to secure their consent to their peculiar social position on rational grounds, as would be done with anybody else?' Women are not, after all, the only people who must accept some disadvantages for the general good; and if they are stupid, so are many men. This he never considers. He is most unwilling to educate women at all, and concedes permission to teach them a little about the world only because their company will otherwise be too boring for their husbands. Even so, it will be best if spouses do not see much of each other. He takes it as obvious that allowing women to think will encourage them to revolt – which, indeed, it is, according to his general view of liberty. His demand is therefore that they shall do their incredibly onerous duty *without* ever seeing the point of it, from mere passive conditioning and a blind fear of public opinion – exactly the motives which he most wished to eliminate for men. '"What will people think?" is the grave of a man's virtue and the throne of a woman's.' 'The man should be strong and active; the woman should be weak and passive' and that mentally as well as physically. About religion, being 'unable to judge for themselves', they must simply accept the creed given to them, even if it is erroneous. Altogether, they need not make choices. Sophie, who has been properly educated, 'knows no course of conduct but the right'. 'The most virtuous woman in the world is she who knows least about virtue.' Sophie has read only two books, and those by chance ('What charming ignorance!').

These views on education are all the odder because, in considering male growth, Rousseau had vigorously stressed that human potentiality is unknown, and must not be read off from existing performance. Men as they are have all been corrupted by bad upbringing. Reformers must allow for this and look carefully for indications of the very different beings which boys can and should become. Over women, however, he drops this idea flat, and describes female nature directly from existing custom – indeed, from the customs of the more depressing sections of the French upper classes. 'Women were not meant to run.' A woman is a being who 'has hardly ventured out of doors without a parasol and who has scarcely put a foot to the ground'. Passive, weak and proud of her weakness she can get her way only by 'contriving to be ordered to do what she wants'. Little girls 'are flatterers and deceitful and soon learn to conceal their thoughts'; they 'always dislike learning to read and write'. 'A man says what he knows; a woman says what will please.' And practically speaking, in spite of their primitive foraging ability, women are a wash-out – 'Women, honour your master. He it is who works for you, he it is who gives you bread to eat; this is he!' A few pages later, he repeats almost verbatim parts of the libertarian manifesto of the *Contrat Social,* with its red-hot denunciation of slavery, and its promise that 'every man in obeying the sovereign only obeys himself'.

2.2 Psychological difficulties

Now all this is not just a sad but exceptional case-history of self-deception. The significance of Rousseau's little disagreement with himself here is twofold. First, indeed, it illustrates the pathology of egalitarianism, the emotional pressures and temptations obscuring the subject. But also, and more constructively, it lights up real conceptual difficulties about equality itself, difficulties which would be there however calm we might be.

First, then, the pathology. Of course this would not be relevant to controversy at all if it was a merely personal matter. And it may at first seem that it is so, because Rousseau's life was so strange. He had good emotional reasons for talking in this way. He was a shy, diffident, lonely, self-made person with plenty of experience of life at the bottom of the heap. As orphan apprentice, servant and destitute wanderer, he had fully felt the miseries of dependence. He climbed out of this slough partly by his own efforts, but also by the patronage of several strong-minded, well-read, argumentative, aristocratic ladies, and of men like Diderot and Baron d'Holbach, who could talk him into the ground. He was grateful, but all help wounded his pride, and increasingly the wounds festered. In middle life he began to see every friend as a patron and every patron as a secret enemy. In his private life – though seldom in his writings – his love of liberty grew paranoid, and he showed increasingly that grim twist of motivation which has wrecked so many revolutions: a resentment of tyranny which springs from a black desire to do the tyrannizing oneself. By way of compensation for dependence on his patronesses, he settled down with Thérèse le Vasseur, an illiterate and by his own account almost half-witted woman who, though often deceiving him, never openly opposed his wishes, and allowed him, though unwillingly, to dump their five children at birth in the Foundling Hospital. The terror of more formidable ladies, however, remained, and the last book of *Émile*, from which I have been quoting, fairly crackles with spite, resentment and fear. Inert though they may be, women, it seems, are still a horrible menace. If female modesty were relaxed, 'the men, tyrannized over by the women, would at last become their victims, and would be dragged to their death without the least chance of escape'. Women ought to accept their servitude because 'it is only fair that woman should bear her share of the ills she has brought upon men', and 'Women are more responsible for men's follies than men are for women's.'

Now this sort of thing, and the rest of Rousseau's tirade, is not just part of his personal case-history, because the attitudes to women expressed here have often been expressed elsewhere, and relied on seriously by people resisting reform. It *is* part of a case-history in being much more extreme than the views which most people – and indeed even Rousseau himself – live by most of the time. In itself, it is neurotic. But when a topic is not thought out clearly, people characteristically deal with it by leaping from one to another of a mixed set of attitudes, some of them often distinctly crazy. Crazy views not properly exorcised by thought are held in reserve, ready to fall back on if more reasonable ones become inconvenient. Chronic ambivalence paralyses thought. Thus the gradual emancipation of women during the nineteenth century was constantly blocked by openly irrational fears and resentments, similar to Rousseau's. His unbalanced character did not produce his misogyny; it only intensified and made him openly express an attitude which others shared. More cautious theorists, who undoubtedly also shared it, held their tongues, but attempts at practical reform always released the bats from the belfry.

Anyone who thinks it quite obvious that equality extends to, and stops exactly at, the species barrier should read the literature of women's emancipation as well as that of colonialism. Thus a member of parliament, opposing the Married Women's Property Bill of 1868, denounced the proposal that a wife should own any property as introducing 'a novel principle of civil equality between the sexes' and creating 'a factitious, an artificial and an unnatural equality between man and woman'. (The measure was thrown out, and did not become law till 1882.) About colonialism, it is striking how often the European emigrants to places like America and Australia disregarded the claims of the local inhabitants, although they themselves had often left home to escape the tyrannies and inequalities of Europe, and held explicit views opposed to these. Their attitude was, in practice, all the same in general often that of the Brazilian farmer who told a journalist investigating the native problem, 'Indians and pigs are the same thing. If either one comes on my land, I don't think twice – I kill them.'

[...]

2.3 Conceptual problems about equality

Let us turn now from the pathology – the emotional temptations infesting the subject – to the solid conceptual difficulties involved by the notion of equality. The trouble here is that the kind of equality put into the calculation is always adapted to what the reformers, on any particular occasion, hope to get out. Equality, like any concept used for practical reform, cannot be left vague. It must be put in specific terms because it is used to resist particular kinds of oppression, to redress particular pieces of injustice. Each kind of oppression has its own public, and the members of that public are those who for immediate purposes must be deemed equal. Suppose that the injustice in question is the arbitrary eviction of tenants, or wrongful dismissal from employment, or the seizure of people's means of livelihood by creditors. Redress for this will rightly be claimed on the grounds that the victims ought not – any more than richer people – to be deprived of their subsistence. But people who do not have a home, or a job, or tools, are left out of this reform; it does not concern them.

This does not mean that the reform is a mistaken one. It means that all actual reforms are limited, and that the notion of equality can only be used *after* one has decided which limitation one wants, for current purposes, to impose. Trade-union negotiations give the clearest example of what happens when equality is pursued as an end in itself, without reference to context – and that not only in South Africa. It is always possible to find a group of 'equals' within which one's own movement will be upwards. The relations between those inside and those outside this group has to be thought out separately in relation to justice, which is a much wider and more subtle concept. When the notion of equality is successfully used in a more general way (as it sometimes was in Athens and in the eighteenth-century revolutions), its users still always have in mind certain particular kinds of unjust privilege which are currently oppressive, such as those of the hereditary nobility. Equality is then defined by birth – but only within one's own country, since it is citizen rights that are in question. Resident aliens will have only limited rights, and there is no general commitment to allow the immigration of foreigners. Moreover, since it is taken for granted that the effective social unit is a household with a male head, women are excluded because they are women, children because they are children, lunatics etc. because they are lunatics etc., and slaves (if present) because they are slaves. With all these reservations – which are scarcely noticed by the people at the right end of them – it becomes possible to make considerable advances towards general liberty and social justice; advances which may, in the end, indeed benefit everybody.

Could this sort of patchiness have been entirely avoided? It is no business of this book to answer that question, but I think we must doubt it. It is hard to see how a large reform could start at the bottom, if only because that is where the scale is vastest. The usual pattern is for things to be improved, with great difficulty, in a certain small area, and for people then to ask, could not this be extended? Thus the theory of liberty and democracy was worked out in Greece, particularly in Athens, with much hard thinking and painful local experiment. This requires some leisure, and leisure means privilege. It was then used to subvert many of the institutions which gave it birth, such as slavery. Similarly, Marx had leisure to sit in the British Museum, supported largely by Engels on the proceeds of his clothing-factory, using the books written by many generations of those similarly privileged, in his efforts to change the world. Gandhi and others may well be right in saying that this kind of act is essentially sinister, and poisons all reform. But it is hard to see how to escape it entirely. What matters is that we do not allow the chance limitations to become part of the system. It is the destiny of any real reformer to be transcended, to have his insights applied in ways which would never have occurred to him, and so eventually to look, to a superficial observer, rather small-minded.

2.4 The importance of the unnoticed background

Let us stand back now to consider more generally what has emerged about the notion of equality. Both its strength and its weakness as a tool of reform depend (I have suggested) on its applying only to a limited, chosen group. To be in a position to demand equality, one must already have picked on a certain area of unfair privilege which one wants, and can hope, to remedy. Indefinite proposals are unreal; practical objectives must be limited. The notion of equality is useful because it has both the kind of versatility and the kind of rigidity needed for this purpose. It is flexible in that it can be variously applied. There are many respects in which the unfortunate can be shown to be equal to the fortunate. By choosing suitably their group, and their kind of equality, innovators can forcibly display the need for reform. The notion is rigid, on the other hand, in absolutely implying a frontier. It allows of no degrees. Unlike the older ideas of charity, hierarchy, fatherhood and the chain of being, it has no place for relations to subordinate creatures. Those who are not equal in the required respect are excluded altogether. Thus, from the rights of man women are simply excluded by definition, because they are not men. If the older ideas were not there to succour them, they would have no standing at all. Similarly, animals are flatly excluded from human rights, often just by definition of the term *human.* Those who notice that this is arbitrary often replace the term human by another, apparently more intelligible one, such as *reason* or *self-consciousness.* These terms, however, do not really change things because they do not have their ordinary meaning here. They are not treated as empirical descriptions, the names of observable qualities which might have degrees, but as marks of status, often with the explanatory tag 'what separates men from the beasts', as if it were absurdly obvious what this was. Empirical observations about the variety of intelligence or of ordinary self-consciousness among different kinds of animals are not allowed to affect them. This happens because they are thought to be necessary barriers to protect the frontier which the notion of equality requires.

Now this notional frontier has indeed been used to very good purpose in establishing the rights of oppressed human groups, particularly in resisting such practices as slavery, colonialism, infanticide and ill-treatment of the deranged. But this is no sort of reason for accepting its negative aspect, the dismissal of animals. This dismissal does not flow from thought, but only from negligence – the kind of negligence which constantly besets reformers when they consider, in passing, cases other than those on which they are actively engaged. This comes out strikingly in cases where ill-used humans are described as being *treated like animals.* If we are told that they were, say, herded into cattle-trucks and transported for days on end without food, rest or water, or that they were kept in a cage without exercise for passers-by to stare at, or that they were hunted down and shot for amusement, we are rightly appalled. But there is no argument leading from the fact that this is wrong treatment for humans to the proposition that it is right treatment for animals. This becomes clear if we consider the earlier cases where the rights of women or poor citizens were defended by insisting that they were not slaves. Nothing follows about whether it is right that slaves should be so treated. This question is simply not being asked. The lit area proposed for reform, on which the notion of equality asks us to concentrate, is always and by its nature surrounded by an area of outer darkness which we ignore. In principle there is nothing to stop us directing our spotlight onto it when we are ready to move on. But notions like equality, rights and even justice tend to imprison our attention in the area which has now become familiar.

Notes

* From *Animals and Why They Matter*, Penguin Books, 1983, Chapters 6 and 7.

'The Significance of Species'

Mary Midgley

Having argued that there are ways in which speciesism is like racism and sexism, Midgley goes on to argue, in the chapter from which this extract is taken,* that there are other ways in which it is unlike both of them, particularly racism. Giving preference to members of our own species, is, like giving preferences to members of one's own family, but unlike giving preferences to members of one's own race, neither always unfair, nor unreasonable.

1 Real and unreal groups

The term *speciesism* was invented, as we have seen, for a particular purpose, as a device to winkle out exclusively humanistic radicals from an inconsistent position. It quite properly followed, as the night the day, the similar invention of the term sexism. *Ad hominem,* for their original purposes, both these explosive charges were well placed and fully justified. Self-righteous revolutionaries who expected their women to type the manifestoes and bring the coffee, but remain otherwise dutifully silent, could scarcely complain if their theory was publicly contrasted with their practice. Their position was not improved if they cheerfully consumed battery pork and chicken. We have already touched on the distressing subject of endemic revolutionary humbug. We have also noticed that the rest of us are probably in no position to get very bloody-minded about it. Humbug, like flu, is extremely common. But it is still dangerous and must be attended to. The more exalted are the principles which people put forward, the more urgently do their inconsistencies need to be pointed out. Moreover, the closer their critics stick to the original wording, the plainer does their point become. That is why the original term *racism* has proved so fertile, spawning in turn sexism, ageism, speciesism, and uglyism to date, no doubt with more to come.

ad hominem move

For destructive purposes, I repeat, these terms are useful. But once the dust clears and the possible inconsistency is admitted, we need something more. To earn their keep, concepts must do more than suggest a surface likeness. What deeper parallels do these ideas show? In the case of speciesism, there appears at once a most awkward and damaging difference. Race in humans is not a significant grouping at all, but species in animals certainly is. It is never true that, in order to know how to treat a human being, you must first find out what race he belongs to. (Cases where this might seem to matter always really turn on culture.) But with an animal, to know the species is absolutely essential. A zoo-keeper who is told to expect an animal, and get a place ready for it, cannot even begin to do this without far more detailed information. It might be a hyena or a hippopotamus, a shark, an eagle, an armadillo, a python or a queen bee. Even members of quite similar and closely related species can have entirely different needs about temperature and water-supply, bedding, exercise-space, solitude, company and many other things. Their vision and experience of the world must therefore be profoundly different.

To liken a trivial human grouping such as race to this enormous, inconceivably varied range of possibilities is to indulge in what revolutionaries call 'patronizing' thinking – a failure to recognize the scale of difference between others and oneself. Overlooking somebody's race is entirely sensible. Overlooking their species is a supercilious insult.

[...]

2 Why is the species-bond so serious?

Questions about the morality of species preference must certainly be put in the context of the other preferences which people give to those closest to them. These preferences do indeed cause problems. By limiting human charity, they can produce terrible misery. On the other hand they are also an absolutely central element in human happiness, and it seems unlikely that we could live at all without them. They are the root from which charity grows. Morality shows a constant tension between measures to protect the sacredness of these special claims and counter-measurers to secure justice and widen sympathy for outsiders. To handle this tension by working out particular priorities is our normal moral business. In handling species conflicts, the notion of simply rejecting all discrimination as *speciesist* looks like a seductively simple guide, an all-purpose formula. I am suggesting that it is not simple, and that we must resist the seduction.

We have seen the difficulties which arise about its first element – the notion that all species other than our own should be treated alike. Singer himself, as it turns out, does not endorse this notion, since he takes account of their differing nervous capacities. What, then, about the more central component of speciesism, the preference normally given to our own species above others? Calling this preference a *prejudice* is treating it as unfair and unreasonable.

Now there are, broadly speaking, two things which can make a preference reasonable, namely value and bonding. There are difficulties about treating this preference as based simply on value. First, it is hard to find an impartial standpoint from which the judgement can be made. Second, there seems to be no attempt to weight the value of the most evil, or even the least capable, of our species against the best and ablest of others. In so far as the preference does depend on value, it can be seen as a direct preference for the value itself, without reference to species. But it is not handled like this. It is automatic. Criminals, however odious, are in general granted a fair trial; it is only in extraordinary cases that people think it in order to 'shoot them down like dogs'. By contrast, the World Federation for the Protection of Animals estimates that, throughout Europe, some five million dogs are destroyed each year merely because they are unwanted, many by animal welfare groups. Similarly, it is strongly argued that the lives of even the most miserably and incurably defective humans, even indeed of unconscious humans, or those anxious to die, may never be ended, that there can never be any question of 'putting them down' or even allowing them to release themselves. But primates may both be killed and experimented on freely. Degrees of capacity on either side of the human species-barrier are not allowed to affect this sharp divide.

J.B.S. Haldane, one of the great biologists of this century, pointed out that this raises real problems. As he remarked, such a proposition as:

> 'John Smith is a complete fool because he cannot oxidize phenylalanine' discloses a relation between mind and matter as surprising as transubstantiation, and a good deal better established. On the ethical side, it raises the problem of human rights in a rather sharp form. Has a hopeless idiot the right to life and care, though he or she is not a rational being nor likely to become one? If so, has a chimpanzee with considerably greater intelligence similar rights, and if not, why not?'
>
> (Introduction to *The Biology of Mental Defect* by Lionel Penrose (1949))

Haldane is certainly suggesting the answer 'yes' to both questions. The solution of current practice, however, is very different for the two cases. As we have seen it is hard to defend this difference on rationalist lines, by first insisting on the high value of human virtue, reason and language, and then building out awkward extensions to cover cases like John Smith's where some or all of these things are simply absent.

3 *The status of natural species-bonding*

Seeing this difficulty, people turn to a quite different line of defence and invoke bonding. An emotional, rather than a rational, preference for our own species is, they suggest, a necessary part of our social nature, in the same way that a preference for our own children is, and needs no more justification. We must look seriously at this position, in which there is, I think, a great deal of truth. The species-bond *is* strong, even outside the institutions which have been devised to protect it. The kind of reaction which makes Crusoe risk his life to save Friday from the cannibals really works. Crusoe was not at all a scrupulous fellow; he had killed and cheated and made his pile as a slave-trader. All the same, he feels instant horror at Friday's predicament, and accepts at once the claim silently made on him by the mere helpless humanity of a stranger. The instinctive bond is a real one. But, as Crusoe's earlier behaviour as a slave-trader, and indeed that of the cannibals, shows, its workings are by no means simple or reliable. Before trying to weigh its moral significance, we had better look at the facts about it.

The natural preference for one's own species does exist. It is not, like race-prejudice, a product of culture. It is found in all human cultures, and in cases of real competition it tends to operate very strongly. We can still ask, however, how far it takes us. Is it an irresistible motive, forcing us to dismiss outsiders from consideration? To prove that it was, we would have to show that the differential response to our own species was a far stronger emotional tendency than our differential response to our own tribe or our own children, because nobody doubts that our duty can sometimes call on us to subordinate tribal or family interest to that of outsiders. It would have to be so strong that all attempts to extend consideration to animals were doomed to failure as unnatural.

This is quite a different kind of point from the rationalist one. It is empirical rather than *a priori*. It rests its case, not on the articulateness or rationality of man as an abstract feature, but on sheer physical kinship and its emotional effect. It would presumably produce different conduct in many imaginable cases. For instance, rational alien beings would be honorary members of our moral community on the rationalist position, but not on this one, while non-rational human beings are a problem for rationalism, but not here. The suggestion is that our nature itself dictates where the border of morality shall fall, and aligns it once and for all with the species-barrier. What about this?

4 *Zoological probabilities*

First, it is plausible enough that our tendency to respond differentially to our own species is a natural one. All social creatures attend mostly to members of their own species, and usually ignore others. This can be clearly seen in such places as the Serengeti Plain, where large mixed herds of grazing animals live together in harmony, but do not acquire each other's habits, nor those of the predators who often roam among them. For any serious social purpose such as mating or fighting or gathering to deal with a danger, each normally seeks out its own group. This direction of attention (which seems necessary to the production of a viable species, standardized enough to use its own ecological niche) is partly secured by imprinting in infancy. So it is often possible for an infant placed in an alien group to grow up imprinted on it, and to imitate many of its habits. This infant, however, is just as bigoted about having only one species as a normal specimen. Even if many models are available for it, it sticks to imitating and loving its parent-substitute and those like it. If brought face to face later with members of its own species, it may transfer its allegiance to them, or more often reach an uneasy compromise between the two. But that is not the same thing as general neutrality.

The option of picking a mixed repertoire of behaviour from many species, of thinking all creatures literally and equally one's brothers, does not seem to be available. The tendency to species-choice as such does seem innate. Moreover, besides imprinting, there are always many detailed positive tendencies which are innate too. The adopted foal or duckling will never be fully integrated into its foster-species because many of the appropriate signals are impossible to it, and it has innate tastes of its own that will set it apart. It may live a reasonably contented life, and be unconscious of missing anything. But it will actually miss a great deal, because a whole range of its social capacities will never be tapped. A solitary duck reared among chickens will never get the clues it needs to perform many of its central behaviour-patterns. It shares some chicken activities, but by no means all. In some ways, too, it keeps getting itself misunderstood. It is therefore a deprived duck, just as it would be if it was kept away from water. Difficulties about mating illustrate this problem. Some species, even quite closely related ones, cannot mate together at all because of behavioural differences. Others can, but the hybrid offspring are not only themselves usually infertile, but unfitted for the full life of either species. Thus lion-tiger hybrids can exist in zoos, but would not have the neural co-ordinations needed for the very exacting, and totally different, hunting patterns of either species. They could therefore not rear young, even if they could produce them, so that if they survived in the wild, their lives would be very incomplete ones.

I think it is important to stress in this way that species-bonds are real, because unless we take account of them, the frequent exclusive attitude of our own species is hard to understand. There does indeed seem to be a deep emotional tendency, in us as in other creatures, to attend first to those around us who are like those who brought us up, and to take much less notice of others. And this, rather than some abstract judgement of value, does seem to be the main root of that relative disregard of other creatures which has been called 'speciesism'. I shall suggest in a moment that this natural tendency, though real, is nothing like so strong, simple and exclusive as is sometimes supposed, and has neither the force nor the authority to justify absolute dismissal of other species. A glance round the variety of human cultures will show that the extremely remote and contemptuous attitude sometimes taken in our own is neither typical nor necessary for *Homo Sapiens*. But before coming to this issue, it may be necessary to justify the suggestion that the reasons for species-exclusiveness in humans are in general of the same kind as those that move other creatures.

5 *The difficulties of species-neutrality*

To see this, we had better go back to our interplanetary situation. The virtuous and super-intelligent Quongs are offering to adopt human babies. Shall we let them? What do we need to know first? The first thing, I should guess, concerns emotional communication. Do the Quongs smile and laugh? Do they understand smiles and laughter? Do they cry or understand crying? Do they ever lose their temper? Does speech – or its equivalent – among them play the same sort of emotional part that it does in human life – for instance, do they greet, thank, scold, swear, converse, tell stories? How much time do they give to their own children? Then – what about play? Do they play with their young at all? If so, how? Then, what are their gender arrangements – meaning, of course, not just sexual activity, but the division into roles of the two (or more) participating genders, throughout life? What singing, dancing or other such activities have they? What meaning do they attach to such words as love? Without going any further, it seems clear that, unless they are the usual cheap substitute for alien beings which appears in films – that is, more or less people in make-up – we shall find that the answers to these questions give us some reasons to refuse their offer completely, even if reluctantly. And these reasons will be of the same kind that applied to the duckling. A human being needs a human life.

Is this sort of objection mere prejudice? Zoology would not say so. It would back our impression that, for a full life, a developing social creature needs to be surrounded by beings very similar to it in all sorts of apparently trivial ways, ways which abstractly might not seem important, but which will furnish essential clues for the unfolding of its faculties. Are there any counter-examples which could show us humans as an exception to this principle because of our flexibility? Stories of wolf-children etc. are hard to evaluate, partly because the actual evidence is slight, partly because all have died soon after capture. It seems impossible that a child should be brought up *from the start* by wolves or any other terrestrial species, because the sheer physical work needed is beyond them. (Mowgli seems to have reached his wolves at about the age of two, which is still remarkably early.) If in this way the thing could be done, the wolf-person would, presumably, have mixed imprinting and have gained some foothold in both worlds, but would be lonely in both – would be excluded from many central joys, and would keep getting himself misunderstood on both sides. Certainly he might gain some kinds of understanding which would be some compensation for this. But the price paid would be terribly heavy – a far deeper variety of 'being at home nowhere' than that which afflicts people brought up to oscillate between two cultures.

A much better way of handling serious inter-species relations is described in C.S. Lewis's delightful novel *Out of the Silent Planet.* This shows a world where three quite different intelligent species co-exist. They live in peace, do business together and respect each other, giving the name *hnau,* rational creatures, to their whole class, and including under that heading, in spite of occasional doubts, the visiting human beings. But most of the time each keeps to its own way of life and its own preferred kind of country. When they do meet, they get on reasonably well, but tend to find each other very funny. They differ considerably in their habits and interests, admire each other's specialities, and do not raise the question whose life is best. This arrangement shows species-loyalty as a quite unpretentious emotional matter, a bond, not an evaluation. And it rightly suggests that it need not determine the borders of social intercourse.

Notes

* From *Animals and Why They Matter,* Penguin Books, 1983, Chapter 9.

'The Moral Status of Animals'

Roger Scruton

In his booklet, the fox-hunting philosopher Roger Scruton discusses, in some detail, the differences between us and the other animals, and outlines his approach to moral thinking. He stresses the point that we, unlike all other animals, are persons – rational beings who form moral communities, have rights, responsibilities and duties, and thereby fall under 'the moral law'. Animals, since they are not such persons, cannot have rights.

However, this does not mean that we have no duties to them. Although our treatment of animals is not (by and large) governed by 'the moral law' (i.e. the calculus of rights and duties), it can be assessed as right or wrong in terms of further moral considerations, namely sympathy, piety and, quite generally, virtue and vice. In the section of the booklet reprinted below,* Scruton discusses a variety of areas of our treatment of animals in these terms.

Non-moral beings

1 The account of moral reasoning that I have just sketched offers an answer, even if not a fully reasoned answer, to the question of animals. In developing this answer, I shall use the term 'animal' to mean those animals that lack the distinguishing features of the moral being – rationality, self-consciousness, personality, and so on. If there are non-human animals who are rational and self-conscious, then they, like us, are persons, and should be described and treated accordingly. If *all* animals are persons, then there is no longer a problem as to how we should treat them. They would be full members of the moral community, with rights and duties like the rest of us. But it is precisely because there are animals who are not persons that the moral problem exists. And to treat these non-personal animals as persons is not to

grant to them a privilege nor to raise their chances of contentment. It is to ignore what they essentially are, and so to fall out of relation with them altogether.

2 The concept of the person belongs to the ongoing dialogue which binds the moral community. Creatures who are by nature incapable of entering into this dialogue have neither rights nor duties nor personality. If animals had rights, then we should require their consent before taking them into captivity, training them, domesticating them or in any way putting them to our uses. But there is no conceivable process whereby this consent could be delivered or withheld. Furthermore, a creature with rights is duty-bound to respect the rights of others. The fox would be duty-bound to respect the right to life of the chicken, and whole species would be condemned out of hand as criminal by nature. Any law which compelled persons to respect the rights of non-human species would weigh so heavily on the predators as to drive them to extinction in a short while. Any morality which *really* attributed rights to animals would therefore constitute a gross and callous abuse of them.

3 Those considerations are obvious, but by no means trivial. For they point to a deep difficulty in the path of any attempt to treat animals as our equals. By ascribing rights to animals, and so promoting them to full membership of the moral community, we tie them in obligations that they can neither fulfil nor comprehend. Not only is this senseless cruelty in itself; it effectively destroys all possibility of cordial and beneficial relations between us and them. Only by refraining from personalizing animals do we behave towards them in ways that they can understand. And even the most sentimental animal lovers know this, and confer 'rights' on their favourites in a manner so selective and arbitrary as to show that they are not really dealing with the ordinary moral concept. When a dog savages a sheep no one believes that the dog, rather than its owner, should be sued for damages. Sei Shonagon, in *The Pillow Book,* tells of a dog breaching some rule of court etiquette and being horribly beaten, as the law requires. The scene is most disturbing to the modern reader. Yet surely, if dogs have rights, punishment is what they must expect when they disregard their duties.

4 But the point does not concern rights only. It concerns the deep and impassable difference between personal relations, founded on dialogue, criticism and the sense of justice, and animal relations, founded on affections and needs. The moral problem of animals arises because they cannot enter into relations of the first kind, while we are so much bound by those relations that they seem to tie us even to creatures who cannot themselves be bound by them.

5 Defenders of 'animal liberation' have made much of the fact that animals suffer as we do: they feel pain, hunger, cold and fear and therefore, as Singer

puts it, have 'interests' which form, or ought to form, part of the moral equation. While this is true, it is only part of the truth. There is more to morality than the avoidance of suffering: to live by no other standard than this one is to avoid life, to forgo risk and adventure, and to sink into a state of cringing morbidity. Moreover, while our sympathies ought to be, and unavoidably will be, extended to the animals, they should not be indiscriminate. Although animals have no rights, we still have duties and responsibilities towards them, or towards some of them, and these will cut across the utilitarian equation, distinguishing the animals who are close to us and who have a claim on our protection from those towards whom our duties fall under the broader rule of charity.

6 This is important for two reasons. Firstly, we relate to animals in three distinct situations, which define three distinct kinds of responsibility: as pets, as domestic animals reared for human purposes and as wild creatures. Secondly, the situation of animals is radically and often irreversibly changed as soon as human beings take an interest in them. Pets and other domestic animals are usually entirely dependent on human care for their survival and well-being; and wild animals too are increasingly dependent on human measures to protect their food supplies and habitats.

7 Some shadow version of the moral law therefore emerges in our dealings with animals. I cannot blithely count the interests of my dog as on a par with the interests of any other dog, wild or domesticated, even though they have an equal capacity for suffering and an equal need for help. My dog has a special claim on me, not wholly dissimilar from the claim of my child. I caused it to be dependent on me, precisely by leading it to expect that I would cater for its needs.

8 The situation is further complicated by the distinction between species. Dogs form life long attachments, and a dog brought up by one person may be incapable of living comfortably with another. A horse may be bought or sold many times, with little or no distress, provided it is properly cared for by each of its owners. Sheep maintained in flocks are every bit as dependent on human care as dogs and horses; but they do not notice it, and regard their shepherds and guardians as little more than aspects of the environment, which rise like the sun in the morning and depart like the sun at night.

9 For these reasons we must consider our duties towards animals under three separate heads: pets, animals reared for our purposes and creatures of the wild.

Pets

10 A pet is an honorary member of the moral community, though one relieved of the burden of duty which that status normally requires. Our duties towards these creatures in whom, as Rilke puts it, we have 'raised a soul', resemble the general duties of care upon which households depend. A man who sacrificed his child or a parent for the sake of his pet would be acting wrongly; but so too would a man who sacrificed his pet for the sake of a wild animal towards which he has had no personal responsibility – say by feeding it to a lion. As in the human case, moral judgement depends upon a prior assignment of responsibilities. I do not release myself from guilt by showing that my pet starved to death only because I neglected it in order to take food to hungry strays; for my pet, unlike those strays, depended completely on *me* for its well-being.

11 In this area our moral judgements derive not only from ideas of responsibility, but also from our conception of human virtue. We judge callous people adversely not merely on account of the suffering that they cause, but also, and especially, for their thoughtlessness. Even if they are calculating for the long-term good of all sentient creatures, we are critical of them precisely for the fact that they are *calculating,* in a situation where some other creature has a direct claim on their compassion. The fanatical utilitarian, like Lenin, who acts always with the long-term goal in view, loses sight of what is near at hand and what should most concern him, and may be led thereby, like Lenin, into unimaginable cruelties. Virtuous people are precisely those whose sympathies keep them alert and responsive to those who are near to them, dependent on their support and most nearly affected by their heartlessness.

12 If morality were no more than a device for minimizing suffering, it would be enough to maintain our pets in a state of pampered somnolence, awakening them from time to time with a plate of their favourite tit-bits. But we have a conception of the fulfilled animal life which reflects, however distantly, our conception of human happiness. Animals must flourish according to their nature; they need exercise, interests and activities to stimulate desire. Our pets depend upon *us* to provide these things – and not to shirk the risks involved in doing so.

13 Pets also have other, and more artificial, needs, arising from their honorary membership of the moral community. They need to ingratiate themselves with humans, and therefore to acquire their own equivalent of the social virtues. Hence they must be elaborately trained and disciplined. If this need is neglected, then they will be a constant irritation to the human beings upon whose good will they depend. This thought is obvious to anyone who keeps a dog or a horse. But its implications are not always appreciated. For it

imposes on us an obligation to deal strictly with our pets, to punish their vices, to constrain their desires and to shape their characters. In so far as punishment is necessary for the education of children, we regard it as justified: parents who spoil their children produce defective moral beings. This is not merely a wrong towards the community; it is a wrong towards the children themselves, who depend for their happiness on the readiness of others to accept them. Pets must likewise be educated to the standards required by the human community in which their life, for better or worse, is to be led.

14 Furthermore, we must remember the ways in which pets enhance the virtues and vices of their owners. By drooling over a captive animal, the misanthrope is able to dispense more easily with those charitable acts and emotions which morality requires. The sentimentalizing and 'kitschification' of pets may seem to many to be the epitome of kind-heartedness. In fact it is very often the opposite: a way of enjoying the luxury of warm emotions without the usual cost of feeling them, a way of targeting an innocent victim with simulated love that it lacks the understanding to reject or criticize, and of confirming thereby a habit of heartlessness. To this observation I shall return.

15 Pets are part of a complex human practice, and it is important also to consider the nature of this practice and its contribution to the well-being of the participants. Even if we fulfil all our obligations to the animals whom we have made dependent, and even if we show no vicious motives in doing so, the question remains whether the net result of this is positive or negative for the humans and the animals concerned. There are those who believe that the effect on the animals is so negative, that they ought to be 'liberated' from human control. This dubious policy exposes the animals to risks for which they are ill-prepared; it also shows a remarkable indifference to the *human* suffering that ensues. People depend upon their pets, and for many people a pet may be their only object of affection. Pets may suffer from their domestication, as do dogs pent up in a city flat. Nevertheless, the morality of the practice could be assessed only when the balance of joy and suffering is properly drawn up. In this respect the utilitarians are right: we have no way of estimating the value of a practice or an institution except through its contribution to the total good of those involved. If it could be shown that, in the stressful conditions of modern life, human beings could as well face the prospect of loneliness without pets as with them, then it would be easier to condemn a practice which, as it stands, seems to make an indisputable contribution to the sum of human happiness, without adding sensibly to that of animal pain.

16 We should also take note of the fact that most pets exist only *because* they are pets. The alternative, for them, is not another and freer kind of existence, but no existence at all. No utilitarian could really condemn the practice of

keeping pets therefore, unless he believed that the animals in question suffer so much that their lives are not worthwhile.

17 This point touches on many of our modern concerns. We recognize the increasing dependence of animals on human decisions. Like it or not, we must accept that a great many of the animals with which we are in daily contact are there only because of a human choice. In such circumstances we should not hasten to criticize practices which renew the supply of animals, while at the same time imposing upon us clear duties to look after them.

Animals for human use and exploitation

18 The most urgent moral questions concern not pets, but animals which are used for specific purposes – including those which are reared for food. There are five principal classes of such animals:

- beasts of burden, notably horses, used to ride or drive;
- animals used in sporting events – for example, in horse-racing, dog-racing, bull-fighting and so on;
- animals kept in zoos or as specimens;
- animals reared for animal products: milk, furs, skins, meat, etc;
- animals used in research and experimentation.

19 No person can be used in any of those five ways; but it does not follow that an animal who is so used will suffer. To shut a horse in a stable is not the same act as to imprison a free agent. It would normally be regarded as conclusive justification for shutting up the horse, that it is better off in the stable than elsewhere, regardless of its own views in the matter. Such a justification is relevant in the second case only if the victim has either forfeited freedom through crime or lost it through insanity.

20 The first two uses of animals often involve training them to perform activities that are not natural to them, but which exploit their natural powers. Two questions need to be addressed. First, does the training involve an unacceptable measure of suffering? Second, does the activity allow for a fulfilled animal life? These questions are empirical, and cannot be answered without detailed knowledge of what goes on. However, there is little doubt in the mind of anyone who has worked with horses, for example, that they are willing to learn, require only light punishment and are, when properly trained, the objects of such care and affection as to provide them with ample reward. It should be added that we have one reliable criterion of enjoyment, which is the excitement and eagerness with which an animal approaches its work. By this

criterion there is no doubt that greyhounds enjoy racing, that horses enjoy hunting, team-chasing and cross-country events in which they can run with the herd and release their energies, and even that terriers enjoy, however strange this seems to us, those dangerous adventures underground in search of rats and rabbits.

21 But this should not blind us to the fact that sporting animals are exposed to real and unnatural dangers. Many people are exercised by this fact, and particularly by the conduct of sports like horse-racing and polo, in which animals are faced with hazards from which they would normally shy away, and which may lead to painful and often fatal accidents. Ought we to place animals in such predicaments?

22 To answer such a question we should first compare the case of human danger. Many of our occupations involve unnatural danger and extreme risk – soldiering being the obvious example. People willingly accept the risk, in return for the excitement, status or material reward which attends it. This is a normal calculation that we make on our own behalf and also on behalf of our children when choosing a career. In making this calculation we are motivated not only by utilitarian considerations, but also by a conception of virtue. There are qualities which we admire in others, and would wish for in ourselves and our children. Courage, self-discipline, and practical wisdom are promoted by careers in which risk is paramount; and this is a strong reason for choosing those careers.

23 Now animals do not freely choose a career, since long-term choices lie beyond their mental repertoire. Nevertheless, a career may be chosen *for* them; and, since the well-being of a domesticated animal depends upon the attitude of those who care for it, its career must be one in which humans have an interest and which leads them to take proper responsibility for its health and exercise. The ensuing calculation may be no different from the calculation undertaken in connection with a human career. The risks attached to horse-racing, for example, are offset, in many people's minds, by the excitement, abundant feed and exercise and constant occupation which are the horse's daily reward, and by the human admiration and affection which a bold and willing horse may win, and which have made national heroes of several privileged animals, like Red Rum and Desert Orchid.

24 But this brings us to an interesting point. Because animals cannot deliberate and take no responsibility for themselves and others, human beings find no moral obstacle to breeding them with their future use in mind. Almost all the domestic species that surround us have been shaped by human decisions, bred over many generations to perform by instinct a task which for us is part of a conscious plan. This is especially true of dogs, cats and horses,

and true for a different reason of the animals which we rear for food. Many people feel that it would be morally objectionable to treat humans in this way. There is something deeply disturbing in the thought that a human being should be bred for a certain purpose, or that genetic engineering might be practised on the human foetus in order to secure some desired social result. The picture painted by Aldous Huxley in *Brave New World* has haunted his readers ever since, with a vision of human society engineered for happiness, and yet deeply repugnant to every human ideal. It is not that the planned person, once grown to maturity, is any less free than the normal human accident. Nevertheless, we cannot accept the kind of manipulation that produced him, precisely because it seems to disrespect his nature as a moral being and to assume a control over his destiny to which we have no right. This feeling is an offshoot of piety and has no real ground either in sympathy or in the moral law.

25 Pious feelings also forbid the more presumptuous kind of genetic engineering in the case of animals. There is a deep-down horror of the artificially-created monster which, should it ever be lost, would be lost to our peril. Yet the conscious breeding of dogs, for instance, seems to most eyes wholly innocent. Indeed, it is a way of incorporating dogs more fully into human plans and projects, and so expressing and enhancing our love for them. And there are breeds of dog which have been designed precisely for risky enterprises, like the terrier, the husky and the St Bernard, just as there are horses bred for racing. Such creatures, deprived of their intended career, are in a certain measure unfulfilled, and we may find ourselves bound, if we can, to give them a crack at it. Given our position, after several millennia in which animals have been bred for our purposes, we have no choice but to accept that many breeds of animal have needs which our own ancestors planted in them.

26 Once we have understood the complex interaction between sporting animals and the human race, it seems clear that the same moral considerations apply here as in the case of pets. Provided the utilitarian balance is (in normal circumstances) in the animal's favour, and provided the responsibilities of owners and trainers are properly fulfilled, there can be no objection to the use of animals in competitive sports. Moreover, we must again consider the human values that have grown around this use of animals. In Britain, for example, the horse race is an immensely important social occasion: a spectacle which does not merely generate great excitement and provide a cathartic climax, but which is a focus of elaborate social practices and feelings. For many people a day at the races is a high point of life, a day when they exist as eager and affectionate members of an inclusive society. And animals are an indispensable part of the fun – imparting to the human congress some of the

uncomplicated excitement and prowess upon which the spectators, long severed from their own instinctive emotions, draw for their heightened sense of life.

27 Indeed, history has brought people and animals together in activities which are occasions of individual pleasure and social renewal. Take away horse-racing, and you remove a cornerstone of ordinary human happiness. This fact must surely provide ample justification for the risks involved. It does not follow that horse-racing can be conducted anyhow, and there are serious question to be raised about the racing of very young horses who, when so abused, are unlikely to enjoy a full adult life thereafter. But, provided the victims of accidents are humanely treated, such sports cannot be dismissed as immoral. Indeed, we have a duty to encourage them as occasions of cheerful association between strangers.

Inflicting pain

28 The same could be said, it will be argued, about practices which are morally far more questionable, and which have in some cases been banned by law in Britain: dog and cock fighting, for example, and bear-baiting. For many people the Spanish bullfight comes into this category. For in these cases pain and injury do not arise by accident, but are deliberately inflicted, either directly or by animals which are set upon their victim and encouraged to wound and kill. We must distinguish three cases:

- the deliberate infliction of pain for its own sake and in order to enjoy the spectacle of suffering:
- the deliberate infliction of pain in order to achieve some other purpose, to which pain is a necessary means;
- the deliberate embarking on an action of which pain is an inevitable but unwanted by-product.

29 The first of those is morally wrong – and not because it turns the balance of suffering in a negative direction. It would be wrong regardless of the quantity of pleasure produced and regardless of the brevity of the suffering. It is wrong because it displays and encourages a vicious character. Spectacles of this kind contribute to the moral corruption of those who attend them. Sympathy, virtue and piety must all condemn such activities, and the fact that they are the occasions of enjoyment and social life cannot cancel the corruption of mind from which the enjoyment springs.

30 ...[T]he utilitarian calculus applies only when it is also the voice of sympathy; wicked pleasures are not better but worse than wicked pains. If dog-fights must occur, it is a better world in which they are observed with pain than one in which they are observed with pleasure.

31 Given the dog-fights and bear-baiting involve the deliberate infliction of suffering for its own sake and with a view to enjoying the result, they must surely be condemned. But not every deliberately inflicted pain is to be compared with these cases. Animals cannot be trained without the occasional punishment, and punishment must be painful if it is to have the desired effect. The punishment is inflicted, however, not for the sake of the pain, but for the sake of the result. If this result could be achieved without pain, then it would be right to choose the painless path to it. If it is far better for a horse or a dog to be trained than otherwise, then it is no cruelty but kindness to inflict whatever pain is necessary to secure this end.

32 The infliction of fear is governed by a similar principle. Many of our dealings with animals involve the deliberate infliction of fear – as when a flock of sheep is shepherded by dogs. But again, it is not the fear that interests the shepherd, but the control of his flock, which can be effectively moved by no other means.

33 Here we come up against a teasing question, however. Just how much pain, and how much fear, are we entitled to inflict, in order to secure our purposes? In answering such a question it is necessary to distinguish the case where the good aimed at is a good for the animal itself, and the case where the animal is sacrificed for the good of others. This distinction is fundamental when dealing with human beings, who can sometimes be hurt for their own good, but rarely hurt for the good of another. But it seems to apply to animals too.

34 Many animals suffer at our hands, not in order to improve their own condition, but in order to provide pleasure to others: for example, when they are killed in order to be eaten. How much pain, and of what kind, can then be tolerated? Most people would say, the minimum necessary. But what is necessary? Animals destined for the table can be killed almost painlessly and with little fear. But religious beliefs may rule this out. Ritual slaughter in the Muslim tradition requires a death that is far from instantaneous, in circumstances calculated to engender terror. Yet the pain and fear are still, in one sense, necessary – necessary, that is to ritual slaughter. Some people might therefore conclude that ritual slaughter is immoral. But that does not alter the fact that it can be carried out by decent people, who neither welcome nor enjoy the pain, and who believe that there is no legitimate alternative, short of vegetarianism.

35 Or take another example: the bullfight, that last surviving descendant of the Roman amphitheatre, in which so many innocent animals, human and non-human, were once horribly butchered. There is no doubt that all I have said in praise of horse-racing as a social celebration applies equally to bullfighting. Nevertheless, in a bullfight great pain is inflicted, and inflicted deliberately, precisely because it is necessary to the sport: without it, the bull would be reluctant to fight and would in any case not present the formidable enemy that the sport requires. The spectators need take no pleasure in the bull's sufferings; their interest, we assume, is in the courage and skill of the matador. Nevertheless, many people feel that it is immoral to goad an animal in this way, and to expose other animals, like the horses of the picadors, to the dire results of its rage.

36 Even in this case, however, we must see the animal's sufferings in context. Only if the spectators' interest were cruel or sadistic could it be condemned out of hand; and the question must arise whether bulls have a better time, on the whole, in a society where they end their lives in the arena than in societies where there is no use for them except as veal. Let it be said that Spain is one of the few countries in Europe where a male calf has a life-expectancy of more than a year. At the same time, it is hard to accept a practice in which the courage of the matador counts for everything and the sufferings of his victim are so thoroughly disregarded. Surely, it might be said, this displays a deficit of the sympathy which we ought to bestow on all creatures whose sufferings we have the power to alleviate?

37 The third case of inflicting pain – in which suffering is the unwanted by-product of a deliberate action – will concern me when I come to consider our relations to animals in the wild. Before moving on I shall consider the remaining cases of animals who are reared and kept for human purposes.

Zoos

38 Some animals are happier in zoos than others. Big cats, wolves and similar predators enter a deep depression when confined, and it is only to be regretted that the sight is not more distressing to the average visitor than it seems to be. It cannot be said of zoos, as I have said of horse-racing, that the suffering of the animals is offset by any vital social benefit. True, there are benefits of other kinds. You can learn much from zoos, and from time to time a species can be saved from extinction by its captive members – though the general reluctance of animals to breed in these circumstances can only be a further sign of how unsuited they are to live in them.

39 The only plausible answer to the problem of zoos is to argue that they should be so organized as to cause minimum distress to their inmates who,

while deprived of many of their natural joys, can at least be assured of a kindly death and a life of comfortable somnolence. The morality of keeping wild animals in these conditions is nevertheless questionable, given that so little of human life depends on it. Some animals, like monkeys and donkeys, become tame in zoos and cease to struggle against their confinement. But what is the point of a zoo if its inmates are tame? And is there not something ignoble in the desire to see a wild animal in conditions of total safety, when the poor creature, raging against the gaping crowd of spectators, cannot punish their insolence with its teeth and claws? The least that can be said is that zoos make no contribution to the store of human virtue.

Livestock, and the eating of meat

40 It is impossible to consider the question of farm animals without discussing an issue which for many people is of pressing concern: whether we should eat animal products in general, and meat in particular. To what sphere of moral debate does this question belong? Not, surely, to the moral law, which offers no decisive answer to the question of whether it is wrong to eat a *person,* provided he or she is already dead. Nor to the sphere of sympathy, which gives few unambiguous signals as to how we should treat the dead remains of living creatures. Our only obvious guide in this area is piety which, because it is shaped by tradition, provides no final court of appeal. In the Judaeo-Hellenic tradition, animals were sacrificed to the deity, and it was considered an act of piety to share a meal prepared for such a distinguished guest. In the Hindu tradition, by contrast, animal life is sacred, and the eating of meat is as impious as the eating of people.

41 In the face of this clash of civilizations there is little that the sceptical conscience can affirm, apart from the need for choice and toleration. At the same time, I cannot believe that a lover of animals would be favourably impressed by their fate in Hindu society, where they are so often neglected, ill-fed and riddled with disease. Having opted for the Western approach, I find myself driven by my love of animals to favour eating them. Most of the animals which graze in our fields are there because we eat them. Sheep and beef cattle are, in the conditions which prevail in English pastures, well-fed, comfortable and protected, cared for when disease affects them and, after a quiet life among their natural companions, despatched in ways which human beings, if they are rational, must surely envy. There is nothing immoral in this. On the contrary, it is one of the most vivid triumphs of comfort over suffering in the entire animal world. It seems to me, therefore, that it is not just permissible, but positively right, to eat these animals whose comforts depend upon our doing so.

42 I am more inclined to think in this way when I consider the fate of human beings under the rule of modern medicine. In comparison with the average farm animal, a human being has a terrible end. Kept alive too long, by processes like the organ transplant which nature never intended, we can look forward to years of suffering and alienation, the only reward for which is death – a death which, as a rule, comes too late for anyone else to regret it. Well did the Greeks say that those whom the gods love die young. It is not only divine love but also human love that expires as the human frame declines. Increasingly many human beings end their lives unloved, unwanted and in pain. This, the greatest achievement of modern science, should remind us of the price that is due for our impieties. How, in the face of this, can we believe that the fate of the well-cared for cow or sheep is a cruel one?

43 Two questions trouble the ordinary conscience however. First, under what conditions should farm animals be raised? Secondly, at what age ought they to be killed? Both questions are inevitably bound up with economics, since the animals in question would not exist at all, if they could not be sold profitably as food. If it is uneconomical to rear chickens for the table, except in battery farms, should they therefore not be reared at all? The answer to such a question requires us to examine the balance of comfort over discomfort available to a chicken, cooped up in those artificial conditions. But it is not settled by utilitarian considerations alone. There is the further and deeper question, prompted by both piety and natural sympathy, as to whether it is right to keep animals, however little *they* may suffer, in conditions so unnatural and so destructive of the appetite for life. Most people find the sight of pigs or chickens, reared under artificial light in tiny cages, in conditions more appropriate to vegetables than to animals, deeply disturbing, and this feeling ought surely to be respected, as stemming from the primary sources of moral emotion.

44 Those who decide this question merely by utilitarian calculation have no real understanding of what it means. Sympathy and piety are indispensable motives in the moral being, and their voices cannot be silenced by a mere calculation. Someone who was indifferent to the sight of pigs confined in batteries, who did not feel some instinctive need to pull down these walls and barriers and let in light and air, would have lost sight of what it is to be a living animal. His sense of the value of his *own* life would be to that extent impoverished by his indifference to the sight of life reduced to a stream of sensations. It seems to me, therefore, that a true morality of animal welfare ought to begin from the premise that this way of treating animals is wrong, even if legally permissible. Most people in Britain agree with that verdict, although most do not feel so strongly that they will pay the extra price for a

free-range chicken, or for free-range eggs. To some extent, of course, people are the victims of well-organized deception. By describing chickens and eggs as 'farm fresh', producers effectively hide the living death upon which their profits depend. But customers who are easily deceived lack one important part of human virtue. Travellers in the former communist countries of Eastern Europe, for example, would do well to ask themselves why meat is so readily available in shops and restaurants, even though no animals whatsoever are visible in the fields. A Czech *samizdat* cartoon from the communist years shows two old women staring sadly into a vast factory farm, full of cows. One of them remarks to her companion: 'I remember the days when cows had souls'; to which her companion replies 'yes, and so did we'. The cartoon was intended as a comment on communism; but it points to the deep connection that exists between our way of treating animals and our way of treating ourselves.

45 Suppose we agree that farm animals should be given a measure of their natural freedom. The question remains as to when they should be killed. To feed an animal beyond the point at which it has ceased to grow is to increase the cost to the consumer, and therefore to jeopardize the practice to which its life is owed. There is no easy solution to this problem, even if, when it comes to calves, whose mournful liquid eyes have the capacity to raise a cloud of well-meaning sentiment, the solution may seem deceptively simple. Calves are an unavoidable by-product of the milk industry. Male calves are useless to the industry, and represent, in existing conditions, an unsustainable cost if they are not sold for slaughter. If we decide that it really is wrong to kill them so young, then we must also accept that the price of milk – on which human children depend for much of their nourishment – is at present far too low. We must, in other words, be prepared to accept considerable human hardship, in particular among poorer people, in order to satisfy this moral demand. It is therefore very important to know whether the demand is well-grounded.

46 Young animals have been slaughtered without compunction from the beginning of history. The lamb, the sucking pig, the calf and the leveret have been esteemed as delicacies and eaten in preference to their parents, who are tough, coarse and over-ripe by comparison. Only if there is some other use for an animal than food, is it economical to keep it past maturity. Mutton makes sense as food only in countries where wool is a commodity. Elsewhere sheep are either kept for breeding or eaten as lambs. Beef cattle too await an early death, as do porkers. We could go on feeding these animals beyond the usual date for slaughter, but this would so increase the price of meat as to threaten the habit of producing it, and therefore the lives of the animals themselves.

47 In the face of this, we surely cannot regard the practice of slaughtering young animals as intrinsically immoral. Properly cared for, the life of a calf or

lamb is a positive addition to the sum of joy, and there can be no objection in principle to a humane and early death, provided the life is a full and active one. It is right to give herbivores the opportunity to roam out of doors on grass, in the herds and flocks which are their natural society; it is right to allow pigs to rootle and rummage in the open air, and chickens to peck and squawk in the farmyard, before meeting their end. But when that end should be is more a question of economics than of morals.

48 In short, once it is accepted that animals may be eaten, that many of them exist only *because* they are eaten, and that there are ways of giving them a fulfilled life and an easy death on their way to the table, I cannot see that we can find fault with the farmer who adopts these ways when producing animals for food. Those who criticize farmers may often have reason on their side; but there is also a danger of self-righteousness in criticisms offered from a comfortable armchair by people who do not have the trouble of looking after farm animals and see only their soft and endearing side. Farmers are human beings, and no less given to sympathy than the rest of us. And a good farmer, rearing sheep and cattle on pasture, keeping dogs, cats and horses as domestic animals, and free-range chickens for eggs, contributes more to the sum of animal welfare than a thousand suburban dreamers, stirred into emotion by a documentary on television. Such people may easily imagine that all animals are as easy to deal with as the cat which purrs on their knees, and whose food comes prepared in tins, offering no hint of the other animals whose death was required to manufacture it. It would be lamentable if the moral high ground in the debate over livestock were conceded to those who have neither the capacity nor the desire to look after the animals whose fate they bewail, and not to the farmers who do their best to ensure that these animals exist in the first place.

Experiments on animals

49 There is no humane person who believes that we are free to use animals as we will, just because the goal is knowledge. But there are many who argue that experiments on live animals are nevertheless both necessary for the advance of science (and of medical science in particular), and also permissible when suitably controlled.

50 It seems to me that we must consider this question in the same spirit as we have considered that of livestock. We should study the entire practice of experimentation on live animals, the function it performs and the good that it produces. We should consider the fate of the animals who are the subject of experiment and the special duty of care that might be owed to them. Finally, we should lay down principles concerning what *cannot* be done, however beneficial the consequences – and here our reasoning must derive from

sympathy, piety and the concept of virtue, and cannot be reduced to utilitarian principles alone.

51 Medical research requires live experimentation, and the subjects cannot be human, except in the cases where their consent can reasonably be offered and sought. It is not only humans who benefit from medical research: all animals within our care have an interest in it, and the assumption must be that it is so conducted that the long-term benefits to all of us, human and animal, outweigh the short-term costs in pain and discomfort.

52 The duty of care owed to animals used in medical research is to ensure that their lives are worth living and their suffering minimized. Even within these constraints, however, there are certain things that a decent person will not do, since they offend too heavily against sympathy or piety. The sight of the higher mammals, subject to operations that destroy or interfere with their capacities to move, perceive or understand, is so distressing that a certain measure of callousness is required if these operations are to be conducted. And that which can be done only by a callous person, ought not to be done. The case is comparable to the battery farm. But it is also crucially different. For an experiment is typically conducted on a healthy animal, which is *singled out* for this misfortune and life of which may be deliberately destroyed in the process. The relentless course of science will always ensure that these experiments occur. But that is part of what is wrong with the relentless course of science.

53 And here we touch on a question so deep that I doubt that ordinary moral thinking can supply the answer to it. As I hinted above, the advance of medical science is by no means an unmixed blessing. The emerging society of joyless geriatrics is not one at which the human spirit spontaneously rejoices. And although discoveries cannot be undiscovered, nor knowledge deliberately undone, there is truth in the saying that ignorance – or at least ignorance of a certain kind – is bliss. Piety once set obstacles in the path of knowledge – and these obstacles had a function; for they prevented the present generation from seizing control of the earth's resources, and bending them to the cause of its own longevity. Medical science may have benefited the living; but it threatens the resources which the dead laid by for us, and on which the unborn depend. Animals were once sacrificed to the gods by people who cheerfully accepted that they would soon follow their victims to oblivion. Now they are sacrificed to science by people who nurture the impious hope that they can prolong their tenancy forever. This may be morally acceptable. But something in the human heart rebels against it.

Wild animals

54 We have no duty of care towards any specific wild animal – to assume otherwise is to deny that it is wild. Duties towards animals are assumed but not imposed. Hence there is a real moral difference between the person who allows his terrier to kill wild rats and the person who keeps tame rats for his terrier to kill. We are surely right in thinking that the second practice is more vicious than the first, even if it causes no more suffering. For it involves the daily violation of an assumed duty of care.

55 On the other hand, wild animals are part of the environment, and our general (and growing) responsibility towards the environment extends to them. And it is surely right that we take their joys and sufferings into account – not to do so is to fail in sympathy and to assume the kind of arrogant relation towards the natural order which sorts ill with our new found consciousness of our responsibilities towards it. However, this introduces a great complication into our dealings with wild animals. For here our concern is not, primarily, for the individual, but for the species. The individual enters our concern only contingently, so to speak, as when a rabbit steps into the headlights of the car that we are driving. Although we recognize a general duty to take account of the individual's interests in such circumstances, our primary moral concern in daily life must be for the fate of species and for the balance of nature on which they depend. Too much concern for the individual may in fact harm the species, by promoting its diseased or degenerate members, or by preventing necessary measures of population control – something that has been witnessed in the case of the Australian kangaroo.

56 Here we should recognize a permanent source of moral confusion in the favouritism that we extend to certain species on account of their appearance, their charm, or their nearness to the species that we have adopted as pets. Beautiful animals like the deer, the fox and the badger take precedence over animals like the rat which instinctively repel us, regardless of their intelligence, relative destructiveness or ability to accommodate the needs of humans. We are deeply concerned about the fate of the elephant and the tiger, but largely indifferent to that of the toad and the stick insect, despite the equal ecological difficulties under which these four species now labour.

57 Moreover, some wild animals are more useful to us than others. Some can be eaten, others can provide clothing, ornaments, oils and medicines. Others are destructive of our interests – killing chickens, rifling larders, undermining houses or even threatening life and limb. We cannot maintain the same attitude to all of them – unless it be some serene Hindu passivism which, in modern circumstances, when the balance of nature depends upon human efforts to

preserve it, can hardly be promoted as in the best interests of the animals themselves.

58 Finally, even if we put sentimentality and self-interest aside, we must still recognize relevant differences between the species. To the extent that our moral duties arise from sympathy, we must inevitably respond selectively – not to do so would be a mark of hardness. Some species can, in the right circumstances, befriend us: the elephant, for example, and the dog. Others, even if they have no affection of humans, deal gently and affectionately with their own kind, as mammals must do with their offspring. Others still, while seemingly devoid of affection, are nevertheless curious towards and interested in the world in ways which excite our concern. And, as I remarked above, there is a great difference between those to whom we are able to relate as individuals and those who, because they cannot learn from their experience, will always be for us no more than examples of their kind.

59 Thus it is only with a certain strain that we can care for the well-being of individual insects, even though we recognize that they suffer pain and fear, and are often hungry and in need like the other animals. And fish too lie beyond the reach of natural sympathy: being aquatic, cold-blooded and slimy to the touch, they exist behind an impassable screen of strangeness. Moreover, we have a great interest in keeping fish at such a distance. For not only are they extremely useful as food; there is a sport in catching them which, while painful and frightening to the fish, is a source of one of the greatest and most popular of human relaxations.

60 In the light of all that, how can we form a coherent moral attitude to animals in the wild? In the absence of any specific duty of care, we must act, I believe, on the following principles:

- we must maintain, so far as possible, the balance of nature;
- we are entitled to intervene in the natural order to defend our own interests. (After all, we too are part of nature);
- in matters such as hunting, culling etc., the interests of all the animals involved should be considered, including the humans;
- our dealings with wild animals should be measured against the demands of sympathy, piety and human virtue. Hence it will be as wrong to take pleasure in the suffering of a wild animal as in the suffering of a domestic animal. It will be wrong to use wild animals in vicious ways. And so on.

61 Each of those principles seems to follow from preceding arguments. But it is worth considering their application to two controversial instances: angling

and fox-hunting. Obviously, a purely philosophical argument will not settle once and for all the complex moral questions that these activities have prompted – the facts are in dispute and feelings run too high. But that does not alter the fact that it is precisely in these controversial areas that a serious moral argument should be put to the test.

62 Angling. There are many ways of catching fish, but angling differs from most of them in that it is primarily a sport, and not a way of getting food. It is also of great environmental significance, since it provides human beings with a pressing interest in maintaining unpolluted waterways and in preventing the destruction of river banks and their flora. It offers a positive contribution to the balance of nature and also to the well-being of the hunted species – conceived, that is, as a species, and not as a collection of existing individuals. By the first of our principles it is unquestionable that angling is morally permissible.

63 The second principle also applies. It is surely permitted to intervene to preserve the stocks of huntable fish, even though this means destroying predators and taking a robust stand against diseases which, in the natural order of things, might have been better left to run their course. It can hardly be regarded as immoral to extract pike from inland waterways – always assuming that the process is carried out with the minimum of suffering. It is true that environmental activists have advocated a return, in these circumstances, to the *real* balance of nature, meaning the balance that would exist, were humans to play no part in producing it. (Some have even advocated the reintroduction of wolves on these grounds, as the 'correct' way to reduce the highland deer population, at present dependent on the arduous work of the deerstalker.) Such proposals are surely unrealistic: for humans would still be taking the initiative in maintaining the balance, and predators would still be instruments of an environmental policy initiated and maintained by humans. Humans too are part of the balance of nature, and the only serious question is whether they maintain that balance or destroy it. Besides, these radical proposals ignore the moral question: the question of how we should treat the animals concerned. Morality involves taking sides; and while nobody could *blame* the pike for its behaviour (since it lies, as a non-moral being, beyond all blame), our vestigial sympathy for its victims ought surely to rule out any special pleading on its behalf. And it is hard to believe that those who would introduce wolves as a means of controlling the deer population have much sympathy for deer. Whether hunted by hounds or stalked by humans, a stag is killed at last with a clean shot from a gun; when chased by wolves it suffers the worst of available deaths: the death inflicted on an animal by a species smaller than itself.

64 The third principle applies in very much the way that it applied to horse-racing. Angling is an abundant source of human happiness – to many people the image of peace and the preferred way of passing their leisure hours. It is also a social institution through which friendships are formed and cemented, neighbours united and the competitive instinct peacefully exercised. From any utilitarian standpoint, it makes a massive contribution to the sum of human happiness, a fact abundantly displayed in our art and literature. If we are to consider the interests of all the animals involved, then we must surely place this fact in the balance, along with the equally evident fact that the angler's quarry is maintained and protected by those who hunt it. The downside is great: for fish caught on a line suffer both pain and fear, as is evident from their behaviour. At the same time, however great the suffering, we should recognize that it is, in an important sense, necessary. Of course, you could kill fish instantly with a gun or a stick of dynamite. But this would be 'unsporting': that is to say, it would give to the fish no chance, and to the angler a cheap advantage which destroys his sport.

65 This indicates an important aspect of our fourth principle when applied to such activities as angling. Traditional forms of hunting often generate and depend upon an ethic of combat, which arises spontaneously in the contest with the quarry. The roots of this ethic lie partly in our piety towards the works of nature. But there is an anticipation too of the human morality of warfare. The hunter tends to have a special respect for his quarry and a desire to offer a fair chance in the contest between them. There are certain things which he feels are owing to the quarry and of which it would be unfair to deprive him. Not that the animals appreciate this chivalrous behaviour. But it is a part of human virtue – a kind of shadow version of justice – to display it, and only a vicious hunter would use every means in his power to trap or kill his prey. Although angling causes more suffering to the fish than an electric current or a stick of dynamite, therefore, we rightly condemn these latter ways of fishing as barbarous.

66 Our fourth principle is therefore satisfied by angling, at least in its gentler versions. The suffering involved is necessary in that it could be avoided only by destroying the sport. And although there may be sadistic people who take pleasure in the pain of the fish and others who are so unconcerned by its sufferings as to make no efforts to minimize them, these people are not entering into the true spirit of the sport. Serious anglers respect their quarry, are gentle when they can be (for example, when extracting the hook), and regard the sport as an equal contest governed by the rules of fair play. It seems to me that there is nothing vicious in this, and therefore no grounds for a moral condemnation.

67 Fox-hunting. The fox is a predator and a potential nuisance, whose charming appearance does nothing to cancel its notorious habits. Foxes are therefore pursued for two reasons – as pests and as sport. There is tension between these motives, since people wish to get rid of pests, but not to get rid of the animals that they hunt for sport. Hence pests have a greater chance of surviving where they are also hunted. On the other hand, it is precisely the *sport* of fox-hunting that is criticized on moral grounds. When a keeper shoots the fox that has been terrorizing his birds, his action seems to arouse little indignation in the public conscience; but when the same fox is pursued by hounds, themselves followed by a crowd of horseback, the strongest protests may be made. It does not seem to me, in the light of the four principles enunciated above, that these protests are really justified.

68 Foxes thrive in copses, hedgerows, and on the edges of pastures, where they can enjoy both cover, and open stretches in which to run down or cut off their prey. To preserve this habitat, is to favour many species besides the fox – rabbits, hares, voles, field-mice, badgers and a host of lesser animals in which people have little or no sporting interest. It is self-evident, in these circumstances, that fox-hunting makes a positive contribution to the balance of nature. Hunting with hounds has made its own very special contribution to the landscape, providing a motive to conserve the coverts, woods, hedgerows and pastures which have fallen victim to mechanized farming in almost every place where hunting with hounds has disappeared. It is also species-specific: properly trained hounds go after no quarry other than the one that they are trained to pursue and furthermore, if they catch it, kill it instantly. Our first principle therefore finds no fault with fox-hunting, and the second principle will apply as readily as in the case of angling.

69 The third principle would also seem to favour the sport. Anyone who doubts that hunting with hounds has been a rich source of human social life and happiness need only consult our literary and artistic tradition, in which this pursuit is celebrated perhaps above all others, as the picture of human joy. From Homer to Trollope hunting scenes provide the high points of intensity in the description of human leisure, while both painters and composers have devoted some of their greatest efforts to portraying or evoking the hunt. The judgement of art is confirmed by those who take part in the sport, and if it were a case of considering human interests alone, there would be no doubt which way the utilitarian calculus would point.

70 Moreover, unlike angling, hunting with hounds generates intense pleasure for animals – for the hounds themselves, and for the horses which excitedly follow them and who are raised to heights of eagerness which quite transcend the daily hedonic diet of their species. Much of the pleasure felt by

those who ride to hounds derives from sympathy with horse and hound – a grateful sense of being returned to the realm of innocent joy in which these favourite creatures are moving.

71 Against this great accumulation of human and animal delight, it would be difficult to count the fear and pain of the fox as an absolute moral obstacle, unless they were shown to be either so great as to outweigh any amount of pleasure, or unnecessary, or the object of some vicious attitude. The questions here are complex, and not surprisingly hunting with hounds remains, and perhaps will always remain controversial – as it already was when Plato, in *The Laws,* wrote in support of it as the highest form of hunting.

72 It is, or ought to be, widely recognized that the death of the hunted fox is, when it occurs, more rapid than its death when shot (unless shot in favourable circumstances by an expert marksman), or its death from any rival method commonly employed to despatch it. Moreover, it is certain. If it is pain that concerns us, then I doubt that we will think it great enough to rule against the sport. It is certainly no greater, and probably less, than the pain of the rat caught by a terrier, or the mouse caught by a cat. It is rather the fox's fear, and the relentless pursuit which enhances it, which raise the most serious moral concerns. If the fox does not run and surrenders to an early and instant death, there can be no sport. Hence he must run, and only fear will compel him.

73 Many people dislike this, not because the fear in question outweighs the pleasure of those in pursuit, but because there is something callous in pursuing a creature so relentlessly. In other words, it is the fourth of our principles that is held to apply, and which motivates those who most seriously object to hunting. It seems to them that the pleasure involved is either vicious in itself, or an expression of a vicious nature.

74 Here, therefore, is where any defence of hunting would have to begin: by showing that the human interest in this sport is compatible with sympathy and virtue.

75 As in the case of angling, however, we must be careful to distinguish legitimate from illegitimate pleasures. Roy Hattersley, writing in the *Guardian,* made the following remark:

> I have long supported whoever it was who said that the real objection to fox-hunting is the pleasure that the hunters get out of it... If killing foxes is necessary for the safety and survival of other species, I – and several million others – will vote for it to continue. But the slaughter ought not be fun.

76 The suffering of the caught fish is not fun, but only the price of fun. To describe it as fun is to imply that the angler takes pleasure *in* the suffering of his quarry, and this is manifestly not true. If there were a sport, exactly like angling except that the fish were lifted from the water and then tortured with

hooks to the amused shrieks of the bystanders, we should regard it in quite another moral light from the sport of angling. Likewise, if there were a sport which consisted of capturing and then torturing a fox, where the goal of the sport was precisely to inflict this suffering, we should all agree with Mr Hattersley's peremptory judgement. But fox-hunting is not like that. Sometimes, no doubt, such sports are abused by sadists; and it might be right for Parliament to examine the matter, so as to ensure that the rules laid down by the Anglers' Association and the Masters of Fox-Hounds Association not only forbid such abuse, but also have the force of law. But the purpose of such a law would be not to forbid the pleasure of those whom Mr Hattersley describes as 'the hunters' (meaning, no doubt, the followers), but to forbid pleasure of the wrong kind. Otherwise all pleasures bought at the cost of animal suffering must be forbidden – from the eating of meat, through horse-racing and dog-racing, to angling, shooting and hunting with hounds.

77 Nor should we neglect the extraordinary role assumed by hunting in the rural community, as farmers open their land to their neighbours, and justify their ownership of the land by briefly renouncing their claim on it. This too is a form of piety, and, like every pious urge, stems from our sense that we are stewards and tenants, not absolute owners, of the world in which we live. It is this attitude, more than any other, that we must foster, if our species is to survive. And if ever we should lose it, our survival would not be justified in any case.

78 The counter-argument should not be dismissed, however, and the case remains open. Its interest lies in showing that the deep moral questions will never be answered by our first three principles alone. Environmental, pragmatic and utilitarian arguments all count in favour of fox-hunting. But the real question of its morality is a question of human vice and virtue. And this is invariably the case in our dealings with wild animals. What really matters is the attitude with which we approach their joys and sufferings. When Jorrocks praised hunting as 'the image of war with only five and twenty per cent of the danger' he was consciously praising the human virtue which it displays and encourages. And no reader of Surtees can doubt that, whatever vices are displayed in the hunting field, sadism towards the fox is rarely one of them.

Notes

* From *Animal Rights and Wrongs*, Demos, 1996.

'On the Side of the Animals: Some Contemporary Philosophers' Views'

In these passages,* a number of philosophers, and one psychologist, briefly state their views. Those of Midgley, Singer and Regan are familiar to you and the passages form useful summaries. Stephen Clark is Professor of Philosophy at the University of Liverpool. His early book, *The Moral Status of Animals* (1977) argued for vegetarianism and against most biomedical research, appealing to the necessity of sparing animals 'unnecessary pain' and recognizing that all living things are part of God's creation. Andrew Linzey holds the world's first academic professorship in the theological and ethical aspects of animal welfare, at Mansfield College, Oxford. He argues that animals do not belong to us, but to God and must be objects of intrinsic value to human beings. Bernard Rollin is Professor of Physiology and Bioethics at Colorado State University, USA. Like Regan he also holds that animals have rights, and in *Animal Rights and Human Morality* (1981) he addresses practical issues about how such rights might begin to be enshrined in actual law. Richard Ryder is the psychologist who, in 1970, coined the word 'speciesism'; his book *Victims of Science: The Use of Animals in Science* (1975) argues that all attempts to justify animal experimentation in terms of benefits to other individuals must fail, just as they would if applied to innocent humans.

Animals and the philosophers

Mary Midgley

With a few impressive exceptions (Voltaire, Schopenhauer, Montaigne, Plutarch) philosophers in the West have until lately shown a rather surprising neglect for questions about how we ought to treat animals. But this neglect is now passing. In the United States (for instance) the number of philosophy students taking courses on this subject has risen in the last decade from none at all to about 100,000 every year. This change stems largely from the publication of Peter Singer's book *Animal Liberation* in 1975, but of course its causes go much deeper. Our civilization is becoming altogether more sensitive on this topic.

Two things seem to have prevented its doing so earlier. One was a traditional Christian objection to nature-worship, which till lately was widely held to put animals beyond the pale of Christian charity. The other was an intense obsession with human dignity, which led to any sense of kinship or sympathy with animals being felt as offensive and insulting. In spite of these obstacles, humanitarian concern for the sufferings of animals did manage to find some expression in legislation during the last century. Interestingly, its champions were often the very same people who made similar struggles on behalf of human beings – Wilberforce, Shaftesbury, and particularly the Utilitarian philosophers, Jeremy Bentham and John Stuart Mill.

Utilitarianism, a very direct moral view which concentrated all ethics on questions of pain and pleasure, happiness and misery, could much more easily accommodate animals than could either the Christian outlook – centring on the salvation of human souls – or the rationalistic one of eighteenth-century philosophers, centring on the dignity of human reason. As Bentham put it, the right question about animals is not 'can they reason?' but 'can they suffer?' Today, nearly everybody feels the plain force of that question, and neither Christians nor dedicated humanists see any necessary conflict between its implications and their own ideals. Philosophers therefore are now occupied largely with details of how to fit animals into our existing moral notions, rather than with trying to keep them out. To fit them in is, of course, not easy because exploitation of them has become ingrained in our institutions. To recognize any duty to them at all involves making changes. But as most people now might agree that some changes must anyway be made, detailed questions of whether animals may properly be described as having 'rights' are not as crucial as they used to be. There is still philosophic work to be done but, as proper philosophic work on moral questions should, it is now leading to action.

A view of animals and how they stand

Stephen R.L. Clark

The commonest moral distinction, historically speaking, is between those creatures that are part of our own community (whether strictly human or not) and those that are outsiders. Creatures with 'moral status' have rights as well as duties; outsiders usually do not. Our own moral tradition has been strongly influenced by 'humanism', the doctrine that all human beings, slave or free, foreigner or native born, have equal moral status. We do not always act on this belief, but it is so entrenched at a verbal level that we usually forget how radical it once was. Behind this doctrine lay the belief that all human beings were all, and uniquely, gifted: humans were quite different from 'animals', because humans had some share in the divine. Utilitarian moralists, who argued that all that mattered morally was to try and produce the best ratio of pleasure to pain amongst all those we affect, included animal suffering in their calculation, thus contradicting the Cartesian view that animals did not even feel pain (let alone the pleasures open to a sophisticated humanity). However, the greatest fear of humanistic moralists until recently was that the barrier between animals and human should be broken down, and humans treated 'like animals', merely as material for some complex utilitarian calculation. That was not how we wished people to be treated, but rather as 'ends-in-themselves' (the expression popularized by Kant). We know now that animals are more like us than we thought, and must, correspondingly be granted a status nearer ours.

What is especially odd is that modern thinkers who are happy to subvert the older humanistic conviction that human beings were of a radically different kind (as being, uniquely, in the image of God) from non-human have been very slow to draw the proper moral conclusion, that we ought not treat creatures of another species than our own with radically less consideration than we show to our conspecifics. If species differences are only racial differences 'writ large', and it is plainly wrong to make such racial differences a ground for radically different treatment (as that it is wrong to beat up 'whites', but not to beat up 'blacks'), we have to concede that if it is wrong to injure humans it must also be wrong to do identical or very similar injury to non-humans.

This is often all that is meant by the claim that 'animals have rights', namely that they have something like the same moral standing as our conspecifics. It is wrong to burn a cat alive, or drown a dog, or evict badgers from the place where they have lived before, or from the only places where they could have a chance of happy lives according to their kind – or, at any rate, it is wrong to do so except with very good reasons of a kind that might seem to excuse similar treatment of human beings. Utilitarian theorists (like Peter Singer) can mean no more than this by talk of 'rights', and would agree that the chance of a considerable net advantage to the general public would often justify us in killing or expropriating or even tormenting not just chickens, cats, dogs and chimpanzees but (potentially) any number of humans. Non-utilitarian thinkers (like Tom Regan) mean rather more by 'rights'.

According to Regan, it is the characteristic of being a 'subject-of-a-life', a being that has a life to live rather than being a mere succession of stray sensations and impulses, that grounds the possession of 'rights'. These rights are not simply those of moral standing, but the more powerful rights of the liberal tradition. State action can only be justified if it does not violate the rights of its subjects, and the 'general good' does not excuse homicide, expropriation or torture. People have a clear right, within the liberal tradition, NOT to be killed, tortured or even robbed even if this (under certain imaginable circumstances) did help others to achieve the best (utilitarian) outcome. Regan points out that there is no identifiable characteristic that literally all human beings have (thus grounding the equivalent rights of all humans) that is not also possessed by some non-human beings. At least those (though he does in practice reserve the class to the higher mammals) must therefore have just the same moral rights as humans do.

My own position is a somewhat different one. How members of our immediate social communities should be treated by each other cannot be decided solely by abstract argument. I would not be willing to concede (as both Singer and Regan must) that humans who were NOT subjects-of-a-life 'in their own right' are beings without rights. They plainly do have positive, legal rights, and their interest will be defended by decent liberals. Non-human members of our communities have claims upon us, some of which are defended by law, and some merely by moral opinion. Those who beat dogs to death do something that society does, and justly may, condemn without waiting to see whether the dog has abstract, metaphysical rights. We are now in a position to understand far more than our forebears about the global community that lies behind our lesser social communities: wild creatures, who are by definition not a part of our society, can be seen as living out their lives within the wider whole which is that 'Great City whose Author and Founder is God'.

The older liberal tradition, developing over the last two thousand years, was founded precisely on a perception of human beings as occupying a place within the global community which allowed them the opportunity to understand and care for creatures of all kinds. What our forebears lacked was a full understanding of the extent to which our welfare depends upon the health of the global ecosystem, and the extent to which our evolutionary cousins can be hurt, harmed and injured in ways analogous to ourselves. The question before us is not simply 'how may we produce the greatest ratio of pleasure to pain' (a wholly vacuous programme), nor yet 'what rights do creatures have before the community formulates me', but how may we best order the communities (social and global) of which we are parts? The answer, I believe, must lie in our taking seriously what we already know, that more matters even to animals than their own pain or pleasure, and that our survival even as a species depends upon being able to maintain or create sustainable and civil ecosystems at household, civil, national and global levels.

The ethics of animal liberation: a summary statement

Peter Singer

Behind our practices of eating animals, hunting them for sport, and using them as tools for research, lies the assumption that the interests of the animals count either not at all, or very little, when they come into opposition with the views of humans.

This assumption, however, cannot stand the light of impartial ethical scrutiny. There can be no ethical justification for refusing to extend the basic moral ideas of equality and rights – which, at least in theory, most people now regard as applying to all human beings – to animals as well.

At first this appears to go too far. Obviously animals cannot have equal rights to vote, or to free speech. But the kind of equality which animal liberationists wish to extend to animals is a special kind: *equal consideration of interests*. And the basic right that animals should have is the right to equal consideration.

This sounds like a difficult idea, but it is really quite simple. It means that if an animal feels pain, the pain matters as much as it does when a human feels pain – if the pains are just as severe. *Pain is pain*, whatever the species of the being experiencing it.

To show what this means, here is an example. Suppose that you slap a horse across the rump with your open hand. The horse may feel something, but because of the nature of her skin, she presumably feels little pain. Now imagine giving a naked baby a similar blow. The baby would feel much more pain. Therefore, if there is nothing more to be said about the slaps – no special justification for giving them – it is worse to give the slap to the baby than to the horse.

But there must be some kind of blow, perhaps with a whip, which would cause the horse approximately the same amount of pain that the slap inflicts on the baby. Then – still assuming that there is no special reason for inflicting either blow – the principle of equal consideration of interests tells us that it would be just as wrong to hit the horse as it would be to hit the baby. The fact that the baby is human, and the horse is not, makes no difference to the wrongness of inflicting the pain.

Many people make a sharp distinction between humans and other animals. They say that all human beings are infinitely more valuable than any animals of any other species. But they don't give reasons for this view. A moment's thought will show that there is no morally important feature which all human beings possess, and no non-human animals have. We share with many other animals the capacity to suffer, and to enjoy life. And if we try to find some higher capacity, like our ability to reason, our self-awareness, or our language, we find that there are some humans – infants, and the profoundly mentally retarded – who do not meet this higher standard.

If it would be absurd to give animals the right to vote, it would be no less absurd to give that right to infants or to severely retarded human beings. Yet we still give equal consideration to their interests. We don't test new cosmetics in their eyes. Nor should we. But we do these things to non-human animals who show greater abilities in using tools, or communicating with each other, or doing any of the other things which use those capacities of reason that we like to believe distinguish humans from animals.

Once we understand this, we may take a different view of the belief that all humans are somehow infinitely more valuable than any animal. We may see this belief for what it is: a prejudice. Such prejudices are not unusual. Racists have a similar prejudice in favour of their own race, and sexists have the same type of prejudice in favour of their own sex. Hence the term 'speciesism' has been coined to refer to the prejudice many humans have in favour of their own species.

Speciesism is logically parallel to racism and sexism. Speciesists, racists and sexists all say; the boundary of my own group is also the boundary of my concern. Never mind what you are like, if you are a member of my group, you are superior to all those who are not members of my group. The speciesist favours a larger group than the racist, and so has a larger circle of concern; but all of these prejudices are equally wrong. They all use an arbitrary and morally irrelevant fact – membership of a race, sex or species – as if it were morally crucial. If we reject racism and/or sexism we must, unless we are to be inconsistent or make arbitrary distinctions, also reject speciesism.

The rights view

Tom Regan

The other animals which humans eat, hunt, trap and exploit in a variety of ways (in sport, entertainment, and science, for example) – these animals have a life of their own, of importance to them apart from their utility for us. They have a biography, not just a biology. They not only are in the world, they have experience of it. They are somebody, not something. And each has a life that fares better or worse for the one whose life it is, a life that includes a variety of biological, psychological and social needs and interests. In these fundamental ways, the non-human animals in our labs and on our farms, for example, are fundamentally like us. And so it is that the ethics of our dealings with them must adhere to principles that are fundamentally the same as those that should govern our dealings with one another.

These principles, according to the rights view to which I subscribe, must begin with the recognition of the inherent value of the individual. Just as the worth of one human being is not to be measured by how useful that person is in advancing the interests of others, so the worth of individual animals is not to be measured in terms of their utility for us. And just as I truly recognize your worth or dignity as an individual only when I come to realize that I am not to use you merely in order to advance my own interests or those of the group I favour, so I truly recognize the worth and dignity of individual animals only if I come to this same realization in their case.

One way to mark this realization and to express the further principles it gives rise to is to speak to the 'rights of the individual'. Among these rights, the most fundamental is the right to be treated with respect. This is a right that should be affirmed no less (and no more) in the case of the non-human animals at issue, than in the case of us humans. These non-human animals no more exist as a 'renewable resource' for us than Jews exist as such a 'resource' for powerful Gentiles, blacks for avaricious whites, or women for chauvinistic men.

This philosophy [the rights view] is categorically abolitionist when it comes to our disrespectful dealings with non-human animals. It is not larger, cleaner cages that are called for in the case of laboratory animals, but empty cages; not more traditional commercial farms, but no commerce in animal flesh whatever; not more humane hunting and trapping, but the total eradication of these barbarous practices.

How we achieve these ends and whether we achieve these ends, are largely political and educational questions. The philosophy of animal rights does not articulate the means to be used. It does articulate the rational foundations of the ends to be sought. And those ends are as uncompromising in their denunciation of human exploitation of non-human animals as the means used to end this exploitation must be imaginative and creative.

A philosophical approach to animal rights

Bernard Rollin

My work in animal rights has proceeded on two levels. In the first place, I have attempted to provide a moral ideal for our treatment of animals, an area virtually ignored by the philosophical tradition until this past decade. Without an ideal, we are, as Aristotle said, in the position of archers attempting to sharpen their skill in the absence of a target. Unlike some philosophers, I have not attempted to create this ideal *de novo*. Rather, I have tried, in Socratic fashion, to get people to extend to animals the logic of the ordinary common sense morality, embodied in our social practice and laws, which we all share by virtue of living in the same sort of society.

In the absence of any morally relevant differences between humans and animals which can justify our exclusion of animals from the moral arena or the scope of moral concern, we must bring to bear on our treatment of animals the whole range of our social moral machinery. Specifically, we live under a moral/legal system wherein the basic object of moral concern is the individual human, rather than the state, *Volk, Reich,* church, etc. We protect the individual from encroachment by the general welfare, by virtue of according rights to individuals – protective fences around certain aspects of what we take to be essential to human nature. These rights are moral notions built into the legal system – thus we protect freedom of speech, religion, and assembly, and guard the individual from torture even when it would be in the general interest to ride roughshod over a given person. But animals too have interests growing out of the nature (or telos as I call it, following Aristotle) which are as central to them as human interests are to us. And if there are no morally relevant differences between humans and animals, animal interests too should be protected by rights, and the legal status of animals must be elevated from that of chattel.

Apologists for the *status quo* sometimes attempt to forestall this conclusion by arguing that animals do not have interests, either because they lack consciousness altogether or lack the degree of consciousness requisite for moral concern. Thus much of my recent activity has been devoted to exploring issues of animal consciousness, with special emphasis on various modalities of pain and suffering.

The second level of my work has involved the attempt to bring this ideal to bear on practical issues. Thus, I was a key architect of recent US legislation which at least begins to provide protection for animals used in research. On this level of activity, I work primarily to get society to maximize the interests of animals consonant with current uses of them, and to upgrade their moral and legal status. In this capacity, I work closely with scientists of all sorts, most notably with veterinarians, to effect immediate and practical changes. Among my victories in this area I take special pride in the aforementioned legislation: in the abolition of the long-time practice of repeated use of the same animals for teaching surgery: in helping to galvanize the research community into using analgesia on laboratory animals, and in helping to pioneer the growing field of veterinary ethics.

It is manifest that significant change in the treatment of animals can occur only when major portions of society have moved from seeing them as cheap, expendable tools for human ends to what Kant called 'ends in themselves'. Towards this end, most of my writing, teaching, and lecturing of late is aimed at those who currently use and abuse animals, rather than at other philosophers. In this way, I hope to accelerate a moral 'gestalt shift' on animals, from which will flow major and enduring social change.

Theology and animal rights

Andrew Linzey

People frequently overlook the Christian history of the humane movement and the RSPCA in particular. It was Arthur Broome, the Anglican clergyman, who called the meeting which first led to the establishment of the SPCA (as it then was) in 1824. He became its first secretary and ended up in prison trying to pay for the Society's debts. The celebrated Victorians who supported the first 'Prospectus' of the SPCA were almost all Christians: William Wilberforce,

Richard Martin, Lord Viscount Deerhurst, Sir John Cox Hippesley, the Rector of Marylebone and three other clergymen. They believed that Christian compassion for animals was a religious duty; it was 'the pure spirit of Christian charity' required by divine benevolence (*RSPCA Records*, vol. 11 (1823–26) p.198). The first Minute Book in June 1832 stated that 'the proceedings of this Society are entirely based on the Christian Faith and on Christian Principles'. One of the 'principal means' of promoting the new aim of the Society was to be the 'establishment of periodical discourses from the pulpit' and the publishing of sermons.

The concept of animal rights is founded theologically on the belief that God has a right to have his creatures treated with respect. Animals have – what I call – *theos-rights* (literally God-rights) because God loves and values them. All animals have an irreducible worth because God created them. When we speak of animal rights we do no more and no less than acknowledge the Creator's rights. We do well to remember that the creation around us is not 'our' world but God's world. It is not our plaything or even our pleasure garden. Human beings own nothing in creation, not even our own life which like all life is a gift and must be returned. Animals do not belong to us but to God. They are subjects of God's creative love and must therefore be objects of value for human beings. Human beings have been given power over creation not to despoil what God has made but to serve it and protect it. We have nothing less than a sacred commission to serve the earth, to honour life and love our fellow creatures. To live a life without any sensitivity or compassion for God's creatures is to lead a deeply impoverished spiritual life.

Once again Christians are beginning to speak out on behalf of animals. 'Animals as part of God's creation have rights which must be respected' wrote Archbishop Donald Coggan (accepting the Presidency of the RSPCA) in 1977. The General Synod of the Church of England, in the same year, passed a long resolution in favour of animals explicitly endorsing 'the due rights of sentient creatures'. The Archbishop of Canterbury, Dr Robert Runcie, in two forceful statements in 1981 and 1982 opposed non-medical experimentation on animals and expressed his abhorrence of intensive methods of modern farming. More recently the Bishop of Salisbury in 1986 described battery chickens as living in 'Auschwitz' like conditions.

The renewal of concern among Christians today is no less significant, I believe, than it was at the beginning of the animal welfare movement in the 1800s. Christians are often forgetful of their history and their theology, and yet it could be precisely these people who pioneered the animal welfare movement in the 1820s who will have a significant contribution to make to the emergence of the animal rights movement in the 1980s and beyond.

Speciesism

Richard Ryder

Speciesism means hurting others because they are members of another species. In 1970 I invented the word partly in order to draw the parallel with racism and sexism. All of these forms of discrimination, based as they are upon physical appearances, are irrational. They overlook the one great similarity between all races, sexes and species – our capacity to suffer pain and distress. For me, pain (in its broadest sense) is the only evil and therefore forms the foundation for all morality.

In my opinion morality is, by definition, about how we behave towards others. (Classical philosophers, in my view, have caused continuing confusion by muddling together the discussion of what we ought to do for others with psychological advice on how to enjoy ourselves). By 'others' I mean all those who can suffer pain or distress, i.e. all those who are 'painient'. (I used to use the word 'sentient' but this is, strictly speaking, too wide in its meaning as I am only concerned with that part of sentience which involves unpleasant feelings; after all, aliens from another planet might be sentient without having any sense of pain at all!)

Painism – the concern for the pain and distress of others – is extended, therefore, to any painient thing regardless of sex, class, race, nationality or species. Indeed, if aliens from outer space do turn out to be painient, or if we ever manufacture machines who are painient, then we must widen the moral circle to include them.

Painience, I believe, is the only convincing basis for attributing rights or, indeed, interests to others. Many other qualities, such as 'inherent value', have been suggested. But, in my opinion, value cannot exist in the absence of consciousness or potential consciousness. Thus, rocks and rivers and houses have no interests and no rights of their own. This does not mean, of course, that they are not of value to us, and to many other painients, including those who need them as habitats and who, without them, would suffer.

Many moral principles and ideals have been proposed over the centuries – justice, freedom, equality, brotherhood for example. But I regard these as mere stepping-stones to the ultimate good which is happiness: and happiness is made easier by freedom from all forms of pain or suffering. (As nouns I will use the words 'pain' and 'suffering' interchangeably). Indeed, if you think about it carefully you can see that the reason why these other ideals are considered important is that people have believed that they are essential to the banishing of suffering. In fact they do sometimes have this result, but not always.

Why am I emphasizing pain and other forms of suffering rather than pleasure and happiness? One answer is that I consider pain to be much more powerful than pleasure. (Would you not rather avoid an hour's torture than gain an hour's bliss?) Pain is the one and only true evil. (What, then, about the masochist? The answer is that pain gives him pleasure that is greater than his pain!) One of the important tenets of painism is that we should concentrate upon the individual because it is the individual (not the race, the nation or the species) who does the actual suffering. I believe, for this reason, that pains and pleasures cannot be aggregated as occurs in Utilitarianism. (One of the problems with the Utilitarian view is that, for example, the sufferings of a gang rape victim can be justified if the rape gives a greater sum total of pleasure to the rapists.) But consciousness, surely, is bounded by the boundaries of the individual. My pain and the pain of others are thus in separate categories; you cannot add or subtract them for each other. They are worlds apart. Without directly experiencing pains and pleasures they are not really there – we are counting merely their husks. Thus, for example, inflicting 100 units of pain on one individual is, in my opinion, far worse than inflicting a single unit of pain on a thousand or a million individuals, even though the total of pain in the latter case is far greater. In any situation we should thus concern ourselves primarily with the pain of the individual who is the maximum sufferer. It does not matter, morally speaking, who or what the maximum sufferer is – whether human, non-human or machine. Pain is pain regardless of its host.

Of course, each species is different in its needs and in its reactions. What is painful for some is not necessarily so for others. So we can treat different species differently but always we should treat equal suffering equally. In the case of non-humans, we see them mercilessly exploited in factory farms, in laboratories, and in the wild. A whale may take 20 minutes to die after being harpooned. A lynx may suffer for a week with her broken leg held in a steel-toothed trap. A battery hen lives all her life unable even to stretch her wings. An animal in a toxicity test, poisoned with a household product, may linger in agony for hours or days before dying. These are major abuses causing great suffering. Yet they are still justified on the grounds that these painients are not of the same species as ourselves. It is almost as if some people had not heard of Darwin! According to Darwin we are related through evolution to the other animals. We are all animals. Yet we treat the others not as relatives but as unfeeling things! We would not dream, I hope, of treating our babies, or mentally handicapped adults, in these ways – yet these humans are sometime less intelligent and less able to communicate with us than are some exploited non-humans.

There is, of course, very good scientific evidence that other animals can suffer like we do. They scream and writhe like us, their nervous systems are similar and contain the same biochecmicals which we know are associated with the experience of pain in ourselves.

The simple truth is that we exploit the other animals and cause them suffering because we are more powerful than they are. Does that mean that if those aforementioned aliens landed on Earth and turned out to be far more powerful than us that we would let them – without argument – chase and kill us for sport, experiment on us or breed us in factory farms and turn us into tasty humanburgers? Would we accept their explanation that it was perfectly moral for them to do all these things as we were not of their species?

Basically, it boils down to cold logic. If we are going to care about the suffering of other humans then logically we should care about the suffering of non-humans too. It is the heartless exploiter of animals, not the animal protectionist, who is being irrational, showing a sentimental tendency to put his own species on a pedestal. We all, thank goodness, feel a natural spark of sympathy for the sufferings of others. We need to catch that spark and fan it into a fire of rational and universal compassion.

Notes

* RSPCA Information, *On the Side of the Animals, Some Contemporary Philosophers' Views,* RSPCA, 1996.

Answers to Exercises

EXERCISE 2

1 The principle of charity tells us to try to find the best – the most reasonable or plausible – possible interpretation of what other people say.

2 In ordinary conversation this amounts to recognizing slips of the tongue and ordinary human muddles and charitably supplying what the speaker must have meant. 'Jason' not 'Jack', 'Tuesday' not 'Monday', etc.

3 If it seems to you, on first reading, that a philosopher has contradicted himself, the principle requires that you look for an interpretation of what he says in which he does not do so, for example, that he is playing devil's advocate against his own position.

4 See p.17.

EXERCISE 3

1 The principle of charity helps you to avoid making weak criticisms and to learn more from what you read.

2 A weak criticism is one that the writer could have easily escaped by quite modest changes in what she said; changes which in being modest, do not affect the main thrust of her argument.

3 I should apply the principle when I am reading an author whose conclusions I strongly disagree with, because this will help me to avoid misreading her and dismissing her as an idiot (which I shall be tempted to do), to avoid making weak criticisms, and to learn about the arguments she has for her conclusions.

4 I shouldn't try to apply the principle when I am reading an author whose conclusions I strongly agree with, because I shall be applying it unconsciously anyhow and, in order to read critically, I need if anything to apply a contrary principle of being grudging.

(What if I am open-minded about an author's conclusions? We'll cross that bridge when we come to it.)

EXERCISE 4

1(a), 2(b), 3(b), 4(a), 5(a) and 6(b).

7 True.

4 and 6 are the only tricky ones. If you got 4 wrong, you were probably thinking 'Well, 4(b) is Mill's view and Mill was a utilitarian'. True, but there is a question about whether Mill's defence of liberty really is a utilitarian defence, or whether 'he is making an impassioned plea for increasing negative freedom as

something good in itself, not simply for the consequences that it supposedly brings with it' (Book 1, p.73). A utilitarian, as such, is someone who believes that actions are right or wrong simply *because* their consequences are beneficial or deleterious. To be consistent, a utilitarian has to take his judgements of right or wrong where the empirical facts about the consequences lead him. If coercion is the most effective means of increasing overall happiness then he must say that coercion is right (cf. 2(b); he must not say that it is wrong even if it has beneficial consequences, like the non-utilitarians in 2(a).

If you got 6 wrong, or could not see what the difference between (a) and (b) was, you probably overlooked that all-important word 'only' in 6(b). 6(a) is a statement of reasonable prudence – a version of 'look before you leap' – which anyone, utilitarian or not, might say. But 6(b) is a statement of consequentialism.

EXERCISE 5

1 (F), 2 (F) (or (D)); 3 (D); 4 (D) (or (C)); 5 (A); 6 (F) (or (D)); 7 (D) (or (C)); 8 (A); 9 (B); 10 (F) (or (D)).

Self-assessment. Where only one answer is given, give yourself a 1 each time you got it right, and a $\frac{1}{2}$ each time you got the mark next to it, and nothing if you were further away. Where a second answer is offered, give yourself a 1 if you got either, and nothing if you didn't. Then I would hope you would get 5/10. I don't believe any of you got 10. 6 or above would be very good indeed.

EXERCISE 6

1 (b); 2 (b); 3 – interesting, and calling for discussion which I will develop on pp.48ff.

EXERCISE 7

1 Only the third. I am not playing author's advocate in the first two cases. I did not have to think of anything for myself on Singer's behalf; all I had to do was refer to what he says. But in the third case I am playing author's advocate. He does not say anything about this sort of case and, on his behalf, I have to think of what he could say.

2 Yes. The amended conclusion goes well beyond anything that Singer actually says, so I am not simply applying the principle of charity. It might even be something he was personally rather unwilling to say, since it might be regarded as a substantial concession. But I can still be regarded as playing author's advocate because I have produced something that still leaves him with a radical, well-supported position.

Singer might not personally like the way I argue on his behalf by producing the amended conclusion. He might prefer to attack the assumption that vegetarians upset and alienate their families to any significant extent. It is pretty questionable, so he might complain that I am not playing author's advocate very well. But, unlike the next case, I am still playing it.

3 No. In this case it is obvious that, far from doing anything on Singer's behalf, I am undermining his whole position.

EXERCISE 9

1 Not this, because of the concession the objection made at the outset (p.62).
2 Not this, because of the argument that can be given for 3's being the right answer.
3 Is the right answer. Read on to see why.

EXERCISE 10

1(a) Yes; (b) no.
2(a) Yes; (b) yes.
3(a) Yes; (b) no.
4(a) No; (b) yes.
5 No, because of 1 and 3.
6 No, because of 4.

EXERCISE 12

The key word here is 'dominion'.

EXERCISE 13

1 It is all right for us to kill animals for our own uses; the commandment 'Thou shalt not kill' does not apply to them. It is also all right for us to keep them alive for our own uses.
2 I would say that he gives two reasons.

(i) Animals are irrational, and dissociated from us by their lack of reason – the premise from Aristotle.

(ii) The Creator subjected animals to us to use – the premise from *Genesis*.

We might further interpret the passage as linking these two reasons. Why did God subject animals to us? Did He have a reason we can understand or is it just a mystery beyond our understanding? It seems He made them subject to us for a reason we can recognize as right or 'just', namely (i).

EXERCISE 14

1 Man is a political animal. Although Aristotle continually speaks of man as a rational animal, this is his, so to speak, official definition. But Aris-

totle did not mean this in the way it is often understood today, namely, it is in man's nature to play the political game – seek to gain and maintain power by Machiavellian means. He meant that a human being is a creature whose nature is to live in a 'state', or, as we would say, in society with laws.

2 (i) Human beings differ from all other animals in having speech.

(ii) Human beings differ from all other animals in having perception (we might say 'knowledge') of good and evil, just and unjust, etc.

3 Singer would (presumably) be pleased to find Aristotle making a point of claiming that animals can feel pain and pleasure.

EXERCISE 16

1 (i) No; (ii) yes, sometimes; (iii) yes.

2 All our duties regarding animals are indirect duties to one another. (Now return to the exercise.)

3 No reason is given for the claim that we have no duties to animals; it is an unsupported claim.

4 It would be wrong of me to kick your dog because this would upset you and it is wrong to upset people.

5 Yes, a reason is given for the claim that we have duties regarding animals; it is not an unsupported claim.

6 The reason given is that we can do wrong acts that involve animals. (Now return to the exercise.)

7 (i) Yes; (ii) yes; (iii) no; (iv) yes; (v) no; (vi) no.

8 An absurd consequence of the claims in this passage is that there is nothing wrong with wanton cruelty to animals if no one is upset by it and no one's property is damaged without their consent. This is a very comprehensive answer. If you got just part of it, that is still a perfectly correct answer. You could also have phrased it as 'An absurd consequence of the claims in this passage is that we have no duties regarding...' and continued, for example, '...our own animals, as long as we can be sure that no one will be upset by what we do to them'.

EXERCISE 17

1 (i) No; (ii) yes, sometimes; (iii) yes. (Kant's distinction between 'duties to animals' and 'duties towards animals' is harder to spot than the distinction between 'duties to' and 'duties regarding' used in the previous passage. He (or perhaps his translator) is careless about it too, slipping into 'Animal nature has analogies to human nature, and by doing our *duties to*

animals in respect of...' But a charitable reading requires taking that as a slip, rather than reading him as hopelessly muddled.)

2 'Our duties towards animals... are indirect duties towards mankind' from the last sentence, or 'Our duties towards animals are merely indirect duties towards humanity' from early on. (Now return to the exercise.)

3 It would be wrong of me to shoot my faithful old dog because by doing so I would damage in myself that humanity which it is my duty to show towards mankind.

4 All of these would be wrong according to Kant.

5 Kant is not open to the same absurd consequences move that we made against the previous passage.

6 No.

EXERCISE 18

1 According to Kant, treating animals kindly, or not treating them cruelly, is a duty we have towards animals because how we treat animals affects or determines how we treat other human beings (and we have a duty to treat other human beings kindly, not cruelly).

2 'Such action' (as looking after the faithful dog) *helps to support us* in our duties towards human beings'. In certain cases we have duties towards animals because 'thus we cultivate the corresponding duties towards human beings'. 'He who is cruel to animals becomes hard also in his dealing with men.' 'Tender feelings towards dumb animals develop humane feelings towards mankind.'

3 The man does not fail in his duty to the dog when he shoots him, because 'the dog cannot judge'. 'Animals are not self-conscious and are there merely as a means to an end. That end is man'. '...animals must be regarded as man's instruments.'

EXERCISE 19

Premise 1	We have 'duties of compassion and humanity' to animals.
Premise 2	'We are not required to give strict justice' to animals.
Conclusion	'A conception of justice is but one part of a moral view.'

Equally good would be:

Premise 1	It is wrong to be cruel to animals
Premise 2	The scope of the theory of justice cannot be extended to include such beliefs.

Conclusion A theory of justice is limited, leaving many aspects of morality aside.

– and similar variants.

EXERCISE 20

1 Kant, Hume and Rawls share the view that our duties regarding animals are different from certain duties we have regarding persons or human beings.

2 They differ in that Kant thinks that our duties regarding animals really amount to duties to human beings or persons whereas Hume and Rawls do not. They think that duties regarding animals are duties of compassion and humanity to animals.

EXERCISE 21

1 (C).
2 (A).

EXERCISE 23

1 According to indirect utilitarianism, respecting the lives of people who want to go on living is a 'well-chosen intuitive principle' (Singer (1993), p.93). As such, we should not depart from it, except when the very beneficial consequences are practically certain. So if the nephew can't be practically certain that he won't get caught (and hence not get the money, make the fortune or benefit all those children) he should stick to it.

2 Appealing to indirect utilitarianism, someone like Singer could, as in 1, say that the nephew should stick to the principle of respecting the lives of those who want to go on living. He will inherit quite soon, and can use what he inherits to benefit others then. Or, appealing to direct utilitarianism, someone could say that it is not clear that killing her now would maximize the interests of those involved. Aunt Bea's remaining interests would be left unsatisfied, and the nephew might fritter away his inheritance and not give any to the children's hospital after all. (Note that the example has made it very likely he will give away some of the fortune he plans to make by saying it will avoid a huge tax bite.)

3 Weak, because nothing could be easier for Regan than his making it explicit (it is implicit anyhow) that Aunt Bea will be mourned by no one.

EXERCISE 24

1 *We* are all intelligent – at least intelligent enough to have written or be reading this article. But no animals are *that* intelligent. Regan's response: nor are many human beings. Do we want to go back to saying that the

severely intellectually disabled lack inherent value, i.e. can be used as resources for the rest of us?

2 We are all human beings – but no other animal is a human being. Regan's response: this is speciesism and (implicit premise) speciesism is like racism and sexism and thereby wrong.

3 We all have immortal souls – as do all human beings – because, for example, we are made in the image of God. Regan's response: this is too controversial.

EXERCISE 25

1 We could try to show that the argument is invalid (or that the premises do not support the conclusion) and we could try to show that at least one of the premises is false.

2 The premises really do look as though they provide conclusively strong support for the conclusion, so the more promising way to set about criticizing Regan would be to attack one of his premises.

EXERCISE 26

Premise 3.

EXERCISE 31

1 Speciesism involves:

(i) drawing a distinction between members of one's own species and others; and,

(ii) sometimes, in some ways, giving preference to the interests of members of one's own species.

2 'Familyism' is not always wrong. ('Familyism' is not the same as nepotism.) But of course it is far from being always justifiable. My example (many others are as good): it is wrong, for example, when impartial justice is required, say, when someone has the job of distributing charitable funds and directs an unequal proportion towards members of her own family.

3 The analogy suggests that the answers to the same questions about speciesism should also be the same; i.e. speciesism is not always wrong, but it is not always justifiable either.

EXERCISE 34

1 Virtue ethics would not give a straightforward answer to the question 'Is it right or wrong to keep a pet animal'.

2 The answer it would give is that the rightness or wrongness of keeping a pet depends on the particular circumstances (of the individual pet-keeper and the way she is behaving).

3 Virtue ethics would, straightforwardly, say it was wrong to treat one's pet in the way a cruel or selfish, etc., person would characteristically treat them.

4 Virtue ethics would, straightforwardly, say it was right to treat one's pet in the way a compassionate, responsible, etc., person would characteristically treat them.

5 Virtue ethics is rather like Singer's direct utilitarianismism in that it says that actions such as keeping a pet can be right or wrong 'according to the circumstances'.

6 It is very unlike Singer's direct utilitarianism because it claims that many actions are intrinsically right or wrong. Acting viciously (cruelly, selfishly, etc.) is intrinsically wrong, acting virtuously (compassionately, responsibly, etc.) is intrinsically right. Moreover, by 'according to the circumstances' virtue ethics does not mean 'according to the consequences', as Singer does.

EXERCISE 36

I would say 'no' to 1, but 'yes, with varying degrees of success' to 3–5. For 2 and 6 see the Discussion.

Answers to the revision test

Chapter 1

1 (i) is absolute dismissal, (ii) is relative dismissal.

2 (i) and (iv). (Many non-utilitarians believe (ii), (iii) and (v). If you ticked (v), look back at the answer to Exercise 4, 6(a) and (b).)

3 (iii).

4 (iii) only.

5 (ii).

6 (iii).

Chapter 2

1 (iii) and (iv). ((i) is also all right.)

2 None. (Not even the development of (vi) was a conclusive objection.)

3 (iii).

4 (ii).

5 (v). (His conclusion is not clearly stated anywhere in the Reading.)

6 (iii).

7 (ii) and (iii). ((i) is also all right.)

8 (iii).

9 (i), (iii), (iv), (v). (Not (vii) because he says that assuming chickens and ducks are not self-conscious is questionable and shaky: they are not *definitely* non-persons.)

Chapter 3

1 (i).

2 (iii).

3 (i), (iii), and (v).

4 (i) and (iii).

5 (i), (iii) and (vi).

6 (i) and (a); (ii) and (c); (iii) and (b).

Chapter 4

1 (a) and (iv); (b) and (iii); (c) and (v); (d) and (vi).

2 (ii), (iii) and (v).

3 (ii) and (iii).

4 (i), (iii) and (iv).

5 (i) and (e); (iii) and (b); (iv) and (c).

6 (a) and (iv); (b) and (ii); (c) and (iii). (Everyone agrees with (i).)

7 (ii) and (iv).

8 (iii).

Chapter 5

1 (i).

2 All are false.

3 (i) and (ii). (Strictly speaking, you can include (iv) because, trivially, if speciesism is always wrong of course it is sometimes wrong. But if you left out (iv) because you took it to imply 'and sometimes it is not wrong' that's fine.)

4 (ii).

5 (i), (ii) and (iii).

6 None of them. (If you ticked (ii) you confused it with 'Moral questions *may* be complex and *may* need to be settled by appeal to a wide range of moral considerations'.)

7 (iv) and (vi).

Chapter 6

1 (i) and (vi) are true; all the others false.

2 (i) and (vi) are true; all the others false.

3 (i) and (iv).

Bibliography

Aquinas (1922 edn) *The Summa Theologiae of St Thomas Aquinas*, 2nd edn, Fathers of the English Dominican Providence (trans), Barnes, Oates and Washbourne.

Aristotle (1998 edn) *Politics*, E. Barker (trans.), Oxford University Press.

Augustine (1877 edn) *The City of God*, Marcus Dodds (trans.), T.T. Clark.

Baird, R.H. and Rosenbaum, S.E. (eds) (1991) *Animal Experimentation*, Prometheus Books.

Benson, J. (1978) 'Duty and the Beast', *Philosophy*, vol. 53, pp.529–49.

Carruthers, P. (1992) *The Animals Issue*, Cambridge University Press.

Clarke, P.A.B. and Linzey, A. (eds) (1990) *Political Theory and Animal Rights*, Pluto Press.

Clark, S.R.L (1977) *The Moral Status of Animals,* Oxford University Press.

Crisp, R. and Slote, M. (eds) (1997) *Virtue Ethics*, Oxford University Press.

Descartes, R. (1966 edn) *Philosophical Writings*, G.E.M. Anscombe and P. Geach (trans), Nelson.

Fox, M.A. (1986) *The Case for Animal Experimentation*, University of California Press.

Fox, M.A. (1988) 'Animal Research Reconsidered: a former defender of vivisection struggles with his radical change of heart', *New Age Journal*, Jan.–Feb.

Godlovitch, R. and S., and Harris, J. (eds) (1971) *Animals, Men and Morals*, Gollancz.

Hargrove, E. (ed.) (1992) *The Animals Rights/Environmental Ethics Debate*, SUNY Press.

Hume, D. (1902 edn) *An Enquiry Concerning the Principles of Morals*, 2nd edn, L.A. Selby-Bigge (ed.), Oxford University Press.

Kant, I. (1948 edn) *The Moral Law*, H.J. Paton (trans.), Hutchinson.

Kant, I. (1963 edn) *Lectures on Ethics (1780–1)*, H. Louis Infield (trans.), Harper and Row.

La Follette, H. and Shanks, N. (1996) *Brute Science*, Routledge.

Leahy, M. (1991) *Against Liberation*, Routledge.

Linzey, A. (1987) *Christianity and the Rights of Animals*, SPCK.

Linzey, A. (1994) *Animal Theology*, SCM Press.

Midgley, M. (1980) *Beast and Man*, Methuen.

Midgley, M. (1983) *Animals and Why They Matter*, Penguin.

Midgley, M. (1996) *Utopias, Dolphins and Computers: problems of philosophical plumbing*, Routledge.

Mill, J.S. (1962 edn) *Utilitarianism*, Mary Warnock (ed.), Fontana.

Mill, J.S. (1985 edn) *On Liberty*, Gertrude Himmelfarb (ed.), Penguin.

Pierce, C. and VanDeVeer, D. (1995) *People, Penguins, and Plastic Trees*, 2nd edn, Wadsworth Publishing Co.

Rawls, J. (1972) *A Theory of Justice*, Oxford University Press.

Regan, T. (1983) *The Case for Animal Rights*, University of California Press.

Regan, T. (1985) 'The Case for Animal Rights', in Singer (1985); abridged in Baird and Rosenbaum (1991).

RSPCA Information (1996) *On the Side of the Animals: Some Contemporary Philosophers' Views*, RSPCA.

Ryder, R. (1983) *Victims of Science: the use of animals in research*, revised edn, National Anti-vivisection Society.

Schopenhauer, A. (1965 edn) *On the Basis of Morality*, E.F.J. Payne (trans.), Bobbs-Merrill.

Scruton, R. (1996a) *Animal Rights and Wrongs*, Demos.

Scruton, R. (1996b) 'Talk on the Wild Side', *Times Higher*, 28 June, p.17.

Scruton, R. (1996c) 'Beastly Burdens', *Times Higher*, 30 August, p.17.

Singer, P. (1973) 'Animal Liberation', *New York Review of Books*, 5 April, pp.17–21.

Singer, P. (1975) *Animal Liberation: a new ethics for our treatment of animals*, Random House.

Singer, P. (ed.) (1985) *In Defence of Animals*, Blackwell.

Singer, P. (1987) 'Animal Liberation or Human Rights', *Monist*, vol. 70, pp.3–14.

Singer, P. (1993) *Practical Ethics*, 2nd edn, Cambridge Unversity Press.

Smart, J.J.C. and Williams, B. (1973) *Utilitarianism For and Against*, Cambridge University Press.

Sorabji, R. (1993) *Animal Minds and Human Morals*, Duckworth.

Statman, D. (1997) (ed.) *Virtue Ethics: a critical reader*, Edinburgh University Press.

Warburton, N. (1996) *Thinking from A to Z*, Routledge.

White, A. (1984) *Rights*, Oxford University Press.

Wiggins, D. (1996) 'From Piety to Cosmic Order', *Times Higher*, 4 October, p.22.

Windt, P. (1982) *An Introduction to Philosophy: Ideas in Conflict*, West Publishing Co.

Wolff, J. (1996) *An Introduction to Political Philosophy*, Oxford University Press.

Index